The Rwala Bedouin Today

Second Edition

The
Rwala Bedouin Today

Second Edition   William Lancaster

WAVELAND

PRESS, INC.

Prospect Heights, Illinois

For information about this book, write or call:
Waveland Press, Inc.
P.O. Box 400
Prospect Heights, Illinois 60070
847/634-0081

Contents

Illustrations

Preface 1997
William and Fidelity Lancaster

Some seventeen years have passed since the final field research was carried out for the original edition of *The Rwala Bedouin Today*. This might be taken to imply that much, if not most, of the material is out of date. In one sense, of course, it is, but an ethnography is never more than a snapshot, a mono-chronic description of how the observer saw and understood a society at a given point in the past. As such *The Rwala Bedouin Today* cannot be altered despite the anachronistic *'Today'* of the title.

What can be done in a new edition is consider points that were raised in reviews and later references, add observations and caveats where the authors are unconvinced by their earlier arguments or analysis, and give an assessment as to how the analysis might, or might not, be relevant in a later period or a wider arena.

One of the points that more than one reviewer raised was the confusing use of abbreviations to denote relationships. It never occurred to us at the time of writing that f. for father, m. for mother, and so on (as used in lectures at Cambridge), was not the standard anthropological shorthand. To amend this naive assumption a table containing all the abbreviations follows:

f. = father, m. = mother, s. = son, d. = daughter, b. = brother, z. = sister, h. = husband, w. = wife, 1/2 b = brother through one parent only, 1/2 z. = sister through one parent only. Thus the meaning of, for example, 'his f.f.m.1/2 b.s.d.h.b'. is that the person to whom it refers is the father's father's mother's half-brother's son's daughter's husband's brother to the other individual in the context.

Another point was that the transliterated spelling of names did not conform to accepted systems. It would be difficult to correct this now so, in this preface and the postscript, the spelling of names has remained consistent with that of the first edition, however unorthodox that may be.

One or two readers objected to the Rwala names of places or things, but such objections only serve to underline the limitations of their own research. Languages are living constructions and change over time and distance, so what word another tribe or group might use is wholly irrelevant and any attempt to be dogmatic is unjustified and does violence to the variousness of Bedu life. Subsequent field research with the Rwala and other tribes has shown that different tribes have different names for parts of the tent, types of wells, clothes, geographical features, and so on. Further, the Rwala now often use a word different from that used in the 1970s for the same object.

It has been said that an ethnography in which the subjects do not recognise themselves is of little value. So it is gratifying to record that all the Rwala who have read the book (there are several unofficial translations around and many Rwala now read English) agree not only with the observations made but with the analysis presented. It is true that we have been taken to task for failing to include more material on, for example, the Doghman or for ignoring the important genealogical information known to Abu So-and-so. When it was explained that we could only write about and analyse such information as we obtained, that the Doghman were few and far between in our orbit at that time and that Abu So-and-so was unknown to us and nobody had mentioned him before, it was generally agreed that, although there was much information that was missing, the overall picture was accurate. The whole point of an ethnography is to extract the fundamental principles of how a society actually works from a necessarily partial body of information. We have, according to the Rwala, been successful in that.

A further criticism that has surfaced from time to time is that we have been 'romantic' about the bedouin and taken what has subsequently been called an orientalist approach. If liking the people with whom one is working, admiring much (though not all) of their behaviour and finding many of their attitudes sympathetic is romanticism then, yes, we have been romantic. If, on the other hand, the accusation of romanticism is a way of implying that we have viewed the Rwala (and bedouin society in general) through rose-tinted glasses and ignored the ugly realities, then the criticism is unfounded. (Some Rwala have complained that we have not been romantic enough – we have not dwelt sufficiently on the hardships of desert life, the dangers and glories of raiding, or their spirited defence of their autonomy.) No anthropological critic has ever been specific as to what particular aspect of Rwala life we have been romantic about. Until that is made clear, the accusation is difficult to refute and the best that can be done is to emphasise that we have consistently analysed Rwala society in its own terms and within its own context. This too is the answer to our orientalism. Orientalism implies the use of Western value judgements or preconceptions in inappropriate settings; at its worst it implies that only an Arab can analyse Arab society. The former we have fought hard and consciously against by trying always to understand and explicate Arab behaviour within its own terms, not European ones. The fact that the Rwala themselves recognise their society and agree with my analysis of it is the best answer to the charge of orientalism. The assertion that only an Arab can understand Arab society we reject unconditionally; understanding other cultures is what social anthropology is all about.

The use of the term 'client' on pages 11 and 123 now causes us acute embarrassment. The nuances of contractual or moral obligation that the term contain in Western use are completely absent in an Arab context. We should have realised that such concepts ran counter to the prevailing ethics of jural equality and individual autonomy. This was even pointed out to us by members of the Sha¹alan family, but at the time we failed to see its significance. In particular the idea of a client tribe is totally inapplicable although it is a description that has frequently occurred in European travellers' and other accounts. While the behaviour of individuals or groups may *look* like a patron-client relationship, in some instances, the premises are different. In fact, the whole area of relationships between tribes needs to be considered, if for no other reason than to clarify this point. Initially we had neither the experience nor the information; we could only relate our observations to the received wisdom of earlier published material. It has since become clear that the subject is complex and important.

There are *lacunæ* as well. For example, we failed to deal adequately with traditional law. We recorded and analysed what we saw on an *ad hoc* basis, but were unaware that a famous traditional judge, who specialised particularly in disputes concerning dogs, lived in H4 (now called Ruwaishid). When we finally heard of his existence in the early 1990s and found time to track him down, he had died. While his specialisation may have been somewhat *recherché* and esoteric, it would have possibly elucidated some of the main features of traditional law. Our rather querulous complaint later that no one had revealed his existence was brushed aside with the remark that we had never asked: we should have known better. How much else we missed remains unknown. However, a preface is not a suitable place to make good errors of omission in a work carried out so long ago. *Now* is not *then* and any addition would pertain to a different time, a different generation, and different political and economic circumstances. The original ethnography sought to elucidate the premises upon which a social organisation of great fluidity was based and the processes by which accommodations were made. Any attempt to recapture the special conditions of the 1970s could be dangerously misleading.

Acknowledgements

How does an anthropologist thank all those who helped him in a long research project? Either by a blanket 'thanks to all', which satisfies no one, or by a long list of names, which is wearisome to the reader. I choose the second (and the uninvolved reader can skip), for it seems ungrateful not to acknowledge all who aided me; without them there would have been nothing.

First, my supervisors and lecturers at university: no teacher is responsible for the subsequent performance of his pupils – all he can do is point the way ahead. If I have strayed I alone am to blame; they did their best.

Secondly, Dr R. V. Short, formerly of Magdalene College, Cambridge: he gave me excellent, non-anthropological advice, which I followed to my own profit if to no one else's.

Thirdly, my wife: while it is trite to say that I couldn't have done it without her it remains, in this instance, perfectly true. Not only did she increase my material comfort but she also gave me the *entrée* into private, family life in a different culture. Over and above this, she provided ideas when I got bogged down and restraint for my wilder flights of fancy. As an anthropologist herself with a different academic background, she saw things differently, which made our work even more stimulating and probably more fruitful. Included in this are my children. They didn't, of course, have much say in the matter but they provided information and an immediate point of contact with other familes. They appear to have enjoyed themselves and I only hope that they feel later that a slightly unconventional start to life was worthwhile.

I cannot hope to name all the Rwala who helped, for the list would run into thousands. Indeed many who took part in discussions were never known to me by name; they were simply passing through. Pre-eminent among my informants were Al-Sha'alan family, more specifically the Emir Mit'ib ibn Fawaz Al-Sha'alan and his brothers (in order of age) Mohammad, Sultan, Nawaf, Nuri, Anwar and Faysal. Without them my best efforts would have come to nought. If I had to pick out the two to whom I am most indebted I would name Mit'ib and Nuri. Mit'ib was a constant source of enlightenment and information, while Nuri was the first to introduce me to desert life and my host of longest standing. Other members of the family who were of enormous help to me in one way or another were Emir Nayyif ibn Nawaf and his brother, the late Nawash ibn Nawaf; Turki ibn Mijhim, his brother Bedr and Mit'ib ibn Manawir; Fa'iz and Majid ibn

Acknowledgements

Faris; the late Al-Aurens ibn Trad, his brother Mohammad and Minwar ibn Khalid; Huweimil and Mit'ib ibn Sagr; Salama ibn Mishrif and Abdul Aziz ibn Afat; the late Fawaz ibn Athub Al-Mijwal; Fa'iz ibn Na'ur, Ali ibn Faiz and Mashbur ibn Hail, all from Al-Zeid; Abdullah ibn Humeidi Al-Mashhur, Abdullah ibn Abbas Al-Datznan and his late brother, Mohammad.

Beyond the immediate members of Al-Sha'alan, my thanks are due especially to Sheikh Freiwan ibn Freih Al-Mu'abhil and his sons Sfug, Fa'iz, Hazza' and Jazza'. Freiwan was more than just an informant, for he took us under his wing. I thank also other members of Al-Mu'abhil, Fajr ibn Harran, Kamil ibn Fajr and Mohammad ibn Thinna. Others who helped in Nathaiyyim are Al-Asmar ibn Addas Al-Nseir, Fedghash ibn Bghaiyith Al-Nseir and his brother Mliyyih, Shumi Al-Nuwasira, Ali ibn Shumi and Msa'ad ibn Bneiyya. Amongst those in Al-Juba mention must be made of Kleib ibn Rashrash, Nayyif ibn Dirzi Al-Doghman, Ashaf Al-Ga'adza'i of Sweir, Mahal ibn Khashm Al-Ga'ga' and Nasr Al-Frejji of Hdeib.

My thanks are also due to all slaves, servants and clients who helped me in myriad ways, and especially those at Goum Nuri, Goum Anwar and Goum Al-Aurens.

Of the non-Rwala I am grateful to Sheikh Nuri Al-Mheid of the Fed'an, Sheikh Rakan Al-Mirshid of the Sba'a, Sheikh Abdul Aziz Al-Maslet of the Jabbour, Sheikh Mahaiyyir Al-Gendal of the Swalme, Sheikh Dahham Al-Fa'iz of the Beni Sakhr and Sheikh Thamir Al-Milhim of the Hessene.

Of the women, special mention must be made of Sita bint Sattam, Al-Jazi bint Kurdi, Maha bint Fawaz, Shamsa bint Faris, Mnih bint Mijhim, Nauf bint Mijhim, Ruh bint Khalid and Anoud bint Al-Aurens, all from Al-Sha'alan; also Mheina Al-Sabte, Bakhita bint Freih and the daughters of Freiwan.

I am deeply indebted to the governments of Jordan, Saudi Arabia and Syria; although I was undoubtedly checked-up on behind the scenes, I was left alone to carry out my research without hindrance or restrictions – no anthropologist could ask for better treatment. Among officials, my special thanks are due to Emir Abdurrahman Al-Sudairi and his son, Emir Sultan.

I would also like to thank Sir John Glubb, Colonel Nigel Bromage and Norman Lewis for so readily supplying information.

Note on Transliteration

As names are variously pronounced and spelt in different dialects and areas, I have relied on commonsense. I agree with T. E. Lawrence that the official system only helps those who know enough Arabic to need no help. I have made no distinction between light and heavy consonants nor between long and short vowels. The apostrophe (') is either a glottal stop or the Arabic *'ain*, a sort of silent growl: the 'gh' is the Arabic *ghain*, a not-so-silent growl. In common place names, like Amman, I have stuck to the conventional spelling. I hope that experts will forgive me.

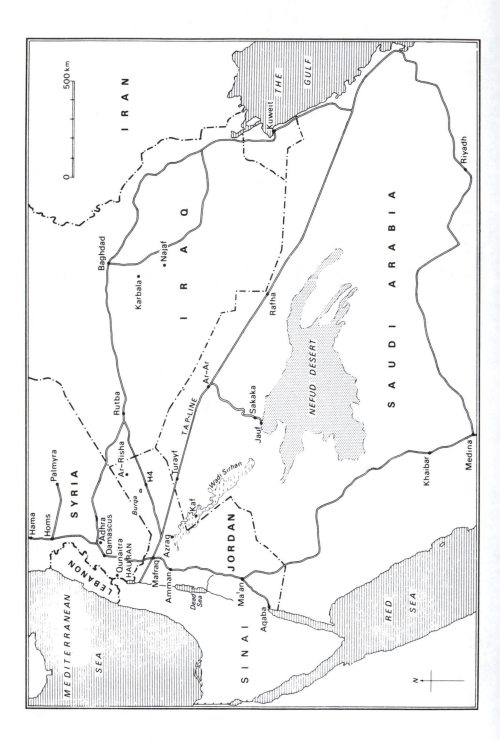

Part I The Present System

1 Methodology

Anthropologists spend much time in determining the constraints that govern choice in the society under study; they are curiously silent when it comes to the question of why they chose the society they did. It seems only fair to the reader and to the society under study that any anthropologist should give an outline of why he chose that society, how he carried out the research and how he got on with them personally. In an inevitably subjective science the attitude of the researcher must be allowed for. I want to know how societies work, how they view themselves and how they maintain themselves. Given these interests, which seem to be the heart of the English pragmatic tradition, I had to make a choice. I already knew and liked the Middle East and had a working knowledge of Arabic. Also, there seemed to be a lack of recent anthropological studies of Arab pastoralists in the Bedu heartland of Arabia.

I have always been interested in nomadic societies, not least in the discrepancies between historians' accounts of the effects of nomads on the civilised world, the presumed logistics of a pastoral life, the apparent rule of sheikhs and yet the equally apparent egalitarianism of many pastoral peoples. How can one reconcile a segmentary political organisation based on an agnatic genealogy with the hierarchic rule of paramount sheikhs, tribal sheikhs, minor sheikhs etc.? What was the position of women? What was the relationship between the desert and the sown? These were the sort of questions I was initially interested in.

The Rwala tribe were chosen for two main reasons. First, they have the reputation of being the 'most' Bedu. As late as 1956 the mimeographed information sheet for newly arrived diplomats in the area (provided by H.M.F.O.) advised that an escort was necessary in the desert as the Aneze tribes were not yet pacified. Secondly, not only are there frequent references to the Rwala in travellers' reports but also there are two writers who knew them well between 1908 and 1936. The first of these is Alois Musil, who travelled with the Rwala extensively between 1908 and 1915; the second is Carl Raswan, who seems to have visited them between c. 1920 and 1936. Musil was a Czech employed by the Austro-Hungarian government and was primarily an historical geographer who escorted parties of military engineers around the desert. His reports on the Rwala are scholarly, accurate and sympathetic. Raswan's contribution is more difficult to assess. His first interest was Arab horses (like Lady Anne Blunt before him) but he published several books about his adventures with the Rwala.

Unfortunately his romanticism is only too apparent, so his reportage is somewhat suspect. From an anthropologist's point of view neither writer is wholly satisfactory, but they do provide names, dates and events that can be checked – one isn't working in a vacuum.

Fieldwork started in spring 1972 in Syria. This was initially abortive, as I was refused permission to work with the Rwala for reasons of military security. (With hindsight I see that this was perfectly reasonable.) Jordan granted me a residence permit with the proviso that it was up to the Rwala themselves whether they accepted me or not; the government would not impose me on them.

The initial intention had been that I should stay with the Rwala while my wife and children would remain in a desert fringe village and observe the interaction between tribesman and settler. This came to nothing. First, there was no suitably positioned house in H4 (the most convenient village), and secondly it was a border and trading town of very recent origin with no agriculture. Also, in the Rwala encampment I was running into difficulties. Quite apart from their natural suspicion it became quite clear that I was to remain a guest and thus debarred from all but public life. In a society where the segregation of the sexes is the norm this posed considerable problems. The solution was proposed by the sheikh's mother. The women were as keen to meet my wife as she was to meet them and a sort of mutual viewing-day was arranged. During the course of this it was suggested that my family should live at the encampment. There were, however, conditions: we must live and behave exactly as they themselves. This suited us very well but it wasn't wholly altruistic. The sheikh's mother distrusted Western influence and wished not only to keep an eye on us but also to ensure that we received a good impression. Her son, too, wanted to keep an eye on us for different reasons and we also served to enhance his reputation for hospitality and generosity.

This all took place at Ar-Risha, a fairly permanent encampment near H4 in eastern Jordan. A one-roomed house was put at our disposal and we moved in. Gradually, with help, we accumulated the necessities of Bedu life – appropriate clothing, bedding, a tent, water-tanks, carpets, coffeepots etc. We were still very much on sufferance but it was felt, at least, that we were trying. By now, as a family man, I had some limited access to the women of the sheikh's family and his mother embarked on a crash course on 'how to become a Rweli'. ('Rweli' is the adjective of 'Rwala'.) Access to the women came about through their own curiosity. They wished to question my wife about such topics as European marriage, miscarriages and the like but my wife spoke no Arabic and there was no one but myself who could translate. This fact helped enormously. While the rules of segregation are said to be more relaxed than in the past, no man except a fairly close relative or a servant, is permitted, under normal circumstances, to visit the sheikhly women. Why then was I? The rumour started to circulate that I was a half-brother to the sheikh. This 'explained' why I was there, why I had access to the women and why we were living as Bedu.

The sheikh's m.b. told me of this rumour and we worked out that the late Emir of the tribe, my putative father, had been in England at more or less the right date for it to be possible. The sheikhly family found it easier to acquiesce than to try to explain to the tribesmen exactly what I was doing, so the rumour was never contradicted. It also rather amused them when old men would say: 'I knew it. He has Fawaz's hands (or eyes or legs).'

While this 'explanation' eased my position socially it also meant that I was neatly trapped in the convention of good manners. Among the Rwala a direct personal question is, at the very least, impertinent. The sheikhly family knew I was a stranger so I was, for a long time, unable to ask direct questions about personal relationships and, as for those outside the family, I, as a member of the Sha'alan family, had no conceivable need to know who someone's wife's father was. Thus for the first eight months or so my field of inquiry was limited to the formal genealogy and tribal organisation, for in my Bedu persona I needed to know about my relationship with other groups. I could also ask impersonal questions of a hypothetical nature and could use straight observation. My wife was in an even worse position; she could not visit widely by convention nor could she converse easily. She was almost entirely limited to observation. This proved extremely fruitful; knowing the main genealogical outlines she was able to work out the majority of the matrilateral links by watching which women visited where, and how often, and what they wore. The accuracy of her deductions was later checked – they were very close to reality. These deductions also had another effect. The fact that we were able to make them convinced the sheikhly family that we really were anthropologists and not Fedayeen, Syrian or government spies.

I had been aware that we were suspected from the beginning (this was shortly after the civil war in Jordan) and the fact that I had originally learned Arabic at the Foreign Office school in Lebanon did nothing to allay their suspicions. This closed to me, for some time, another obvious line of inquiry – economics. I had carefully avoided government officials and embassy staff as far as possible, so I had only heard the vaguest of rumours of how the Rwala at Ar-Risha made their living. They had few sheep, no camels and no gardens – in fact no visible means of support. It soon transpired that the vague rumours I had heard were substantially correct – they made their living by smuggling. This was an open secret but I could hardly inquire deeply into it without giving rise to exactly those suspicions I was trying to allay.

Time and familiarity overcame these initial problems. The next stage was to continue the research among camel-herders. For this we needed visas for Saudi Arabia. The process of obtaining them involved fairly frequent visits to the Saudi Embassy in Amman. While pursuing this we stayed at the sheikh's flat. This gave us an opportunity of observing the sheikh's function *vis-à-vis* the government. We were also able to see how city life affected their normal living-patterns.

After eighteen months in Ar-Risha and Amman (and a spell back home), we obtained our Saudi visas. We settled in Nathaiyyim, a small encampment on the northern edge of the Great Nefud in the province of Jauf. Although some of the inhabitants were distant cousins of the Sha'alan, they led the life of ordinary tribesmen. Nathaiyyim was chosen as a base because it was a frequent watering-place for camels and because the senior man was a highly respected historian and genealogist. It was a contrast to Ar-Risha, for it was not on a sheikhly scale. While I could not shed my Bedu identity, I was not expected to behave in a particularly sheikhly manner, even if my finances had permitted it, for the whole episode was viewed as an extension of my education in being Rweli.

Our intention of migrating with the camel-herds never really came to fruition. Our second year in Ar-Risha was without rain and the only grazing was in Saudi Arabia, for which we had no visas. While we were in Saudi the only rain was in the heart of the Nefud or in Iraq. Iraq was closed to us for political reasons and the Nefud was virtually impassable to wheeled vehicles and no one nowadays has any spare, trained baggage-camels. However, a herding group stayed for some months at Nathaiyyim and I made a few short trips with them, but with that we have had to be content. In seven and a half years we have never managed it; the rains have always been where we weren't and the herds have always moved on before we could make the necessary arrangements (mostly obtaining visas) to catch them up.

In all we have spent rather over three and a half years with the Rwala, nearly all of it in the desert, and I have spent about another four months with them on my own. Throughout this time we have avoided the company of Europeans and officials as far as possible and in the towns we have always stayed with tribesmen. By the end of our first visit conditions had eased in Syria and we were able to stay with the Emir in his family house in Damascus. My own family thoroughly enjoyed themselves, although there were times of physical discomfort and the children are fond of their adoptive uncles, aunts, grannies and cousins. We hope to remain in close and frequent contact.

My own bias should by now be clear and it is, in part, due to my awareness of my emotional involvement that the publication of my findings has been so long delayed. I hope that it does not obtrude in the analysis. If one is following Barth's injuction to observe micro-events one gets caught up in a dilemma. One has to live as a member of the society and know the personalities on an intimate basis. Inevitably one becomes emotionally involved; one just likes some people more than others. How then does one detach oneself and view the society dispassionately? Having one's family helps, for there is always the possibility of a retreat into one's real identity where ideas can be formulated and discussed, but time seems necessary also, so that a more balanced perspective can be achieved.

The long-drawn-out nature of the research has conferred two main benefits. First, if I had relied on the observations and material from the first eighteen months, my analysis would have been very different and,

I can now see, wrong. Later in the fieldwork we were taken for granted and had become part of normal life, so we could be fairly sure that what we were seeing was spontaneous and not put on for our benefit. This material has enabled me to reinterpret my earlier observations. Everything has been checked and double-checked during our everyday life in the desert by the actions and behaviour of ordinary people leading their normal lives. Secondly, such a long period has enabled us to observe changes taking place. This is particularly important in the relationship with, and reaction to, the non-Bedu world. I cannot pretend to have been only an onlooker in this. As a representative of (or at least someone familiar with) the non-Bedu world, I was used as an information source. Such information and advice as I could give was obviously coloured by my own attitudes and prejudices, but the Rwala are so self-assured that I very much doubt if I affected the course of events. Still, it has happened. I make no apology for this intrusion into the material; I have obligations towards the Rwala as well as towards research.

The way in which my material is written up will obviously reflect my academic background. Briefly, I am firmly rooted in the English pragmatic tradition. In particular, I have been influenced by Barth, especially in his ideas concerning process (as opposed to institution) and in the value of analysis in terms of 'assets and options'. These I have found fruitful.

2 Background

(a) The tribe and the physical environment

The Rwala are the largest tribe of the Aneze confederation. Actual figures are unobtainable but they are undoubtedly the most numerous tribe in the northern Arabian desert and probably the largest to acknowledge a single Emir in the entire peninsula. Their own estimate of their numbers sometimes rises to one and a half million, whereas estimates made by the French mandate government in 1935 gives only 35,000. My own estimate, based on an accurate count of some sections of the tribe and then extrapolated on a comparative basis, seems to indicate a figure between a quarter and half a million. Another count bears this out. In the early 1960s there was a heavy concentration of Rwala tents at Ar-Risha and an air photograph, taken by West German television, is said to show some 12,000 tents. I have not been able to track the photograph down and have had to rely on the information of one of the locally-employed members of the film crew, an American–Armenian. Allowing five persons per tent, this gives a figure of 60,000. As the photograph was taken just after the Emir and the tribe were expelled from Syria it seems reasonable to suppose that the majority were those who had been in Syria. The tribal section of the Frejje was the only one to move in force in Syria at that date. Even so, it cannot have been all of them, as many were in Saudi Arabia at the time. At the most it can only have been half of them and it was probably far less; the logistics of herding are against a larger proportion. By all accounts the Frejje are the largest tribal section of the five that make up the Rwala, so if we take each other section as being half the size of the Frejje we get four sections of 12,000 tents and one of 24,000. This gives a total of 360,000 Rwala. This was in the early 1960s: natural increase might not have altered the figure all that much but the period coincided with the opening of Saudi Arabia (where most of them live) and an enormous investment in government health clinics, hospitals and medical care. The Saudi Ministry of Planning reckoned an average of over six people per household in 1978, whereas I have been working with five, so a figure of between a quarter and half a million is probably not too far out.

The Rwala are divided into five tribal sections, the Murath, the Doghman, the Ga'adza'a, the Frejje and the Kwatzbe. Until 1958 virtually all of them herded camels except for the Frejje, who have, since the 1920s, herded sheep as well. The territory in which the Rwala were usually to be found in the past was bounded in the south and west by the southern and western edges of the sand desert called the Great Nefud. It continued up to Azraq via the Wadi Sirhan and along the mountain edge to Damascus and Homs. In the north the boundary was a line drawn roughly between Homs and Palmyra, although this fluctuated rather, and in the east it was a line running south-east from the east of Palmyra to Rutba and just inside the present Iraqi border to the eastern edge of the Nefud. In all it is an area about 500,000 sq km in extent. In no sense did the Rwala own this vast territory nor did they have exclusive rights to it; various tribes used (and still use) different parts at different times of the year. The Rwala nomadic cycle was in the south, in the Nefud, during late winter and early spring, moving northwards up the Wadi Sirhan until Golan was reached in high summer. In the autumn and early winter they moved off eastward, gradually working south towards the Nefud. It must be emphasised that this was a tendency only, the predominant move being north-west in summer and south-east in winter, or as they say 'west for summer and east for winter'. Some groups, like the sheep-herding parts of the Frejje, stayed north for most of the time, while others, like the Murath, tended to remain in the south. Again, some groups sometimes spent the summer around Karbala and Najaf in Iraq, while others went to Khaibar in the extreme south-west. The idiosyncratic nature of their migrations was not only a response to uneven rainfall but also a result of personal histories and personal preferences. It is also apparent that the Rwala only exceptionally migrated as a tribe; they were too large. Now that only about half the tribe actively herd and there are four international borders within their territory, the pattern of migration is even less clear-cut. Although the majority are to be found within their traditional bounds, individual members of the tribe may be anywhere from the Turkish border to the United Arab Emirates.

The area that they inhabit is described as arid steppe or semi-desert. Except for the Nefud, there is little sand, most of the area being of a gravelly nature patchily covered by drought-resistant shrubs and, when rain falls, grasses and wild flowers. Over the whole area the average rainfall is well under 10 inches (25 cm) per year and probably under 5 inches (12½ cm) in the recent past. In any case, it is so scattered as to be relatively meaningless as a figure. In most years sufficient rain falls in two or three places to provide for the whole population. Permanent water is in short supply. In the past when the herds followed the rains this was not very important, but now, with settlement taking place, many of them are dependent on new wells. The only large, permanent body of water is at Burqa, near H4 in eastern Jordan, with old wells in the north of their territory in what is now Syria, wells (brackish) along the Wadi Sirhan and wells along the northern edge of the Nefud and at Jauf. The rest of the territory had no permanent water at all. Water was not the only constraint on their migration pattern, temperature too was a factor. Those with sheep tended to stay in the north, for the fat-tailed sheep does better there than in the south. The camel-herders tried to stay in the south during the winter because the cold in Syria can take a heavy toll of newborn camel calves, which are dropped in January. Even in the Jauf depression the temperature can sink to freezing in winter, while in summer it can rise to 45°C or even higher. In Syria the winter is longer and colder with north winds sweeping off the Anatolian highlands and the summer is much cooler. At all times of year the variation between day and night temperatures is marked, drops of 25°C at night being common.

(b) The social environment

The individuals in this section and the next are referred to by initial and figure or by group name only. This is done partly to confer relative anonymity and also to emphasise the fact that structure is the important feature, not personality. Personality obviously affects choice of action but family structure limits the number of choices; a man might prefer path *A* to path *B* and his choice is related to his personality but, because of family structure, paths *C, D* and *E* are closed to him.

However much or little the Rwala may have changed, the layout of their encampments remains much the same whether they are temporary herding-camps or fairly permanent bases. The encampment at Ar-Risha in 1972–3 is an example. It is a fairly permanent encampment in that it has buildings as well as tents but this should not be taken to mean that it has a permanent population. Of the 500 or so family units at Ar-Risha in 1972 only about 8 remained in 1979; the other 200 were newcomers. Strictly speaking, Ar-Risha is an area and the encampment was known as Goum *F5*, that is 'the people who have clustered around *F5*'. The term 'goum' is not geographical nor genealogical but indicates a conglomeration of people with an identity of interest. *F5* was not the leader but simply the most influential man within the group. (This distinction is examined later – I sometimes refer to people as 'goum-leaders' for convenience, as it is tedious to repeat a long phrase, but it must be remembered that 'leader' is always in inverted commas.) The actual layout of the tents and, to a lesser extent, the buildings is genealogical. (See Figure 1.)

The most conspicuous tent and house belonged to *F5*, a member of the sheikhly family. *F5* was from Al-Nuri subgroup of the Sha'alan, as were *B1* and *B2* (*F5*'s brothers) and *F5*'s f.b.s. The other subgroups, Al-Mohammad,

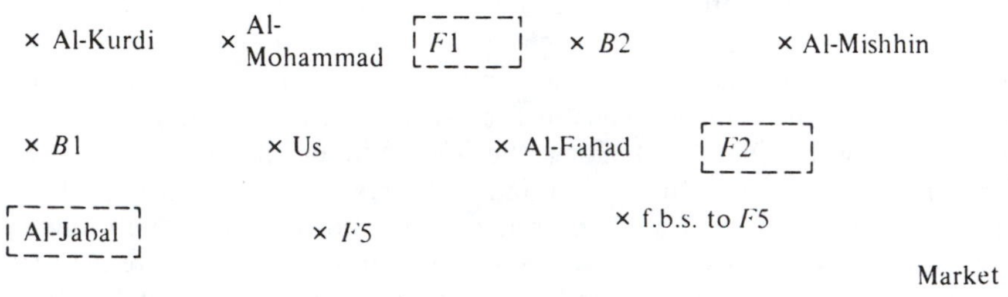

× Al-Kurdi	× Al-Mohammad	F1	× B2	× Al-Mishhin
× B1	× Us	× Al-Fahad	F2	
Al-Jabal	× F5	× f.b.s. to F5		
				Market

Figure 1. Physical layout of Goum *F5*. The inner family.

Al-Kurdi, Al-Fahad and Al-Mishhin were also from the Sha'alan and were genealogically equidistant from Al-Nuri and from each other. In no case was any subgroup complete. $F5$'s other brothers were in Amman, Riyadh, Damascus and America; two of Al-Kurdi lived in H4 and one in Ar-Ar in Saudi Arabia; another member of Al-Mohammad lived in Turayf in Saudi Arabia as did two of Al-Mishin; the second member of Al-Fahad lived in Kuwait.

At first glance the layout doesn't look very genealogical. Why were the Al-Nuri more scattered than the other subgroups? If genealogy had been followed strictly, Al-Nuri should have been encamped far closer together. At this micro-level, however, the layout was partially determined by a continuing economic and political process. (This is why only parts of each subgroup were here. The others were elsewhere, exploiting different options and expressing different assets.) $B1$ lived a long way out because he was not politically or economically involved in Goum $F5$ at all. He had to live somewhere and was *persona non grata* in Syria at that time. $B2$ lived where he did largely because of the changes brought about by time. When $B2$ built his house, $F5$ had had a far larger retinue of slaves and servants, all of whom had needed to be fairly near $F5$. As their number had declined, so $B2$ appeared to be further away, although the distance was only about 200 metres. The f.b.s. lived closer to Al-Fahad than to $F5$ because his wife came from Al-Fahad. As a whole, Al-Fahad lived equidistant between $F5$ and $B2$ (who were full brothers) because $F5$'s mother came from that group and because his m.b. was his deputy and managed $F5$'s day-to-day business affairs; $F5$ dealt more with policy. Al-Mohammad lived close by because his sister was $F5$'s wife and he was, moreover, a f.b.s. through a uterine link: i.e. $F5$'s father and Al-Mohammad's father were uterine half-brothers.

All the above, except for $B1$, worked as an economic unit. Al-Mishin and Al-Kurdi, who were physically more distant, worked separately or as parts of different networks. They were dependent on $F5$ politically, however. When two of Al-Kurdi retired and moved to H4 the remaining tent moved closer to Al-Mishin, into which an Al-Kurdi sister was married; they also took to working together to some extent.

Interspersed between these tents and houses were groups from other tribes. Between $B2$ and Al-Mohammad was a group from Al-Fwaré tribe. They were involved in a feud and were under $F5$'s protection; as a result they were almost surrounded by Sha'alan. The other group of Fwaré were not involved and so were less enclosed. (Al-Fwaré are a Syrian tribe, predominantly shepherds; parts of them have long been clients of Al-Sha'alan.) The group from Al-Jabal (a mountain tribe) were also originally protection-seekers, but they had stayed on for economic reasons. The *suk* (market) was a totally separate entity in social terms. The traders were nearly all Syrians and non-tribal, together with a few ex-slaves. All were personally under $F5$'s aegis and most had had a long association with the family, in some cases stretching back two or three generations. Scattered among the dwellings of Al-Sha'alan were the tents and houses of servants and ex-slaves. They mostly lived near their employer but some had bought houses, which meant a move, while some had built houses before their employer moved to a different site.

A note on servants and slaves is needed to avoid misconceptions. In 1972-3 the vast majority of servants were Syrian nationals and non-tribal. Practically all of them had been involved in a killing in defence of honour. Rather than spend some years in prison while compensation was sorted out they preferred to slip over the border and work as servants for Al-Sha'alan and others. They were a very fluid population. Ex-slaves are more difficult to explain adequately: 95% are of black African origin, and there is a sprinkling of Kurds, Armenians and Arabs. They were technically freed some time after the First World War by the British and French mandate authorities, but their status was uncertain when they moved, with or without owners, to Saudi Arabia, where slavery was not abolished until 1956. The first essential, as far as Rwala slaves are concerned, is to rid the mind of preconceptions. 'Slave' in this book denotes a social category and very little else. A slave, then as now, was a member of the tribe and although he was owned he could not be given away or sold against his will. The majority were household servants, bodyguards or companions, and like any other member of a household they were entitled to food, clothing, shelter, protection and gifts. They could own property and trade on their own account and were fully protected by the laws of blood-feud, even against their owners. Many rose to eminence and positions of great influence – for instance one of the governors of Jauf under Al-Sha'alan was a slave – and

Plate 1. Slave girl making bread

several became managers of their owners' agricultural holdings. The main differences between a slave and a free man was that the slave had no honour of his own except among other slaves. He only reflected the honour of his owner and it was because he had no honour that he was unable to marry a free Bedu girl. Equally no free Bedu could marry a slave girl nor, among the Rwala, could a slave concubine be taken; to do so was (and is) to demonstrate that self-gratification comes before honour. Those Bedu families who countenance this practice are despised on that account. Nowadays slaves are free and, in law, equal; they still have no honour and they have lost much of the reflected honour and the protection of the past. Their behaviour towards their former owners is still much the same as it always has been.

To return to Goum *F*5, this group of relations, clients and dependants (some thirty-five households in all) by no means comprised the whole of the goum, for there were four other separate encampments in the vicinity. (See Figure 2.) Immediately to the west was a large but fluctuating group from the Frejje. This group was divided into smaller subgroups seen, on the ground, as discrete clusters of tents, sometimes three, sometimes four. The two largest of these subgroups were again divided into micro-groups. All these groupings were based on the degree of genealogical closeness to each other. Group *A* was comprised of two micro-groups *a* and *b*; so was group *C. Aa* and *Ab* were physically separated, but by a smaller distance than that which separated them from group *B*; *Aa* and *Ab* were more closely related to each other than either were to group *B*. At various times

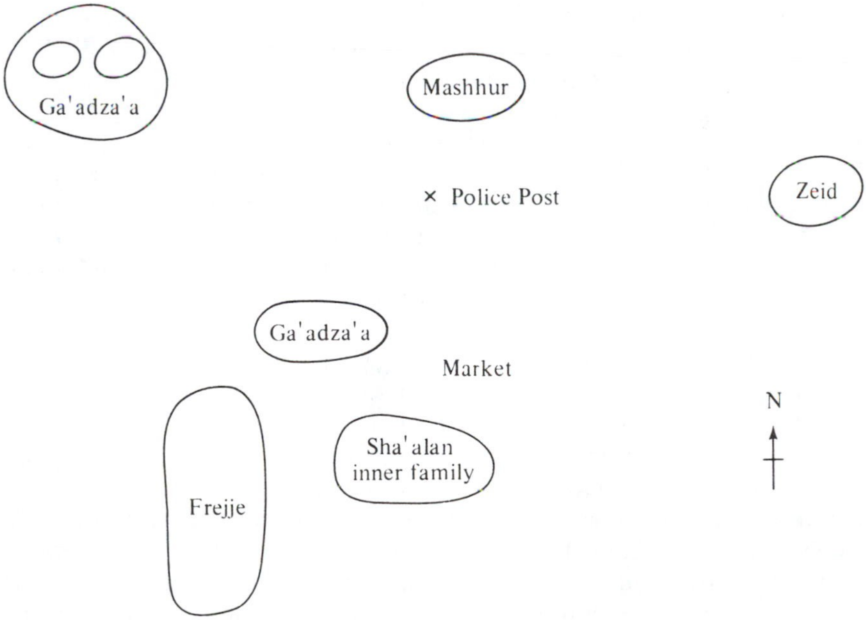

Figure 2. Goum *F*5

many of these groups contained tents of non-group members who, however, were more closely related to their 'hosts' than to any other group. Again it must be emphasised that no group ever contained all its members; each group had close relations who were not part of Goum *F5* and led totally separate economic lives in other areas.

North-west of the Frejje tents was an encampment of Ga'adza'a. Not so large as the Frejje, this comprised only two subgroups. A third subgroup lived close to the *suk*. This was for convenience as, for some reason, nearly all the young men were working elsewhere, so grandparents, who couldn't drive, needed to be near the shops and the children needed to be within walking distance of the school. A lone family from the Doghman camped with the Ga'adza'a – I never discovered exactly why.

Some 3 km north of *F5*'s tent was a group of three tents on their own. These belonged to three families of Al-Mashhur section of the Sha'alan. Genealogically the Mashhur are the most distant group of the Sha'alan to be acknowledged as such. In detail, this little encampment consisted of an elderly man, his b.s. and a rather distant cousin for whom the former were his closest relations at Goum *F5*.

North-east of the *suk* was another small group of tents, sometimes two, sometimes three or more. These were part of Al-Zeid, a group of Sha'alan cousins more distant than the Kurdi or the Mishhin, but closer than the Mashhur.

The Kwatzbe tribal section had no representatives, nor, apart from the Sha'alan, did the Murath.

The number of tents and individuals fluctuated wildly but the number of families economically involved with Goum *F5* was usually around 500 in 1972. In the summer this number swelled in some years by 3000 or more, as herders came in for water.

From its inception in 1962, Goum *F5* was geared to smuggling. Over the years the continuing rapprochement between Syria and Jordan, particularly in the mid-1970s, has made smuggling a more politically sensitive occupation and the growing determination of the Syrian government to stamp it out has made it more hazardous. Initially a retaliation by the Sha'alan for the sequestration of their land by the Ba'athists, and intended to provide themselves with an alternative source of income, it has now become an activity organised by *F5* for those tribesmen who prefer the danger, excitement and profits of smuggling to other more pedestrian occupations. It is now just one option among many and as an asset the smuggling is seen by some as distinctly double-edged.

This spatial arrangement in accordance with genealogical relationships is not confined to temporary tented encampments. At Sweir, a new agricultural settlement, the same feature is apparent. Since I have known it, Sweir has grown from 40 to 400 households. Initially a settlement of tents, it is now predominantly houses, all inhabited by members of the Ga'adza'a. Each subgroup within the section has its own 'quarter', separated from the next subgroup by an empty space. If the increase continues, these spaces are going to be filled up and the genealogical precision is going to deteriorate as families move or sell their property. What will happen then no one seems to know. Formally it will have no effect whatever, as relationships remain irrespective of dwelling-patterns, but in practical terms there might be a reduction of solidarity simply because the women and children will find it more difficult to visit each other. Even in 'encampments' that are tribally mixed the same pattern is apparent. At military camps, for example, all members of the Rwala will be together and the Rwala will stay closer to members of the Fed'an tribe (who are also Aneze) than to members of the Shammar or Ateiba. On the outskirts of larger towns and cities it is the same story; the original tented suburb, the subsequent shanty-town and then the new quarter will be inhabited by members of one tribe subdivided by section into streets or groups of houses on a strictly genealogical basis.

The system only starts to break down when those with sufficient means move into a richer part of a town or city. Close relations may not have the money to move too or there may not be a house available. What will happen to family or tribal solidarity under these circumstances it is too early to say.

(c) Assets and options

Having considered the spatial arrangement of the social environment, the next step is to see how an encampment works. The example taken is a rather extreme one but it highlights many principles. It also illustrates other aspects of Bedu life, which are examined later, for example the function of the sheikh.

Goum $F5$ is not the only goum in the area. Just outside H4 is the goum of $T1$ and an hour's drive north-east, right on the Syrian border, is the goum of $B6$, a half-brother to $F5$. $T1$ is a cousin of $F5$ and the senior (and most influential) member of Al-Sattam group of the Sha'alan. $T1$ had originally settled there in about 1934 when he was employed by the Iraq Petroleum Company to guard their new pipeline and its personnel against marauding Bedu, principally $T1$ himself. In 1948 the pipline ceased to operate (its outlet was Haifa) and $T1$ became redundant. He had by this time built himself a house, dug a well and started a small market garden. He may already have started smuggling but he now extended his operations. In particular he became involved in the traditional hashish trade to Egypt, for the creation of Israel had forced the route inland. In 1962-3 came the exodus of the newly destitute Sha'alan from Syria, who settled just north of $T1$, intent on making a protest against the Ba'ath regime and a living at the same time. $T1$'s reaction was miscalculated; fearing that they were trying to take over his own particular lines he did all he could to stop them, but without success. In 1967 $T1$ suffered a setback for, with the renewal of the Arab–Israeli war and Egypt's loss of Sinai, the direct land

link to Egypt was severed and the hashish trade greatly reduced in consequence. By this time *T*1 had *B*5 and *B*6 working for him as well as *F*5's
brother-in-law from the Mohammad. *B*5 and *B*6 were full brothers and z.s.
to *T*1 while the Mohammad man was *T*1's f.b.d.s. who soon married *T*1's
daughter. The following year (1968) *T*1 suffered another reverse when a
convoy of hashish was surprised in Syria by a Customs patrol. In the
ensuing gun battle *T*1's eldest son was killed and *B*5 badly wounded,
although he managed to escape back into Lebanon. When *B*5 recovered he
decided that hashish smuggling was becoming too dangerous and politically difficult, so he asked his m.b. for his accumulated profits. *T*1 refused,
saying that the brothers had worked for pay only. Aware that in a previous
argument of this nature *T*1 had shot and killed three of his own f.b.s., *B*5
and *B*6 cut their losses and set up their own goum, Goum *B*6 as it is now.
They left hashish firmly alone and concentrated on smuggling cigarettes
and luxury goods into Syria. This led to an argument, though not immediately. Originally Jordan had cordially disliked the Ba'ath and had
happily turned a blind eye to the Sha'alan's activities. While this continued and while the borders were wide open, the two goums of *F*5 and
*B*6 did not compete and there was plenty of profit for all. As soon as the
Jordanian government started to crack down on the free transit of goods
from Saudi to Syria a considerable problem arose. The original arrangement had been made between the authorities and another brother who
had since left: who was to take over the franchise? *F*5 claimed that he had
taken over the original goum and had thus inherited the franchise. *B*6
claimed that as his brother *B*5's representative he was the senior member,
as *B*6 was older than *F*5. What it really came down to was, who was to be
recognised as the Emir's deputy in Jordan? *T*1, who might have seemed
the obvious candidate in terms of age and length of residence (as well as
wealth and personal prestige), had fatally weakened his position during the
civil war of 1970-1 by sitting on the fence while the rest of the Sha'alan
had openly supported King Hussein – not just in words but to the tune of
over a thousand fully equipped fighting men.

None of this was known to me when we arrived except for vague
rumours that *F*5 and *B*6 weren't on speaking terms. It soon turned out
that these rumours were only a pale reflection of the truth. No Sha'alan
member of Goum *F*5 (with one exception) ever visited Goum *T*1 or Goum
*B*6; nor did any Sha'alan member from the latter two ever visit Goum *F*5.
Very occasionally *F*5 and *B*6 would meet at a predetermined time and
place with an equal number of armed retainers. (What went on at these
meetings, which were concealed from me, I never discovered.) Why did
most Sha'alan back *F*5? Why had the split developed in the way it did?
The unequal sizes of the goums had nothing to do with it; this was an
internal family squabble and no one else would interfere. In fact ordinary
tribesmen continued to visit all three goums freely. The answer lay in a
close analysis of the participants' personal genealogical relationships using
bilateral and affinal links, i.e. their genealogical assets and options. On

normal patrilineal grounds the struggle was between half-brothers, so other members of the Sha'alan all had equal links with both sides and thus should have been neutral. But they were not: the majority backed $F5$, so the differentiation could only lie in their matrilineal and/or affinal links.

Taking Goum $F5$ first, $F5$ had the backing of his full brother $B2$, his f.b.s., the representatives of the Kurdi, the Mohammad and the Mishhin, as well as his mother's family, the Fahad. He also had the tacit backing of his elder half-brothers $B1$, $B3$ and $B4$. The reason for their support cannot have been that $F5$ would have made a better deputy than $B6$; if anything the opposite would be true – $F5$ was impetuous, rash and overfond of the dramatic gesture: $B6$ was cautious, respectable and diplomatic. That $F5$ should be supported by his full brother seems reasonable, but why should all the other half-brothers join him, at least on the diplomatic front? ($B5$ and $B6$ were supported by their full brothers $B7$ and $B8$, but as they were high-school students in America throughout they don't enter into it.) $F5$'s wife comes from the Mohammad and two of her full sisters are married to $B3$ and $B4$. Another full sister is married to $F5$'s m.b. from the Fahad. His f.b.s. is married to $F5$'s m.z. from the Fahad, as is $B1$. The preferential links of the Mohammad and the Fahad are fairly clear. The representatives of the Mishhin are full brothers whose mother comes from the Fahad as well, $F5$'s m.f.z. All the affinal and matrilineal links of the Kurdi are towards those who supported $F5$.

As for $B6$, his support came only from his full brother, $B5$, and from $T1$, his m.b. This is the crux – of all the brothers only $B5$ and $B6$ had close links with $T1$ and his brothers. The only counter-weight to the closely-knit supporters of $F5$ was the wife of $T1$, who was full sister to $B2$. None of the Kurdi, the Fahad or the Mishhin had any extant links with Al-Trad ($T1$'s part of the Sattam Sha'alan) other than the formal patrilineal ones – nor did any of their former links produce offspring. Nor did $B5$ and $B6$ pick up any support through their marriages; they married uterine half-sisters from Al-Khalid (the other group from the Sattam Sha'alan). The Khalid are f.b. children to $T1$, but since the feud between them, mentioned previously, the relationship between them has been strained and their support for $T1$, and therefore for $B5$ and $B6$, has been lukewarm. Any support that they might have given was offset when $B2$ married another girl from the Khalid, a half-sister to $B6$'s wife.

One figure who doesn't fit neatly into the picture is the representative of the Mohammad. His sisters were all married to supporters of $F5$; he himself was married to $T1$'s daughter and his mother came from the Khalid. This man supported $F5$ (they were great personal friends from childhood) but his structural position was equivocal. He was the only man who could move freely between the three goums and he was instrumental in effecting a settlement – he acted as go-between.

This quarrel is all water under the bridge by now. $F5$ won in the end, or perhaps it would be truer to say that $B6$ decided that he had more profitable options elsewhere and so changed course. The split is covered over now but it is still there and it plays a large part in working out where children in the next generation are going to marry – a constant topic among the women. The interest in the whole episode lies in the way that the matrilineal, matrilateral and affinal links were used as assets by the protagonists in gathering support. *F*5 had greater assets than *B*6 and so opinion swung in his favour. There is no evidence that anyone thought he would make a better deputy for the Emir, it was just that the job was an option open to him in preference to *B*6. He had the assets to exploit it: *B*6 hadn't.

While this is a rather dramatic and, perhaps, atypical example of assets and options at work, other situations can be analysed in the same way.

The development of Nathaiyyim is a case in point. In 1973 Nathaiyyim was just a valley, similar to hundreds of others, with a little pocket of poor soil surrounded by rocky outcrops and sand-dunes. There was no water, it was on no through route, it was just a name. The first question is why did Freiwan al-Mu'abhil decide to settle at all? And, secondly, why there? After the drought of 1958–62 he was left with eleven camels in very poor condition, none in milk and none pregnant; two more died soon after. This was below what is reckoned to be a viable subsistence herd, especially as they were in such poor condition. It would have taken at least three years before the herd even approached viability so Freiwan decided to switch to sheep. With their far higher breeding-rate and the fact that they were relatively cheap at the time sheep made a better option. After a few years, however, Freiwan lost an asset – labour. He was by now well into his seventies and not really up to taking the sheep out to graze every day in all weathers. His sons were all gainfully employed in what looked, at that time, like good jobs with prospects. One was in the border police, one a trained welder with Trans-Arabia Pipeline (T.A.P.-line), a third in the National Guard and the fourth a trainee electrician with T.A.P.-line. A job with this company was a good option then, and it wasn't till the Lebanese civil war and the closing down of the pipeline's outlet at Sidon that people realised how vulnerable it was. Freiwan's elder daughters had just married and his younger children were too young to do the herding. Also the grazing, after a few reasonable years, declined as more people took up the same option. Trucking the sheep further out was a possibility but he could not drive and again his sons were unavailable. By 1971 he was living in his tent at Kassara (a new settlement that had grown up around the police post on the new road) with his wife and his younger children. His sheep were being herded for him by a cousin who had a truck. The eldest son, now in his forties, left the police and decided, with the new emphasis on agricultural development, to take up land and farm. He persuaded his father to do likewise. Nathaiyyim was chosen because the soil seemed suitable; it was far enough off the road to be undisturbed, yet near enough to be convenient. It was also quite near Sakaka, the administrative capital of Jauf district, where Freiwan's wife had settled relatives (her mother came from the Muwaishir family who have a certain standing in the district), and she owned, through them, some land there. A further factor was

Plate 2. Sheikh Freiwan ibn Freih Al-Mu'abhil Al-Sha'alan

that historically the valley 'belonged' to the Mu'abhil, although the basis of this claim was far from clear. The son got the government to drill him a well, obtained a soft loan from the development bank and a peasant, on a sharecropping basis, from Syria and started his farm. Freiwan followed suit next year.

It is always difficult to determine motives with any precision but this case is tolerably clear – Freiwan's assets and options were very limited and given that he didn't want to retire, settlement at Nathaiyyim with the developmental climate in Saudi Arabia at the time seemed his best bet. The first time my family went to Nathaiyyim, the encampment (for there were no houses yet) consisted of Freiwan, his eldest son, a group of Zuwaiyyid Nseir tents, three Doghman, one Ga'adza'a and a few from the Hawazim tribe. What constrained them to join Freiwan? The Hawazim were simply there for the water and soon moved on. The Doghman should have been at Gara, an oasis just south of Sakaka with an exclusively Doghman population, but they were at feud with someone there; Nathaiyyim was just physically convenient. The Ga'adza'i was there for a similar reason; he had a job in Sakaka but wanted to be near his relatives at Sweir; Nathaiyyim was between the two in terms of time. He soon moved to Sweir when a road was built to it. The Zuwaiyyid Nseir contingent consisted of three brothers, the son-in-law of one of them and a cousin who was, although a contemporary, also a son-in-law to one of the brothers as well as being related in several other ways. The three brothers were really passing through, although they stayed for some months. The eldest herded camels (with his son-in-law and his son), the second herded sheep with a hired herder, while the third tagged along not doing much as he was nearly blind. The cousin had no herds; he had a job in Kassara. Apart from its convenient location, these Zuwaiyyid Nseir had come to Nathaiyyim because Freiwan was the most closely related Murathi (their tribal section) in the immediate area. Freiwan's stepmother had been their f.z. and he was thus well known to them. This was their stated reason for choosing Nathaiyyim in preference to any other well or embryo settlement and I have no reason to doubt it. They quite clearly saw the marriage link as an asset that could be exploited.

This sort of asset became even more obvious the next time we stayed at Nathaiyyim some three years later. Only Freiwan and his eldest son remained of the original inhabitants. The Zuwaiyyid Nseir, some of whom had been thinking of settling there permanently, had left, owing to a row over the allocation of land. I never managed to acquire an even faintly unbiased account of this and it was a rather touchy point. The most plausible explanation was that several other families more closely related to the Mu'abhil had also wanted to settle and that there hadn't been enough land for all; but this wasn't the whole story. Be that as it may, Nathaiyyim now consisted of some twenty-two tents; thirteen from the Sabte, five from the Jabr and four from the Mu'abhil, as well as Freiwan and his son. All these groups are subgroups of the Muwasserin (but see pp. 26-8).

The Sabte tents were divided into two subgroups, one called the Fuweiris Sabte, the other the Firhan Sabte, Fuweiris and Firhan being brothers some four generations ago. Freiwan's wife comes from a branch of the Fuweiris Sabte and his son is married to a woman from the same branch, while one of his daughters is married into a collateral branch. The two branches of the Fuweiris and Firhan Sabte are not only closely related in the male line but also extensively intermarried and thus closely related in the female line as well. In fact for most purposes they are regarded as one group and I have broken them up for analytical reasons. Both these branches of the Sabte are comprehensively intermarried with another section of the Muwasserin, the Jabr. At least three groups of the Jabr were represented at Nathaiyyim and they all had close, patrilineal links to another Jabr group in Sakaka, where their senior member was a man of some influence. It must not be thought that the entire group of the Mu'abhil or the Sabte or the Jabr were at Nathaiyyim; each group was only a subgroup and there were other Mu'abhil, Sabte and Jabr elsewhere. Apart from these multiple links through women, nearly all the families at Nathaiyyim (except Freiwan and his eldest son) herded or transported sheep or both; that is to say the sons of those encamped permanently did the work, reappearing from time to time. The co-operation in these activities was extensive, with trucks, tankers and personnel being borrowed and loaned. This co-operation was by no means exclusively along patrilines; a record of who co-operated with whom would not reveal much differentiation in co-operation rates. While the reason for the choice of Nathaiyyim may well have been economic, the reason given to me was always 'because we are very close' (genealogically). When it was pointed out that the patriline of the Jabr were not particularly closely related to the Mu'abhil the riposte was a long list of marriages that, although often at several removes from the participants, showed that the two groups had preferential links through women, at least to account for their presence to their own satisfaction. It must not be supposed that these links were the only links any group had that might secure them preferential treatment: they undoubtedly were not. Their importance lay in the fact that they were the operative links that allowed them to be at Nathaiyyim. In the case of the two groups of Sabte, marriage links probably did account for their presence at Nathaiyyim. It may also have accounted for the Jabr, except that it was their links to the Sabte, not the Mu'abhil, that had decided them to stop there, even though their explanation was couched in terms of links to the Mu'abhil. This supposition is strengthened by the fact that there was another group of Jabr only 3 km distant at another small encampment. In theory both groups of Jabr should have camped together but each separate group had preferential links through women to the other inhabitants of the two encampments. Jural responsibility for a woman lies with her natal family throughout her life and emotional ties between brother and sister are stronger than those between husband and wife. So wishing to be near a sibling is often the real reason that a choice of encampment is made: however, as most people have several siblings, as do their spouses, the choice may well be economic but couched in relationship terms, even though those relationship terms may extend well beyond the patriline. Friendship, and still less economic considerations, are rarely sufficient grounds on which to base co-operation or agglomeration and straight patrilineal relationships do not give a very wide variety of choice, but relationships through women cut across patrilines and markedly extend economic or political options. Each relationship is thus an asset that can be used to legitimise an economic choice.

This use of 'assets and options' as an analytical tool was forced on me by the evidence. Early attempts to determine why certain people lived closer or co-operated preferentially always broke down over the reason given and its discrepancy with genealogical fact. The usual explanation was 'because we are *ibn amm*' – that is f.b.s. in either an actual or a classificatory sense; but so widely is the term used that it could be applied to any Rweli, any Bedu or even any human being. Inquiring into the definition of *ibn amm* often showed that while two men might well belong to the same patriline, they often did not. Nor did such an inquiry account for the observed fact that others more closely or more distantly related to them also camped or co-operated with them. The example of the competition between the Sha'alan brothers showed that links through women mattered and the composition of camping- or herding-groups showed that this practice was not confined to the sheikhly family. However, it also became clear that there was no pattern of prescribed links through women either. Links through a m.b or a f.z. crop up slightly more frequently than others but not markedly so and certainly not to the exclusion of other links. Links through stepmothers, sisters or daughters are commonly given. The only exception to this general rule is that uterine brothers with different fathers are regarded as being peculiarly close, although proximity or co-operation by no means always follows such a relationship. I attempted to classify degrees of relationship but the task had to be abandoned. How do you correlate a f.z.d. step-m.b. as against a m.½b.d.h.b.? Which is closer? It proved impossible to determine, especially when the close intermeshing of families became apparent. Any man or woman has a myriad of relations if any of these sorts of links are followed through and in all probability there are several or even many pathways that can link two co-operating individuals together. The multiplicity of pathways is very striking in the sheikhly family and fairly impressive elsewhere. Obviously in practical terms most co-operation takes place between members of the same named patrilineal group, for they have more, and closer, links to each other than to any other group but many links cross patrilineal group, tribal section or even tribal lines. The Zuwaiyyid Nseir have links through women to the Wald Suleiman and the Beni Sakhr; the latter are not even an Aneze tribe. The Mu'abhil have similar links to the Wald Ali, the Swalme and the Shammar tribes. The Jabr have a link to the Amarat. These links are all known and are kept up, sometimes, after a lapse of time by another marriage. There are almost certainly others unknown to me that could easily be resurrected if the need arose. It is impossible to classify such relationships as other than assets, for this is how they are used. Involvement in a feud, for example, might make removal to a distance advantageous, so you go on a visit to your m.z.s. who is from another tribe. Or your m.f.f.b.s.d.s. might be in a position to get you a job, so you go to visit him. (This is a true instance although the man was also f.f.b.s.s. to his visitor – the other link went through another tribe and gave the visitor a preferential link over all his other cousins who had the same f.f.b.s.s. relationship.) Each relationship opens up an option that may be peculiar to the individual *vis-à-vis* his patrilineal group. Equally, an individual's asset may be exploitable by his group as a whole, as in the case of the Sabte who used the marriage links of one branch to rationalise their settling in Nathaiyyim.

Choice is not determined by the institution of the patrilineal genealogy, although it will probably be used to 'explain' the choice to an outsider. A closer look at the 'explanation' reveals its weakness and a closer look at micro-reality shows that practical considerations lead to the use of all sorts of relationships, which are seen and used as assets giving access to a wider variety of options than would otherwise have been the case.

3 The Bedu System — the Generative Genealogy

The Rwala view the system in which they operate as being made up of groups ultimately descended in the male line from a common ancestor. At its widest, of course, this system gives rise to a fundamentalist belief in Adam and Eve and the Brotherhood of Man. That they are aware of these implications is demonstrated by men who wish to remain anonymous stating that they come from the *Beni Adam*, i.e. the human race. A man concealing his identity in this way is automatically suspected of the deepest treachery, but no one denies his humanity and he is still entitled to the standard hospitality for any unknown guest. On the whole the Rwala don't concern themselves much with the larger distinctions of race or colour, contenting themselves with their interaction within the Arab world. For them Arabs are divided into two categories, Bedu and non-Bedu. In general, non-Bedu are seen as further away genealogically although nobody bothers about the exact relationship. All other Bedu are considered closer, but again the exact genealogical relationship is ignored beyond the confederation level; for the Rwala this is the Aneze confederation of tribes. Interaction with non-Aneze tribes was, in the past, limited to hostilities with the powerful, like the Shammar or Beni Sakhr, or potential or actual clientship with lesser tribes like the Fwaré or the Umur; other, more distant, tribes with whom they may now interact are in a sort of limbo. For practical, everyday purposes the only supra-tribal grouping that is recognised is the confederation and this is thought of in genealogical terms. The Rwala position themselves as in Figure 3.

The descendants of Ma'az are unknown. The only time I heard this 'explained' was to account for a man from the Harb tribe who was living with them at the time. The Harb were said to be descended from Ma'az, an assertion that surprised the Harb man although he didn't deny it. None of the names represent real people: they are specifically the names of groups. Thus Rweli and Mislim are groups that make up the Zayyid group, they are not two brothers whose father was Zayyid. One man claimed that the name Rwala came from an old arabic word, *rowol*, meaning a collective or 'gathering-up'. I have been unable to trace this word further, but it is undeniable that *Jlas*, which is the name of the group to which the Rwala belonged before moving north into Syria, is a plural that means 'participants in a social gathering'. It is unlikely that the Rwala actually 'see' the genealogy in this particular form; in fact they probably don't. I have cast it in this form because it is clearly a segmentary system and it is our usual

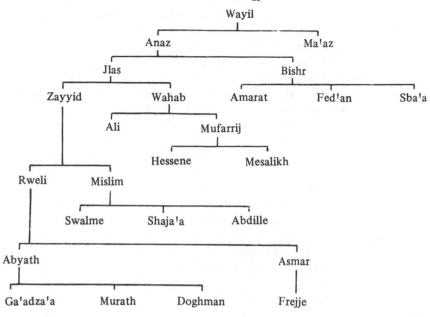

Figure 3. Tribal genealogy of the Rwala

practice to lay it out in this manner. (Cf. chapter 12.) What they care about is that the Fed'an are 'closer' than the Harb, that the Hessene are 'closer' than the Fed'an, that the Swalme are 'closer' than the Hessene and that all the Rwala are 'closer' than the Swalme. Similarly, within the tribe the Murath and the Doghman are closer to each other than they are to any other tribal section because they used to form the Jum'an, but they and the Ga'adza'a are again 'closer' than any of them are to the Frejje. (The Kwatzbe are a special case and are considered later.)

At this level there is a conceptual break. From tribal section upwards the genealogical terminology is figurative only. Murath may be called the son of Abyath but nobody pretends that either Murath or Abyath were real people, nor that there was a father-son relationship between them. Murath is simply the name of one of the groups that makes up the inclusive group of Abyath. Below the level of tribal section there is a gap. The various groups that make up the Murath are descended from Murath in some vague sort of way, probably in a figurative sense, but they are simply seen as groups making up a larger group. No one of the named groups that make up a tribal section is 'closer' to another than to the rest. It is as if Murath had several 'sons' who were the ancestors of the present-day named groups. This is entirely metaphorical and is put in purely as illustration; the Rwala specifically do not see it like this. In practice there is a complete gap at this level. On no occasion did anyone attempt, even as a joke, to invent 'ancestors' to fill in between tribal section and lower groups. This is significant, as it was only at this level that this was observed. Above and below this gap invention was commonplace, motivated by misguided helpfulness or by a desire to have some fun, but never was there an attempt to bridge the gap, even figuratively.

The portions of the genealogy on either side of the gap are different. Tribal section and more inclusive groups are one of the 'givens' of the system. It is possible to alter and manipulate this part of the genealogy but it is difficult and it is a major political act. The portion of the genealogy below tribal section is highly manipulable and entirely pragmatic and is exclusively concerned with actual living groups on the ground. The difference in manipulability above and below the gap is one of degree and the real importance of the gap seems to lie in the concept of equality that it engenders. A named group within a tribal section remains just that; it is simply one of many similar groups and because there is no genealogy there is no possibility of claiming supremacy, primacy or superiority over any other group. The suppression of the genealogy at this point makes all groups on the ground jurally equal. This jural equality is fundamental to the system and is mainly expressed in the allocation of responsibility: each and every named group below the gap is responsible for the behaviour of its own members. This group I refer to as the minimal section or the five-generation 'ibn amm' and it consists of all those descended in the male line from an ancestor five generations distant. (I have, at this point, to use the two terms, for the minimal section is the same as the five-generation *ibn amm* to the outsider, although the minimal section may well be divided internally into several five-generation 'ibn amms' as far as its own members are concerned. This becomes clearer later.) A man from minimal section *A* of the Murath kills someone from minimal section *B* of the Doghman; no one is involved except the members of the two minimal sections. The Murath, as a collective, is not involved nor are all the Doghman. The break in the genealogy ensures that this must be so, for nobody can assert that two minimal sections from the same tribal section belong to the same five-generation 'ibn amm' (the corporate vengeance unit) because by definition the patronymic ancestor, Murath or Doghman, is more than five generations away; he must be, for no one can 'remember' the genealogy between an individual and the ancestor of the tribal section.

Thus, looked at from the outside, each minimal section is discrete and unequivocally belongs to one or other of the tribal sections. This places them in the overall Bedu system. With this position established beyond query the levels of minimal section and below can then be manipulated to fit political or economic reality without threatening the system as a whole. This is possible because the composition of the actual groups on the ground (minimal sections and below) concerns nobody but themselves. These groups can split, subdivide or coalesce as they think best but it will not affect their jural identity as members of the tribal section and thus of the tribe.

This coalescing and splitting can be shown within the Murath. The Sha'alan are one of the minimal sections who make up the Murath. Sha'alan, the patryonymic ancestor, is said to have had several sons as did his eldest son, Gherir. (See Figure 4.) For reasons that needn't be gone into here, the descendants of Fneikh, Jabr, Salim, Suleiman and Daghai'ir opposed the descendants of Gherir and Rothan and became known as the Muwasserin, 'the bound-together'. The Muwasserin did not flourish numerically; the descendants of Mneif, on the other hand flourished mightily and it is from him that the present sheikhly family descend. In fact it is only Mneif's descendants who are now known as the Sha'alan. What has happened to the descendants of Mneif's brothers? They have not increased greatly in number but together with the Muwasserin and the Rothan they make up a group roughly equal in numbers to the Sha'alan. This whole Group (Muwasserin, Rothan and the descendants of Mneif's brothers) is becoming known as 'the Muwasserin' as opposed to the group of the Sha'alan. Within the Muwasserin the old names still survive, i.e. *vis-à-vis* a member of the Sabih, a man is Mu'abhil or Fneikh or Jabr; but *vis-à-vis* the Sha'alan he is simply Muwasserin. This type of coalescence has taken place within the Muwasserin itself. The Sabte are really the descendants of Salim and Suleiman, but the Sabte are never differentiated except by members of the Sabte itself.

It has been possible to see this process because it is fairly slow and its progress can be determined by the attitudes of members of different generations. For Freiwan, the eldest Mu'abhil, aged about seventy-six, the Muwasserin are a discrete group descended from Gherir's brothers only; he, himself, still belongs to the Sha'alan, for this was political reality when he was young. His son, aged about fifty, is uncertain and open-minded, while his grandsons say that they are part of the Muwasserin. Freiwan is a recognised authority on genealogical matters. No one else in the Muwasserin knows the genealogy in such detail or is so passionately interested in it: they know that they are a member of (for example) the Sabte or the Mu'abhil, who are now part of the Muwasserin and, as Muwasserin, are closer to the Sha'alan than any other group. This is, for them, enough: all their economic, political and social life takes place within the Muwasserin or with members of similar groups tied to individual members of the Muwasserin through women. Much of Freiwan's social, political and economic life took place among members of the Sha'alan and his political influence inside the Murath came from this association and his skill as a mediator. This skill depended on, and developed from, an encyclopaedic

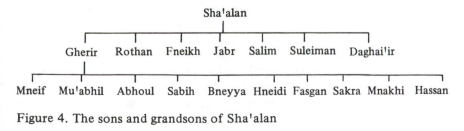

Figure 4. The sons and grandsons of Sha'alan

27

knowledge of political history expressed in genealogical terms. It is perfectly clear that Freiwan's detailed knowledge of the inter-relations between groups is based partly on the known genealogy, but where there are lacunae he 'explains' political reality in genealogical terms, thus completing the genealogy. And there are few who can contradict him. However, even he cannot halt the rationalisation of genealogical reality by the application of pragmatism. Despite his insistence that the Mu'abhil are Sha'alan and not Muwasserin, his grandsons know full well that, despite genealogical evidence, the Mu'abhil are part of the Muwasserin, because that is how they see it working.

Initially the whole genealogical organisation below minimal section appears confused to the inquirer, but it soon becomes apparent that it is merely fluid. To the casual observer the situation is clear and static and most of the Rwala are casual observers. This comes about because each individual knows his own minimal section personally but has no need to know the details of any other minimal section. For instance, for a member of the Muwasserin, it is very simple: so-and-so is from the Muwasserin, someone else is not. Within the Muwasserin some groups are 'closer' to him than others, but he knows this (and so do they) without recourse to the genealogy. To the outsider who bothers to inquire (in practice this is only the anthropologist) the membership and the relationships are in a constant state of flux and the difficulty in understanding them arises simply through the difficulty of explaining an essentially political and/or economic system in genealogical terms. The very terms used are general and imprecise and depend for their exact meaning on the context in which they are used.

There are only four expressions used to explain groups. The largest group to have its own word is the tribe. In fact it has two of the four words - *kabila* and *ashira* - although there seems to be no essential difference between their meanings. *Ashira* is usually used for a larger unit than *kabila*, i.e. the Rwala refer to themselves as an *ashira* more often than as a *kabila*, while a tribal section is sometimes called a *kabila* but never an *ashira*. (There is no word in general use for 'confederation'; the Rwala refer to the Aneze confederation either by name or as 'the tribes of the Aneze'.) The more usual term for the tribal sections is *fakhdh* (plural *fukhudh*), which means, literally, 'thigh'. Sometimes the minimal section is called a *fakhdh* as in 'the *fukhudh* of the Murath', but normally they are called *ibn amm*. Literally *ibn amm* means f.b.s. but it is also used in a classificatory sense as well. (The term *ibn khal*, m.b.s., doesn't concern us here as the genealogy is couched in patrilineal terms only.) So below the level of tribal section there are only two words that can be used to describe groups and of these only *ibn amm* can explain relationships. In fact *ibn amm* is used to explain any relationship in the male line and is therefore highly contextual. (The width of the possible contexts can be gauged by the fact that both World Wars are 'explained' in terms of relationship – the French and the English are *fukhudh* who are *ibn amm* as opposed to the Germans. This gives rise to the belief that the English and the French must be more closely related to the Arabs, their allies, than to the Germans. The fact that the English, French and Germans are all European while the Arabs are not is glossed over in this context and if it is pressed home the result is appalling semantic confusion.) The problem of context is largely confined to the anthropologist, for members of a group will know what context they are talking about and if it is an internal context no member of another group would be taking part anyway. Any companion from another group that I might have with me while I was trying to determine exact relationships within a group, was invariably as muddled as I. For instance the Frejje tribal section (*fakhdh*) is composed of some eleven groups (*fukhudh*). Two of these groups form an intermediate group that is also called a *fakhdh*. The only way to explain the relationship between these groups is to use the word *ibn amm*. The two groups that make up the intermediate group are called the Suwalha and the Sabah, while the intermediate group is the Muharrag, of which the Suwalha and the Sabah are the constituent parts. No other intermediate groups were known to my informants from the Muharrag so they could not determine whether all the other groups were at the level of the Muharrag or at the lower level of the Suwalha and the Sabah. Greater clarity could only be achieved by determining jural responsibility in terms of actual named groups and actual named people with their genealogies within each group. This made it clear that minimal section and five-generation 'ibn amm' were not, in many cases, the same. A minimal section might consist of two or more five-generation 'ibn amms' or the two levels might coincide.

It is at this point that any analysis based on the concept of 'institution' breaks down. A Rweli will say, talking in general terms, that the minimal section is the smallest corporate group and it is the minimal section that is jurally responsible for its members. He will, if pressed for details, say that the minimal section is the same as the *khamseh*, the vengeance unit descended from a common ancestor five generations back, although *khamseh* is not a term that they themselves use. In the example above, for instance, Muharrag was not the jurally responsible group, the Sabah or the Suwalha were, although the founding ancestors, Sabah and Suwalha, were in fact more than five generations distant. Further probing revealed that, although Sabah and Suwalha were conceived of as the founding ancestors, and were so regarded by outsiders, the two groups were actually further subdivided in terms of vengeance if a killing took place. In other words there are at least two conceptual levels of jural responsibility operating at the same time, depending on the context. In the case of a killing (the most usual case of jural responsibility), say by a member of the Sabah, there are two contexts; the context of the bereaved group, who only know that the Sabah killed one of their members, and the context of the Sabah who know that only part of the Sabah are responsible, for the group is composed of two subgroups, closely related but with founding ancestors of five generations back who are not identical.

Both these conceptual levels are defined in terms of *ibn amm*. The first level is the formal genealogical minimal section, which is institutionally (and theoretically) the smallest corporate group and is so described to outsiders. The second level is the vengeance group, which may or may not have a name, but is the actual group that is jurally responsible for its members. This latter group I refer to as the five-generation 'ibn amm'. In later illustrations I give a name to these five-generation 'ibn amms', taken from their founding ancestor (real or fictional) five generations ago: this is for clarity only as the Rwala do not necessarily use these names themselves. For outsiders the minimal-section name is sufficient, while members of the group concerned know who they are talking about without the need for an identifying group name. The formal nature of the minimal sections is clearly shown by a consideration of the lists of them compiled by Musil (see Appendix 2) in 1914. Lists that I collected in 1973 are almost identical although at least two generations separate them. If Musil's groups were minimal sections as well as five-generation 'ibn amms', i.e. if the two levels coincided at that date, it is obvious that mine cannot. Despite this, and this was discussed with the Rwala, the Rwala claim that the lists I collected were the smallest corporate groups that were jurally responsible for their members.

To understand how the system works (as opposed to how it is said to work) it is necessary to follow Bedu practice and start from ego and work upwards. I have taken, as an example, a part of the minimal section of the Nseir, who are one of the minimal sections that make up the Murath tribal section. I take this group in preference to the Sha'alan because the formal genealogy of the Sha'alan is known in detail whereas the genealogy of the Nseir is not. The Nseir can thus be analysed for the process that is taking place. It would be possible to do this for the Sha'alan but as they use both conceptual levels at once, depending on their immediate aim, the analysis becomes extremely complicated and very difficult to comprehend.

The minimal section of the Nseir is divided into a number of five-generation 'ibn amms'. Each five-generation 'ibn amm' is again subdivided into a number of three-generation 'ibn amms'. These latter have no names and are really economic units whose members co-operate very closely with each other. They tend to be brothers or patrilateral parallel cousins plus their descendants; they are not the corporate group that makes up the jurally responsible group (that is, the five-generation 'ibn amm'). (I do not use the word 'lineage' for any group for a number of reasons. To call a minimal section a minimal lineage would be misleading, for a minimal section is a discrete group of actual people who cannot trace a complete patriline to the tribal section; they just know that they are part of that tribal section. To call an 'ibn amm' (five- or three-generation) a lineage would be equally misleading for, as will be shown as the analysis proceeds, an 'ibn amm' can be formed in a number of ways, of which direct descent in the male line is just one. Over and above these objections, the word 'lineage' is often qualified by 'senior' or 'junior'. This runs totally counter to the Bedu concept that all minimal sections are equal and all five-generation 'ibn amms' are equal irrespective of size or the actual details of their genealogy.)

The five-generation 'ibn amm' under consideration is called the Zuwaiyyid Nseir to distinguish it from other five-generation 'ibn amms' also belonging to the Nseir. This group is divided into five three-generation 'ibn amms' that have no names, although for ease of identification I give them qualifying names drawn from their real or supposed founding ancestor. Three of these three-generation 'ibn amms' are in the process of coalescing. Their actual genealogy, in so far as it is known, is shown in Figure 5.

Turub, Khizmi, Khazzaiyyim, Shaja' and Fa'iz were real people and it is assumed that they were the sons of Zayyid, although Fa'iz probably wasn't. Each is the founding ancestor of a three-generation 'ibn amm'. We are concerned with the descendants of Turub, Khazzaiyyim and Fa'iz; the descendants of Khizmi and Shaja' rarely interact with those under consideration and I never to my knowledge met any of them. The Turub (my convenience name for the descendants of Turub) are numerically weak and consist only of Ayyish and Hneittir. The Fa'iz are fairly weak too, there being only five adult males (Freij may be dead; no one was certain). The Khazzaiyyim are not much better off. At a slightly earlier date, of course, all three groups were weaker still, as the present generation, who are all young, didn't exist. When these three groups were all herding, three or four years ago, they worked as a herding unit. Each adult male had his own herd and tent but they worked co-operatively. This co-operation was fostered by intermarriage – a decisive act that almost entirely excluded the Khizmi and the Shaja'. The earliest of these marriages seems to have been between Bghaiyyith and the daughter of Thahir ibn Fa'iz. Judging by the age of the eldest son (Fedghash) this must have been about sixty years ago. Since then there has been a whole series of intermarriages. Ayyid ibn Fedghash is married to the daughter of Ayyish of the Turub; Hneittir ibn ibn Maram is married to a daughter of Fedghash; Mlih is married to the daughter of Adda ibn Thahir; Sayyil ibn Nazil is married to a daughter of Al-Asmar ibn Adda; Al-Asmar is married to a daughter of Nazil; Shallah ibn Adda is married to the daughter of Fedghash; Adda ibn Thahir was

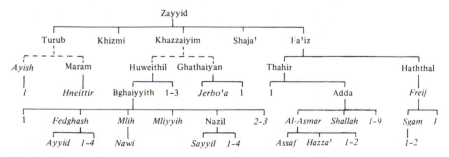

Figure 5. Genealogy of the Zuwaiyyid Nseir. The names of those who are still living are italicised.

married to the daughter of Freij ibn Haththal. Freij was married to a daughter of Huweithil. This is not the sum of the marriages but they are far and away the most intermeshed series. There are a few marriages to other groups from the Zuwaiyyid Nseir; for instance Sgam ibn Freij and the children of Ghathaiyyim are married into other three-generation 'ibn amms' of the Zuwaiyyid Nseir. The names of the groups into which these latter were married are the Firhan and the Dweirij. However, no one could fit these marriages into the Khizmi or the Shaja', though presumably it must be these groups that are involved. Firhan may be a five-generation 'ibn amm' like the Zuwaiyyid, while nobody knew who the Dweirij were at all.

Three factors emerge from this welter of facts and doubts. First, no one knows more than their own three-generation 'ibn amm', and those with whom they intermarry extensively, in any great detail; secondly, relationships between three-generation 'ibn amms' are not necessarily dependent on the genealogy (i.e. there is no genealogical reason why the Khizmi and the Shaja' were excluded); thirdly, the mechanism for organising the relationships between the groups is intermarriage. The genealogy is part truth, part fiction, for there is no reason why these three-generation 'ibn amms' should intermarry more frequently with each other than with either of the other two apart from personal preference and, probably, proximity. In fact Khizimi and Khazzaiyyim were almost certainly full brothers, as the one name is the diminutive of the other (a common practice) and it is acknowledged that Fa'iz probably wasn't a brother to the others at all. Yet Khizmi's descendants are excluded from marriage while Fa'iz's are welded in. On the other hand the working patterns show, through preferential co-operation, that the Turub, the Fa'iz and the Khazzaiyyyim are very closely related indeed; they 'must be' because they co-operate. Conversely, those three-generation 'ibn amms' that don't co-operate closely can't be as closely related. This argument is then clinched by the statement: 'We must be more closely related because we intermarry more frequently' and it is well known that the Bedu always marry their *ibn amm*. Within these three three-generation 'ibn amms' the process is not yet complete, but it is easy to see that Turub and Fa'iz will 'become' sons of Khazziyyim (or some other combination) and Zayyid will disappear because the pattern of marriage will show the sonship of Turub and Fa'iz to be true. The important group is the actual working, living and inter-marrying group on the ground, whether it is the minimal section, the five- or three-generation 'ibn amm' or any composite of parts of these groups. The more distant genealogical relationships are largely forgotten and so the genealogy can be reordered to fit pragmatic reality. This reality is then 'explained' in genealogical terms and 'proved' by hindsight.

This type of proof (which I call the 'must-have-been' argument) is clearly shown by the rumours of my parentage to which I referred earlier. Because I was on familiar and familial terms with the sheikhs I 'must have been' their brother or I wouldn't have been able to behave as I did. It was even more apparent at Nathaiyyim. Because my wife visited and was visited by Freiwan's wife they 'must have been' closely related, for only close relations visit at all frequently. As Freiwan also visited my wife in my absence and I, similarly, visited his, the relationship must be such that we were all close to that degree of consanguinity that disallows intermarriage. The exact relationship was never formulated but it was proved by our behaviour and this was the only acceptable explanation.

There are other instances of this sort of genealogical realignment. Among the Sha'alan the process is more difficult because the formal, real genealogy is known for some fifteen generations, but there is one simple instance that springs to mind. It was frustrated by my asking awkward questions, but probably only temporarily. Figure 6 shows the relevant part of the genealogy.

The present sheikhs are descended from Hazza'; the Trad and the Khalid are descended from Hamad and the Bender are descended from Faysal. Hazza', Hamad and Faysal were all brothers. The Zeid and the Mijwal are descended from Zeid and Mijwal, the f.bs. of Hamad, Hazza' and Faysal. All these named groups, i.e. the Hazza', the Hamad, the Bender, the Zeid and the Mijwal, are roughly five-generation 'ibn amms'. In real life the Bender were the odd ones out, for they didn't interact with the others at all. Nobody mentioned them and it was a long time before I met any of them. All the others I knew well, including the Mashhur, who were descended from Abdullah's brother, and therefore further away genealogically. But no member of the Bender ever appeared, although I had discovered that some of them lived at H4, which was nearby. I had, by this time, collected up and sorted out the main lines of the Sha'alan genealogy and I couldn't understand why none of the Bender came to visit. When I asked I was always told: 'they are Sha'alan, but from a long way away [genealogically]'. When I pointed out that this wasn't true I was told that I had got the genealogy wrong. As this portion of the genealogy had been checked with several reliable genealogists who all agreed and as it squared with Musil's account of 1910, this seemed unlikely. So I pursued the matter. In the presence of three of the Hazza' I asked various Hazza' women. They fully agreed with my genealogy and told the men, unequivocably, that they they were wrong. The men were, by now, beginning to doubt their own assertions, so we all went off to ask some of the Hamad.

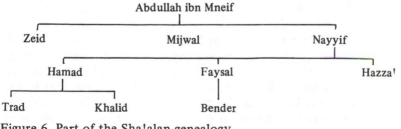

Figure 6. Part of the Sha'alan genealogy

They, too, agreed with my genealogy and produced the clincher in the shape of an elderly slave woman who had belonged to Bender himself. The men of the Hazza' admitted defeat. It was clear, by this time, that the Hazza', for motives unknown to me, were trying to push the Bender beyond the genealogical limit of normal interaction. In other words they were trying to manipulate the genealogy to fit in with the working arrangements of groups on the ground. That they were unsuccessful was not primarily due to my untimely intervention, but because the real genealogy was too well known to allow such manipulation. Unlike the Zuwaiyyid Nseir genealogy there were no convenient lacunae that could be suitably filled in. Their initial argument for their assertion that the Bender were more distant than the other groups was, however, the same: 'we don't intermarry or interact with the Bender, therefore we "must be" more distantly related'.

The 'must be' argument is extraordinarily strong. Some time ago one of the Sha'alan girls was married to the sheikh of the Jabbour tribe. The Jabbour are a tribe on the banks of the Euphrates north of Deir-ez-Zor and well beyond the normal range of the Rwala. While trying to find out the reason for this unusual marriage I was told that it was said that the sheikhly family of the Jabbour were really a branch of the highly respected family of the Milhim, the sheikhly family of the Hessene tribe. That the Jabbour should have asked a respected family from another tribe to become their sheikh is not inherently improbable; it has been known to happen. However, I had met the sheikh of the Jabbour and he had denied the story. While I was discussing this with a group of the Sha'alan, a young man burst out: 'But it must be true; she couldn't have married him otherwise' – and every one present agreed.

Recapitulation

The genealogy above the level of minimal section is cast in segmentary form. That is to say, any named group can be structurally opposed or complemented by a similar group at the same level. Thus the Aneze confederation is structurally and conceptually opposed to the confederation of Shammar tribes, even though in practice the two confederations as such have never opposed each other. Conflict was carried on at a lower level, mostly for logistic reasons. Similarly, within the Aneze the Dhana Bishr are conceptually opposed to the Dhana Mislim and it is vaguely assumed that both groups are roughly equal in number. In reality this is a simplification owing to the similarity in name (*dhana* being an old word for 'offspring') and genealogically these two groups are not equivalent. Again, owing to logistic problems these two groups never opposed each other and actual opposition seems to have been confined to tribal level, that is, the Rwala opposed to the Fed'an. In this there is a marked similarity with the level of minimal section, but there is one major difference. At tribal level it is known that logistics affect the practicalities of opposition, following strict known genealogical lines. That is, the Rwala should not oppose the Fed'an, it should be the Jlas opposing the Bishr, because it is physically impossible to gather all the larger groups together owing to problems of communications and grazing, amongst others. At minimal-section level, however, there is no conceptual framework for combining all the Murath, say, because there is no genealogy between the two levels. As each tribal section consists of several minimal sections, not just two or three, and all minimal sections are equal and equally related to each other there is no possibility of their combining into two groups that oppose each other. At tribal level the problem is logistic: at minimal-section level it is structural. Below minimal-section level there is fluidity, as minimal sections (five- and three-generation 'ibn amms') realign their internal structure and genealogy in accordance with political, economic or social reality within a framework of segmentation. As all minimal sections are equal, nobody outside that section has the right to interfere in their affairs, so minimal sections are free to follow up their own assets and options. The fact that the minimal section is theoretically the jural corporate group, while in practice the five-generation 'ibn amms' are, provides room for manoeuvre. Such manoeuvrings can be justified by the 'must be' argument, although no one outside the 'ibn amm', except for the anthropologist, is remotely interested. The difficulty for the observer is that the process, although essentially politico-economic in motive, is invariably couched in segmentary, genealogical terms and is described by the participants in terms of institutions that quite patently don't fit. As political and economic motives change with time, so the genealogy must change to accommodate changing assets and new options and so there is no true genealogy – truth is relative to the pragmatic needs of the group involved. Thus a society that appears to be constrained by the past (for this is how we see genealogies) is in fact generating the very genealogy through which it 'explains' the present, and, as we shall see in the next chapter, using that genealogy to generate the future.

4 The Generative Genealogy and Marriage

I have shown that the personal genealogies of 'ibn amms' that make up a minimal section can be manipulated. I have also mentioned briefly that marriage is one of the major ways in which this manipulation is achieved. Taking this line of argument further, I shall show how internal generation of the genealogy, as expressed through marriages, is used to maintain the groups on the ground (the five- and three-generation 'ibn amms') as viable units and how the future of the group is, as far as possible, insured and directed. The macro-genealogy (tribal section and upwards) generates and maintains the framework of society at large; the micro-genealogy generates the future development of the autonomous groups that make up that society.

The Zuwaiyyid Nseir are a case in point. The three three-generation 'ibn amms' that I considered in the previous chapter are in the process of coalescing to generate a single three-generation 'ibn amm'. By intense preferential marriage they are ensuring a dense web of bilateral inter-relationships that prove, by the 'must be' argument, that they are very closely related in the male line, i.e. the formal genealogy. The argument rests on the premise that marriage between close patrilateral parallel cousins is the norm, therefore frequent marriages between two groups means, *ipso facto*, that they are closely related. The corollary to this is that if two or more groups intermarry frequently the offspring of those marriages are, in fact, very closely related, albeit bilaterally. By the time the process has continued for a generation or two the more distant genealogical details are forgotten and the f.f.fs. of the groups will have 'become' brothers: there will be no one alive who can deny it with any authority and the facts of the marriages will prove it to be true.

It seems probable that the process of generating a genealogy is unconscious in cases like that of the Zuwaiyyid Nseir. As is shown later the actual constraints on choice of marriage partner are often as much to do with economics or reputation as they are to do with deliberate political manipulation. Whatever the exact motives, the net result is that the genealogy so created generates its own future. The deliberate use of marriage to produce a desired genealogical pattern is, however, in evidence among the Sha'alan. It will be remembered that there was a split among the brothers over the question of being the Emir's deputy. The row was resolved and everything calmed down. The women, however, have decided that such a dangerous split must be minimised and that the generative genealogy must be used to bind the two factions together. A whole series of marriages have been arranged between the main protagonists' children so that the offspring with few bilateral links back into the family can be welded in and so reduce the possibilities of the split developing again in the future. Whether these marriages will in fact take place is open to doubt, as the eldest of the children is only seven years old and the whole emphasis in the relationship between the brothers has already changed and will probably change again. Such a deliberate use of the generative genealogy is rare, because for most families there are not many options profitable enough to be worth quarrelling about in this manner. For the Sha'alan the generative genealogy is of rather limited use because the formal patrilineal genealogy is too well known to be tampered with, so that the 'must be' argument cannot be used with success. However, to the outsider who doesn't know the detailed genealogy the end result is the same: in both cases the generated genealogy corresponds to the pattern of co-operation between groups on the ground and the stranger is not to know that among the Sha'alan it is unratified. In some ways the Sha'alan have the advantage by working with the generated genealogy but remembering the real genealogy because, if anything goes wrong, the generated genealogy can be put smartly into reverse and the real genealogy emphasised. Both these possibilities can be illustrated.

It will be remembered that the split among the Sha'alan brothers was between groups of half-brothers. i.e. along lines developing from the generative genealogy. An attempt by a local government official to exacerbate the split was foiled by a quick reversion to the formal genealogy, which emphasised the brotherhood rather than the halfness. Inside the family the row still went on, but publicly it was simply denied.

Still talking about the same quarrel, the opposite can also be demonstrated, but this time from the inside. It also demonstrates the way in which the generative genealogy can work down through the generations. The row was between two groups of half-brothers from the Hazza'. One set of half-brothers was backed by their own group and their cousins the Mohammad, the Kurdi and the Mishhin. The other group of half-brothers was only backed by their mother's group, the Trad Sattam section of the Sha'alan. By normal standards they should also have had the support of their mother's first cousins, the Khalid Sattam, but this was never forthcoming. The real reason for this was that there had been a feud between the Trad and the Khalid, which had resulted in three deaths among the Khalid and one among the Trad. The feud had been resolved, but not very satisfactorily, and the Khalid still felt aggrieved. The official reason was, however, different. Sattam, the patronymic ancestor of this branch, had had children by two wives; the Trad were descended from his Sirhan-tribe wife while Khalid was his son by his Fed'an-tribe wife, who was called Turkiyya bint Jed'an Al-Mheid. Turkiyya's daughter, Khalid's full-sister, married the f.f. of the Sha'alan brothers and by another marriage was also the ancestress of the relevant part of the Mohammad three-generation 'ibn amm'. This relationship was heavily emphasised by the Khalid as their reason for giving their f.b.ss. no practical help. In fact the links between these groups (who are called, on occasion, 'the family of Turkiyya') are far stronger than this owing to a very complex and continuing series of marriages between them and Turkiyya's natal family, the Mheid. The Trad have no such links at all. It should be emphasised that Turkiyya was, by all accounts, an exceptionally strong-minded woman; furthermore, one of her daughters was still alive and, at eighty-seven or so, very active, so there was still a real link to the past, which could be used to rationalise present behaviour.

There is no question here of manipulating the genealogy but the arguments used are exactly the same as if manipulation could take place.

The importance of affinal links does seem to decline quite sharply when the original participants and their immediate descendants are dead. This is true of marriages across tribal or tribal-section lines as well as marriages within a minimal section or ibn amm. It is particularly true for the Sha'alan, who cannot rearrange their genealogy. But whether Sha'alan or not, the commonest marriage of all is between descendants of a common f.f.f., i.e. a patrilateral parallel second cousin. (Despite the strength of the formal theory that f.b.d. is the preferred partner, it is actually exceedingly rare; I know of two among the Sha'alan, both of which rapidly broke down, and none at all among tribesmen.) By using a fairly simple model (see Figure 7) it is possible to see how the generative genealogy actually works.

A marries twice: first he marries his f.f.b.s.d., then he marries his f.f.b.d.d. Both of these are extremely common marriages. His son, $B1$, marries from his father's family, while $B2$ marries from his mother's family: again, a very common occurrence. All the C generation marry more-distant cousins, except for $C2$ who marries his f.f.b.s.d., i.e. A's brother's son's daughter. In the next generation $D1$ and $D2$ are going to be very isolated because $D3$–$D8$ are going to be more closely related, as $C2$'s wife is also related to $B2$'s wife. In other words there will be multiple matrilateral links between $D3$–$D8$, while $D1$ and $D2$ will only have the formal patrilineal links. The whole group will be on the point of splitting into two or more three-generation 'ibn amms' at this point, so the marriages of the D generation become crucial. If the group wants to split, then $D4$ marries $C3$'s daughter and $D1$ and $D2$ are effectively frozen out. Or, if the group does not want to split, the children of $C1$ and $C2$ marry their f.f.b.s.ds. and the group

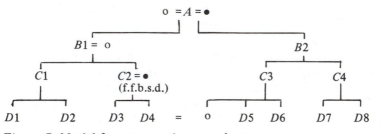

Figure 7. Model for a generative genealogy

becomes a solidary unit once again. If the splitting occurs, then the descendants of *C2* will 'become' the descendants of *B2* in course of time, because 'we always marry our *ibn amm*'.

The situation, in this very simple model, is similar to that which was used to rationalise the Khalid supporting the family of Turkiyya. Another similar situation occurs within the Mu'abhil. The Mu'abhil are, to outsiders, a five-generation 'ibn amm', but they are really, i.e. for vengeance purposes, two five-generation 'ibn amms'. Each five-generation 'ibn amm' is divided into a number of three-generation 'ibn amms'. One of these three-generation 'ibn amms' called Al-Jasir, is being further split by the generative genealogy. One part of the Jasir marry back into the rest of the Mu'abhil, while another part does not. This latter part can, if desired, be pushed out entirely or it can be drawn in by a series of marriages with the rest of the Mu'abhil. This is the generative genealogy at work.

The generative genealogy does, however, raise problems, especially for the Sha'alan. Owing to the former practice of multiple sequential marriage, which is still carried on in some degree today, an age-difference of twenty or thirty years between half-siblings is not uncommon. This makes generation level very difficult to determine and can have dramatic effects if it ever becomes essential to define the exact extent of the five-generation 'ibn amm', as in the case of feud. It is not impossible for two men who work together and are much the same age to belong to different vengeance groups, the one being more inclusive than the other. The problem is compounded by a rule (which seems peculiar to the Rwala) that states that 'a man follows his son into the sixth generation'. Thus, a pair of full brothers, only one of whom has sons, might well belong to slightly different five-generation 'ibn amms'. When this rule is mixed with a normal generation-lag between say a man and his f.f.b.s. who is also his w.b., the difference in a five-generation 'ibn amm' can span three entire generations. For ordinary tribesmen the matter is of little moment, for the generative genealogy can rearrange the levels to fit pragmatic reality; among the Sha'alan this is impossible. The question never really came up while I was there, which was perhaps just as well as there was no consensus as to when a man follows his son into the sixth generation. At birth? At puberty? At his marriage? And what about the f.f.? Does he follow his son as well into the (for him) seventh generation? The system does have an advantage, though. In the case of a killing the avengers have to be very careful to take their revenge on the right person or a very close relative, otherwise they might find themselves with a totally different feud on their hands as well as the original one.

The advantage of working both systems, that is, the formal genealogy and the generative genealogy, is that it multiplies bilateral pathways for any individual. This is of importance for the sheikhly family as will be shown when I consider reputation range and the role of the sheikhs as mediators. It is sufficient here to point out how extraordinarily extensive a network of this sort is when the generative genealogy cannot be ratified.

(It also shows why I avoided demonstrating the generative genealogy by using the Sha'alan as an example.)

The late Emir married nine remembered times; here is a list of his wives with their relationships to him.

1. f.f.b.d.
2. f.f.b.d. (m.f.f.b.s.d.).
3. f.w.b.d.
4. m.m.f.b.s.d. (from a different tribe).
5. From another tribe; exact genealogy unknown but already related in the female line.
6. f.f.b.s.d. (f.d.d.).
7. f.f.f.b.s.s.d. (m.f.s.d.).
8. f.f.b.s.d. (m.m.b.s.d.d.).
9. Unrelated.

The late Emir's half-brother only married twice.

1. f.f.b.d. (½b.½z.).
2. f.f.b.s.d. (f.f.b.d.d.).

The present Emir married only once. His wife is his f.f.f.b.s.d. (m.f.b.s.d.: m.f.f.b.s.s.d.: f.m.b.d.d.: f.uterine½b.d.).

One member of the family is related to his wife by no fewer than eleven different pathways without going further than five generations back and without counting affinal links.

Members of the Sha'alan in the course of their daily lives and interactions, quite consciously take these relationships into account. What must be considered is not only how these relationships affect them personally but also how their interaction with a second party will affect subsequent interactions with a third party whose inter-relationships with the second party must also be considered. Given the multiplicity of pathways by which relationships may be traced, it is easy to see how pragmatic actions can be justified by appealing to genealogy.

Thus pragmatic groupings can, for the ordinary tribesman, be accounted for by manipulating the genealogy while the Sha'alan make the same sort of use of the generative genealogy, but by appealing to bilateral relationships. Of course this should not override the formal genealogy, and in important instances it wouldn't, but for everyday use relationship through women can easily justify many interactions.

A *caveat* must be entered here. Owing to the form of words used, it might be construed that the Rwala are using a bilateral genealogy. Certainly they make use of bilateral relationships to justify working relationships, but this is simple pragmatism. If A and B work together they say that this is so because they are *ibn amm*, real or classificatory, and this can be shown on the formal genealogy. But A works with B rather than C because A and B share a common m.m. and because A is married to B's sister. In other words, nearly all men live, work and marry within their 'ibn amm' or minimal section, i.e. within their patriline, but choice within that patriline is often governed by other relationships. The Sha'alan, especially, appear to be bilateral but this is because their generative genealogy can never (or only very rarely) 'become' their formal genealogy.

That the bilateral genealogy is apparent rather than real is shown most clearly by considering women's feasts. Women, at any encampment, may well come from many different patrilines or even different tribes and it might well be supposed that, in the absence of any one patrilineal relationship to give the women a social structure, a bilateral one might have developed. The most obvious place to look for this would be at a women's feast, where their position as individuals is not subordinated to their social position as wives, as is the case in the arrangement of tents. At first glance it appears that there is a bilaterally determined structure. Convention demands that women closely related to the guest sit closest to her and demonstrate their closeness by not bothering to dress up particularly. Those less closely related sit further away and dress more elaborately. Initial observations show that degree of closeness is determined bilaterally, thus a m.b.d. to the visitor will sit closer than say a f.f.b.s.d., although the m.b.d. and the visitor come from different tribes. My wife attempted to analyse these bilateral relationships by observing where people sat and what they wore. She tried to determine why each person sat where she did and why each person had decided to sit there. Absolutely nothing came of it. Most of the people present were already so closely intermeshed that each had several pathways to demonstrate her degree of closeness. Over and above this, no one knew which pathway anyone else might be using to justify her position and manner of dress or even what pathways might be available to her. So each ego could interpret any other's position in many different ways. These different interpretations might well not be genealogical at all. For instance a woman fairly closely related to the guest in patrilineal terms but distant in matrilateral terms might be wearing a new dress to show that, although fairly closely related, she didn't know the guest very well. Equally she might be using the occasion to show the guest that she was highly regarded by her husband and that he was doing well. If both came from a different tribe from the hostess, this would essentially be a signal for transmission to the woman's natal family and nothing to do with degree of closeness. However it might be interpreted by the hostess as simply showing off, while to a neighbour it might show the opposite of the intended signal, that the woman had put on a new dress because she had nothing else except a dirty working overall.

A system that is open to so many different interpretations, not only by the anthropologist but by the participants too, cannot really be regarded as a system at all. Matrilateral relationships (or any others for that matter) are never organised in the same way that patrilineal ones are; they are simply used in an *ad hoc* manner. If this is true for the women, it is even truer for the men, for they never have the complementary and possible antagonistic ties to natal family as opposed to son's natal family. If men do have a tie to another patriline it is in purely pragmatic terms, although those terms may be expressed bilaterally.

Bilateral ties are certainly used but they never constitute an alternative, organised system. The generative genealogy, although it may work bilaterally, in that men who are more closely related through women 'become' brothers or father and son, is never seen to do so. After all, the whole point of the generative genealogy is to make sense of pragmatic groups in strict patrilineal terms. When taxed with using bilateral relationships in this manner, men readily admit to it but only as an exception and anyway 'if they were not actually brothers, they must have been very closely related [patrilineally] or the relationship between them couldn't have existed'.

5 Marriage and Reputation

The generative genealogy determines, in large measure, the organisation of groups on the ground. Whether the pragmatic groups can be justified by the formal genealogy depends on whether it is remembered or forgotten. The Zuwaiyyid Nseir forget their formal genealogy and then manipulate it to justify the present: the Sha'alan remember theirs and justify their actions by resorting to secondary relationships. However, both types of justification are the result of the same process - marriage. So it is hardly surprising that exactly who marries whom is carefully considered, for all are aware that the results of the marriage will play a large part in determining the future of themselves, their own children and the group as a whole.

The Rwala say that marriage is 'for the sake of the children'. At first I took this to mean that the purpose of marriage was orderly procreation. Of course it is, but the statement also means that each marriage is a new departure point in the generative genealogy and that the bilateral links can be either an asset or a hindrance to the children of that marriage. Thus a man chooses a wife (or a father chooses a husband for his daughter) with an eye not only to the assets, political or economic, such a marriage might bring, but also to how the children will benefit from this particular mother (or father) in the long term. Politics and economics are important but the political arena changes rapidly and economic assets can be very transitory so the most important consideration is the reputation of the family of the spouse-to-be.

Reputation is based on how closely a person demonstrates Bedu virtues - honour, bravery, generosity, political acumen and mediatory abilities. In the past when all men were economically equal (this is examined and explicated later) the only way of distinguishing one man from another in terms of worth was by his reputation. Wealth had little meaning as the only wealth was camels, which were acquired, over and above subsistence needs, simply to gain a reputation as a successful raider and then given away to demonstrate the raider's generosity - success in raiding and generosity were the main features in building a reputation. Thus it is possible, indeed logical, for there to be a category of those who excel in acquiring high reputation. Jural equality notwithstanding, some men became more influential than others and so sheikhdom could develop. Unable to express their position by material possessions (for this implied a lack of generosity) sheikhs could only distinguish themselves by maintaining their high reputation, which in practice came down to displaying every Bedu virtue to the fringe of excess (and still does to some extent today). There are limits to these virtues; over-generosity leads to the inability to fulfil normal obligations; over-braveness leads to death and excess political acumen leads to the double-cross. The sublime is but a short step to the ridiculous and sheikhs teeter on the brink. But for the ordinary Bedu the aim is not to excel but to be sufficiently successful to be regarded as a *rajul tayyib* – a 'good man': a man who demonstrates bravery without rashness, generosity without ostentation, political sensibility without double-dealing, honour without false pride, (*amour propre* rather than *orgueil*), and an ability to mediate between his fellows. In other words he has to fulfil the normal roles with modest success.

A man's reputation will have been in the making since childhood, and it is, in part, a reflection of his upbringing by his mother (which is regarded as forming character) as well as his use of the assets and options that his immediate family and his three-generation 'ibn amm' have made available to him. Did he always look after his younger siblings? Was he generous or mean with sweets? Did he protect those smaller and weaker than himself? Did he try to mediate in squabbles? Did he succeed? Did he shirk work? Or did he only seek out the easier or more glamorous tasks? Has he built up the basis for his own future economic network or did he rely entirely on his father's? Is he too quick to take offence or too complacent? And so on. Males of all ages lead a life exposed to the public gaze and memories are long. A man's public life starts at about the age of two when he begins going through to the men's side of the tent on his own. Thus his early reputation is based on his willingness to fulfil the role of son. A man whose father has a good reputation starts with an advantage. By definition his father must be fairly successful and therefore has an active social and political life, so the son partakes, from an early age, in the normal activities of life and has more opportunity to learn how to behave under a wider variety of circumstances than others. He also has more opportunity to hear men discussing affairs and thus gather information that will be useful to him when he makes his own way in the world. There is, however, a corresponding drawback; his defects, as well as his good qualities, will be known to a far wider audience. But whether his opportunities are wide or limited his reputation is of his own making – it is on his own public behaviour that he is judged.

A girl's reputation is rarely as public, but it is equally important. The Rwala say that honour comes through women and while they are thinking primarily of sexual honour the phrase includes all female virtues such as the ability to run the household economically and efficiently, obedience, cheerfulness, hard work and the loving upbringing of children. It also includes the virtues of generosity and bravery. Quite apart from personal generosity a girl should materially aid her father's, brother's or husband's reputation for generosity and hospitality. This means that she must not only provide food in more than adequate quantities for visitors (by borrowing from neighbours if need be) but must develop the difficult skill of acting host in the man's place if guests arrive unexpectedly when her menfolk are absent. She must feed and entertain the visitors on her own, but in such a decorous manner that she may not later be reproached. The virtue of bravery is highly prized. It is perhaps more akin to fortitude and hiding the emotions in public than physical bravery. The stoicism of Rwala women is extraordinary. One elderly woman related how her eldest son was killed in a riding accident while she was entertaining guests. This was not allowed to affect her treatment of her guests at all. On another occasion she had overnight visitors. Two of her children died during the night (probably from 1918 influenza) but this was concealed from the guests for the remainder of their stay and they only discovered much later. Her correct behaviour enhanced not only her own personal reputation but that of her husband and her natal family. In fact, it is stories like this that give the Rwala the reputation of being 'very Bedu' among slaves and peasants. This sort of behaviour is by no means confined to a 'golden age' in the past. Recently a woman was divorced by her husband, over the telephone without any warning: the reason was her husband's political ambitions and had nothing to do with her. As a result she had to abandon her children, aged four years, two years, and six months, with little prospect of seeing them again for years and with even less likelihood of herself marrying again. I met her two days after her divorce: she was chatty, cheerful and dressed up in her best (because she was visiting) and it was only slight lines of strain around the eyes and mouth that belied her manner. (This story has a happy ending. The husband's ambitions came to nought and the couple are now happily remarried.) Neither of these women is exceptional and they illustrate quite well the sort of qualities that enhance a woman's reputation.

In part a woman's reputation is important because the upbringing of daughters devolves on her almost entirely. Girls just do not have the wide-ranging public life of boys, so their social models are restricted to their mother and other close female relations. For this reason, if no other, the reputation of a woman's family is of great importance.

The first real test of reputation (male and female) comes at marriage. Neither sex, unless the circumstances are exceptional, can live an independent life unless married. Women have no jural identity and therefore only exist in their father's or brother's shadow. Men cannot lead independent lives until they have a tent of their own and they cannot run a tent unless they have a wife. (In theory, of course, a man could run a tent on his own with a divorced or widowed mother. I know of one or two young men who have done this but only for a short period until they got married. The pressure to get married is enormous, through convention and through the demands of the generative genealogy as transmitted through other members of the 'ibn amm'. I did come across a group of five elderly brothers who had never married; they were regarded with something close to disdain and even their closest relations neither knew nor cared where they lived.) Thus the choice of spouse is a public statement of reputation. It is, indeed, more than this, for it is also a declaration of the future direction of the generative genealogy. The whole future of the group thus pivots around marriage.

Neither party to a proposed marriage will wish to lower his or her reputation, so marriage tends to take place between individuals and groups with roughly similar reputations. This is the first constraint on choice of marriage partner. As neither partner, in the case of first marriage, will have had their reputation tested much yet, the constraint is really formed by the reputation of the 'ibn amm' groups involved. The general ranking of groups is fairly widely known, particularly in the minimal section, so a single marriage can be seen publicly as a measure of a group's maintenance, rise or decline in reputation. (The collective reputation is not confined to small groups. Aude, sheikh of the Howeitat, by the reputation he acquired while allied to Col T. E. Lawrence, enhanced the reputation of the entire tribe according to the Rwala. The circumstances were, however, exceptional.) This is not to say that there is a sort of central scale of reputation to which one can refer; in fact, different groups probably have contradictory scales, which will be confined to those groups with whom they interact most frequently. A man will think of a 'suitable' group into which he might marry and fear of lowering his reputation or suffering a public rebuff will limit his choice to those groups that he considers to be more or less comparable in reputation with his own. As so often when considering an unconsciously held, self-evident truth, it is easier to understand by looking at cases that are atypical and go against the general belief – that is at marriages that violate the principle of equality of reputation between marriage partners or at marriages that may have been proposed but haven't taken place because of this constraint.

A man from the Hazza¹ three-generation 'ibn amm' fell in love with a girl of settled, semi-peasant origin. There was nothing against the girl except this – her parents were respected, well-to-do landowners and her father was the sheikh of a recently-settled part of a Bedu tribe. However, she was unsuitable in terms of general background for a Rwala sheikh. As the man was fully adult the marriage could not be prevented although his close relations tried their best to dissuade him. The consequences for the children of this marriage have been marked. The daughter, an exceedingly pretty girl, cheerful, competent and of high personal reputation, has not been allowed to marry into the Sha¹alan. Several young men have been attracted but their fathers forbade the match, nor would the girl's half-brother (the father is now dead) give his consent. He was quite clear as to the reason: 'If she married into the Sha¹alan and the marriage went sour for any reason, she would have her mother cast in her face.' She has subsequently been married elsewhere – to a business man of similar mixed parentage. Another man has a poor reputation, apparently from childhood; he is quarrelsome, self-indulgent and mean. His daughters, too, have poor reputations, partly inherited, partly acquired. They are unhelpful, rude to

their mother, lazy and constantly bickering. (This is from personal observation.) According to their cousins, they are also forward with young men
at school (they live in a city) and go out of the house unescorted by a
brother or male slave or even alone. At least two are above marriageable
age but no husbands or inquiries have been forthcoming; in fact it is widely
known that their close relations have refused even to consider marrying
them. The eldest girl is married to a f.f.b.s. who has a similar low reputation. I knew this man's father and brother for a long time before I knew of
his existence. I never discovered why his reputation was so low, for his
family refuse to discuss him – for them he no longer exists. He is said to
be working as a labourer in Kuwait, which is an unlikely occupation for a
close member of a very influential family. While pursuing this topic my
wife asked, apropos two particular women, whether they had always been
bad-tempered and complaining or if it was because they had been married
to men of low reputation. The answer was immediate and unanimous; 'Oh,
they were married to those men because no one else wanted them – they
were always like that.'

The inference is clear – like marries like. Although all these instances
have concerned unsuitable marriages or low reputations (because they are
easier to see) the principle applies to both high and low – a suitable marriage is between people of similar reputation.

Given the long-term consequences of marriage, influencing, as it does,
the generative genealogy of the whole group, it is hardly surprising that
marriages are very carefully arranged. There seem to be two main processes that can lead to marriage – love and parental choice. Love, as the prime
mover, is the rarer of the two and it is unusual for a marriage to be conclu-
ded on these grounds alone. If it is, it means either that the marriage is
suitable and the parents give their consent or that the couple have to elope.
In this case it is said that most elopements are subsequently regularised; if
they are not the couple disappear altogether.

It might be thought that love would be difficult where the sexes are
fairly rigorously separated, but girls help with the herding and watering of
animals and this provides opportunities for meeting. More common is love
by report. This may strike Western ears as odd but the ability of Bedu
men and women to fall in love by proxy is very marked. Again parental
consent is needed and perhaps it is more common when a marriage that
has been arranged cannot take place at once for some reason or another.

The initial impetus nearly always comes from the man, at least in formal terms, even though the instigator may be the girl's father or, far more
likely, brother. Patterns of herding and camping are usually confined to
small groups, most commonly composed of closely-related three-generation
'ibn amms'. Even at the bigger camps, around the wells in summer, the
lay-out of tents in genealogical order means that the nearest tents will probably be those of the group with which one herds, so that when a man
sees or hears of a girl and falls in love with her, it is likely that she will be
related to him already through her father or mother or both. Equally if he

hears of a girl at second hand, he will probably hear of her through her brother or f.b.s. and this man is likely to belong to a group with which his own family have regular contact, otherwise he would not know the brother well enough for such confidences. Both relationship and close co-operation imply a similarity of group reputations, and obtaining more information so that the two families can make a decision need present little difficulty. However formal family consent must be given.

The straight arranged marriage is commoner. There is no age at which marriage should take place as such but a man usually starts to think seriously about marriage between the ages of twenty and twenty-five, while a girl is considered marriageable from about fifteen or sixteen years old. Most girls are married before they are twenty. It is usually the case that everyone concerned, the man, the girl and both sets of parents, has been thinking vaguely about marriage for some time. It is one of the main topics of casual conversation and teasing, so all the parties concerned will have some rough idea of the direction in which to look for a spouse. A certain division of labour is apparent in the process. The men will have a fairly good idea which groups are suitable in terms of reputation and politico-economic assets, while the women are in a better position to find out, if they don't know already, the actual details of reputation of individuals and their bilateral genealogy. (I am using 'bilateral genealogy' here as a convenient short-hand for 'assets and options that the individual might have available through his or her mother's family'.) This automatically restricts the choice somewhat: only close groups can seriously be considered, for the men won't have the necessary information about a group with which they don't interact and the women will not be able to gather information easily about the details of an unrelated or distant group. Obviously this is not an absolute constraint; there are many channels of information available for the determined. However, unless there is a pressing reason for a particular match it is easier to consider partners who are closer in. This constraint and the usual camping-pattern means that the new link is likely to be between two groups who are already connected by marriage. This makes the choice of individual easier, for all the necessary information can easily be collected. It will be fairly generally known which groups have men and women available and the parents just have to find the most suitable partner. The degree of existing relationship determines who actually makes the inquiries. In many cases, if the marriage is to be between close '*ibn amm*' few actual inquiries need to be made, but should they be necessary it is usually the father of the man who makes investigations into the overall suitability of the group, while the mother is better placed, either herself or through female intermediaries, to find out about such vital matters as the girl's or man's full siblings and their bilateral genealogy. In other words, women are equal partners, or even dominant, in determining the direction in which the generative genealogy moves.

The normal constraints on marriage choice make it clear that the majority of marriages will take place between 'ibn amm'. Real 'ibn amm' marriage, i.e. f.b.s. or d., is very rare because the two families are so close already that a further link is redundant. The next generation out, that is f.f.b.s.s. or d., is the most popular, for the three-generation 'ibn amm' will be in danger of dividing in the next generation, so this is the time to concentrate it if that is desired. This practice means, of course, that partners are likely to be closely related through both their parents, sometimes closer though men, sometimes through women. Quite apart from these considerations, the closer the group the easier it is to obtain information about them and the more certain one can be of their reputation; this is undoubtedly a further constraint on choice though it is difficult to assess its importance. That the girl's reputation is of prime importance is shown by the man who told me that the ideal wife was one's sister, for only then could one be absolutely sure of her reputation. Needless so say, such a marriage is prohibited and I have never even heard of a case.

I have only considered the practical reasons why 'ibn amm' marriage is preferred. There are theoretical reasons too. These cannot be gone into in detail here, but an outline of the argument, which will be published elsewhere, is included.

The problem of 'ibn amm' marriage arises because of the dual function of the five-generation 'ibn amm'. In practice a known, named, five-generation 'ibn amm' is necessary so that the subgroups of which it is composed can fit themselves into the overall Bedu system genealogically. The five-generation 'ibn amm' is also, in theory, the same as the vengeance unit. For the tying-in function, change of name cannot be too fast because the rest of the tribe could never keep up with it, the tribe is too large; but equally the name must change to reflect the changing level (and personnel) of the vengeance unit. There are two obvious ways of aligning the two functions. One is that it should be very strictly patrilineal, so that a named five-generation 'ibn amm' consists of a number of named true patrilines, each of which is a vengeance group. This is what the Rwala say that they are doing. It is quite clear that they are not. The other way of aligning the functions is by amnesia; that is, simply forgetting intermediate ancestors. This the Rwala do in part. Given the premise of equality, the strict patrilineal path cannot be followed, because it gives rise to remembered generational differences, which in turn give rise to the concepts of senior/junior collateral branches. Such concepts are inadmissible. At the same time amnesia is impossible because any group needs to know its degree of closeness or distance from any other group for decisions concerning co-operation. If you camp and work with your close cousins and need to agglomerate at certain times with more distant cousins so that the environment can be exploited efficiently, you have to know your ancestors in order to work out with whom you should, or should not, be co-operating. The system must remain patrilineal but groups must remain equal and able to work efficiently at differing levels according to ecological needs. In other words the genealogy must be remembered and forgotten at the same time. As has been shown, this is precisely how it works. However, this raises another

49

problem: how do you decide which bits to remember and which bits to forget? Put another way, when faced with five groups of cousins, all equally related to you, how do you decide which ones to choose to co-operate with and which to discard? For you must co-operate to survive. Even if a purely pragmatic choice is made, it has to be justified in genealogical terms, so the genealogy has to be fudged to fit reality. The easiest way to do this is to change one existing relationship into another; a son becomes a brother or an uncle a father. This is fine provided your complementarily opposed segment, the groups you are shedding, don't contest it. So you have to have a private way of fudging the genealogy. This is only possible through women, for men and the patrilineal genealogy are very public indeed – they must be so that you can demonstrate how you fit into the total system.

Preferred marriage within the patriline and especially at the level of f.f.b.s.d. fulfils all the conditions very nicely. You remember the necessary parts of the genealogy to fit yourself into the overall society, while at the same time you generate the lines of division that will later be used to justify the shedding of a subgroup. It is much easier for a son-in-law to become a son, for he must have been more closely related or he wouldn't have been a son-in-law in the first place. Equally a subgroup to be excluded becomes more distant because you don't marry with them. They cannot complain that they are really closer because they can never demonstrate it. Women become the means whereby the real is made to conform to the ideal; this discrepancy cannot be admitted without putting the whole system at risk, and the only women over whom you have sufficient control are those belonging to your own patriline, because a woman does not change her allegiance on marriage, she remains part of her natal group. How the marriage pattern arose in the first place is immaterial; the result is that reality conforms to the theoretical, groups remain patrilineal, discrete and equal and each group maintains control over its own future.

To return to practicalities, whether a man chooses his own wife or leaves it to his family, he nearly always acts through a mediator, usually his f., b., f.b. or f.b.s. Similarly the girl is not directly involved either, her agent being a similar relation. The girl's relations check the suitability of the suitor and his 'ibn amm'. The girl, herself, should also be consulted about her willingness to marry this particular man. This is not required but it is usually observed. An enforced marriage does not reflect well on the girl or her family nor does it do credit to the suitor – his natural sense of honour should lead him to abandon the suit. Enforced marriages are rare and can give rise to women taking violent action. In two cases, in the past, the women committed suicide (the only examples of suicide that I came across) and in other cases the women have murdered, or attempted to murder, their unwanted husbands. In all these cases the girl's father or brother had refused to let her leave her husband. The killing of a husband is a new development. Now that official Shari'a law is enforced, women have made the discovery that if they kill their husbands it is their father or brothers who pay the penalty. While this happened in the past the offending father or brother was not removed from the scene as he is today. As far as I know no Rweli woman has been involved in such a killing, although every woman knows about them and appears to approve of the new departure.

When a match has been decided, upon the grounds of general suitability and politico-economic assets, the two agents (usually the fathers) start negotiations over the financial aspects. There are no generally accepted rules about these; different tribal sections and even different five-generation 'ibn amms' follow different practices. Nor does there seem to be much consensus within even smaller groups. Some say that *siyag* (bride-price), which is the payment from the groom's family to the bride's family, is essential, others say that it isn't; some say it is a new practice imported from the towns; others say it is an old practice dying out through town influence.

The same uncertainties arise over *jihas* (bride-gift), the present from the groom to the bride, which remains hers absolutely. Even the practice of the groom giving a wedding feast is not uniform and this has nothing to do with economic factors. There are several contributory causes to this confused state of affairs. The form of wealth is wider; in the past the bride-price was computed in terms of camels and, presumably, reflected the ability of the groom to support a family. But as most marriages took place between *ibn amm* who co-operated there was little point in transferring so many camels from one herd to another as the herds were worked together and were likely to be raided together. Anyway, the rights of ownership made a physical transfer difficult because many camels were jointly owned or partly owned or the groom had a right to every third female calf and every second male calf of one particular beast. How, if animals are a self-generating form of capital, can you equate a camel now with a putative one in three or four years time? The first camel might have increased to three in that time, but equally one or other initial camel might have been raided before the transfer actually took place. Then as now, little transfer seems to have taken place. *Siyag* is not so much a transfer of wealth or compensation for loss of labour or even payment for breeding capacity as a public statement of the value that the family puts on the girl. If the groom is prepared to pay a high *siyag* it is a public statement about how much he and his family value the new relationship with the girl's family. Low bride-price cannot exist, for no family will say publicly: 'Look, we have a poor reputation; who will take this terrible girl off our hands?' Thus bride-price, of itself, is inflationary. In practice this doesn't matter, for in many cases, perhaps the majority, it is asked for, and agreed to, but never paid, and never expected to be paid. It is simply a means of making a public statement. It also provides a way of discouraging unwanted suitors – by asking a prohibitively high price and then insisting on pre-payment. This aspect is important, as it is more graceful than saying 'no', which implies that the suitor's reputation is poor. A high bride-price is only a measure of how much the family value the girl; or that is what the suitor is led to believe. Bride-price is a legal requirement under Shari'a law, but outside Saudi Arabia there is a growing practice of abandoning *siyag* altogether in favour of a high *jihas*. This was initiated by the Sha'alan; for reasons of prestige their demands for *siyag* became so enormous that no one could begin to pay it. Nowadays the *jihas* is the only payment demanded and this is specifically to insure against divorce and to ensure the girl's creature comforts. Typically a Sha'alan girl receives a furnished house in Damascus, Amman or, formerly, Beirut, two or three cars plus chauffeur, clothing and jewellery commensurate with life-style – the whole in 1977 coming to about £100,000. Among the ordinary Rwala the common practice seems to be to demand a *siyag* if the marriage is outside the 'ibn amm', but to ask for a *jihas* if the marriage is inside. Often the bride's family will return the *siyag* in the form of presents to the girl, furnishings for a house or tent, which traditionally the bride has always brought as her trousseau so to speak. Among *ibn amm* the bride-price is always computed and agreed upon but rarely paid, for very often the debt is cancelled by another marriage between the two groups in the opposite direction, a repayment that may be delayed for years. Under Shari'a law such exchange marriages are discouraged and actually forbidden if there is no bride-price. The Rwala don't take the formal aspects of religion very seriously, especially when they run counter to accepted practice, and under these circumstances they simply lie to the religious sheikh who performs the ceremony, if they bother with a ceremony at all. Bride-gift is very variable. In one recent exchange marriage between close cousins the two couples deliberately kept the *jihas* small so that the maximum money could be spent on feasts for the whole encampment. The present arrangements about marriage are very fluid and pragmatic; once again the gap between what they do and what they say they do (or ought to do) is marked.

The confusion over marriage feasts is more explicable. Until ten or fifteen years ago, according to informants, marriage feasts among ordinary tribesmen were rare. The big feasts were those given at a boy's circumcision and they might last for days and be accompanied by singing and dancing. Such feasts are now a feature of marriages, while circumcision has become a private, family affair. Nobody could even suggest a reason for this development and neither can I.

In practice the differing views on *siyag*, *jihas* and feasts rarely seem to prevent a desired match. Although a lot of time may be spent haggling, the actual redistribution of wealth seems rather unimportant, the main functions of any individual marriage being the forging of links between groups or the strengthening of the solidarity of a single group and the increasing of options for the group as a whole. The lack of concern over payment points to this conclusion as well. I have never heard of a case where non-payment or undue delay led to the breakdown of a marriage or gave rise to a lessening of co-operation.

The interaction of reputation, assets and options and the changing attitudes towards prospective partners, as well as the functional switching of *siyag* into *jihas* can be seen if an example of the course of negotiations is followed. The prospective groom came from the Mu'abhil: the prospective bride from the Nsir minimal section. Both 'ibn amms' had good reputations, as did both individuals, although possibly the Mu'abhil had slightly more prestige owing to their closer relationship with the Sha'alan. There was no known marriage link between the two 'ibn amms'. The bride was said to have been courted previously by a wealthy and influential member of the Sattam Sha'alan, but to have turned him down. The reasons were unclear. For the prospective groom there were the following advantages. The girl had a high reputation and her father was well known to him; the Nsir (or the relevant five-generation 'ibn amm') lived mostly around Turayf and had a certain influence there; Turayf was the place where he wished to settle and make a career. The Mu'abhil already had extensive internal marriage links within their five-generation 'ibn amm' and within the Muwasserin, their minimal section, so the groom was more or less free agent to forge new links where he would. For the Nsir the advantages were not so obvious. True the Mu'abhil have a high reputation and the young man was a promising business partner, but it was not apparent that the Mu'abhil, as a group were going to approve the match. If the Mu'abhil were to resent the marriage then much of the profit (economic, political and social) would evaporate. Because of this uncertainty the girl's father asked a prohibitively high bride-price. As mentioned earlier this is a graceful way of turning down an unwanted suitor without specifying the grounds. However the young man persevered and it became evident that the Mu'abhil came to approve of the match. There was a little opposition from the Mu'abhil at first, which took the form of counter-suggestions that the young man resolutely turned down. The group seem to have swung in his favour because the Nsir were particularly strong in small entrepreneurship, in which the Mu'abhil were lacking at that time. This was the more important because during this period it became evident that T.A.P.-line was running down its operations and that the long-term future of those employed by them were uncertain. The young man and one of his brothers worked for T.A.P.-line, as did several other members of the Mu'abhil. With this doubt about the group's approval resolved, the bride-price was reduced to a more manageable figure and further negotiation reduced it still further. The final seal of approval came when the bride's father agreed to turn the whole of the bride-price into bride-gift by handing over the whole sum to the girl in the form of a furnished house. The money still, of course, had to be found and the whole of the Mu'abhil rallied round, groups of cousins providing the cash for certain rooms. The marriage took place, celebrated by a week of feasting. Some eighteen months later the house still wasn't complete (a second storey was being added) nor was it yet fully furnished, but everyone was satisfied with the arrangement and the relationship between the two 'ibn amms' was prospering, metaphorically as well as financially. It is interesting to note that whereas formerly the distance between the Mu'abhil and the Nsir was stressed, it was now their closeness to which attention is drawn. As the patronymic ancestor of the Nsir was Nasr, the brother of Sha'alan, it is entirely possible that this is the beginning of a new twist in the generative genealogy whereby the Nsir 'become' part of the Muwasserin, the minimal section to which the Mu'abhil now belong.

From the foregoing descriptions the process of choosing may appear very cold-blooded but it is rarely so. Where the majority of marriages take place within an 'ibn amm' that already co-operates, the members of which are already related, the bride and groom will have known each other since childhood despite the fact that at the onset of puberty the two sexes draw apart. Even where this is not the case, young men and women nearly always say, with apparent sincerity, that they married for love. In many cases this is probably perfectly true, for even in a society where the sexes are segregated, opportunities for meeting can usually be effected. In herding-groups, taking the animals to water or 'happening' to meet while out with the flock are easily engineered. In a more permanent encampment it is a bit more difficult and contacts are more fleeting. It is curious how often the cars of personable young men break down in front of a tent where a marriageable girl lives: a spanner or something may be borrowed and the car or truck driven slowly backwards and forwards until all is well. It is extraordinary how eager the marriageable girls are to help with the food at a feast at precisely the moment that the young man of the tent comes through for some tea, water or to see how things are going. Feasts are a good opportunity for seeing and sizing up a prospective partner. Young men carry the trays of food through to the men's side and they come through to the women's side at fairly frequent intervals 'thinking' it is ready. When the trays are ready the host's son comes through with his helpers and it is strange how often he decides that the food needs re-arranging. It is at this point that the young girls who have been sitting quietly together, giggling, 'discover' that their veils are out of place and the accompanying flapping draws instant attention to them at exactly the moment when their faces are uncovered and the maximum number of young men are present. Women, of course, can always peer through the gaps in the dividing curtain of a tent to have a look at any male visitor; this is denied the young men. In the past there was a further opportunity, which is now said not to exist. A young man who was attracted to a girl contrived meetings while out herding. If all went well and his suit was looked on with favour by the girl's parents, he might slip into the back of the girl's tent at night (or she would slip just outside) when everyone else was asleep. They could then converse in low tones. In theory both he and the girl could be killed, but provided his intentions were known to be honourable and the girl's parents approved of him, the girl's family would pretend to be asleep. Middle-aged informants say that this custom ceased when they were young, but the young nowadays seem fully conversant with the practice, so I doubt if it has lapsed entirely. As neither of my daughters were of marriageable age and I am, alas, too old, I cannot confirm or deny the custom from personal experience.

Whatever the shifts and contrivances there may or may not be for clandestine meetings, the negotiations are carried out by the families, although in a far less formal manner than the bare outline might suggest. Again the flavour of the negotiations is best acquired through an example. The girl was from the Mu'abhil; she was about sixteen years old, pretty, intelligent and competent. She was not yet married, when I last heard, but in the four years that I knew the family, there were at least seven possible suitors considered. Only once did negotiations reach a formal stage. The first suitor came from the Hazza' Sha'alan. In the biological genealogy this may seem to be some way away, but the young man was f.z.d.s. to the girl. The young man brought up the possibility of marriage himself; this is unusual but the two families used to herd together in the past and the young man's father's father and the girl's father were old raiding-partners and friends. In any case he happened to be passing through on business. He started by sounding out the girl's father who raised no objections and indeed even seemed to welcome the idea. However when it was mentioned to the girl's mother it was turned down as impossible, for she had been 'milk-mother' i.e. wet-nurse, to the young man, which meant that the young couple were 'milk-siblings' and therefore debarred from marriage. So the arrangement came to nothing. No negotiations had taken place, no announcements had been made and no feelings were hurt. (The girl's mother, however, decided to take her position as 'foster-mother' seriously; she started looking for suitable girls from her own natal group for her foster-son – and now found one.) The father, perhaps reminded of the advantages of marrying back into the Sha'alan, started to investigate the possibilities of the Zeid Sha'alan. There are no direct close links between the Mu'abhil and the Zeid except through another five-generation 'ibn amm', who are linked complexly with both. On the face of it, this didn't look very promising, but the girl's father was elderly and thought of himself as part of the Sha'alan rather than the Muwasserin. More practically, he and the senior members of the Zeid were raiding-partners and close friends in the past and both had a connection with the Ikhwan even though they were never actually members. This pseudo-link is peculiar to them and part of the Mashhur. A further point in favour of the match was that neither group took part in internal sheikhly politics any longer and they would have complemented each other nicely in the economic sphere. A difficulty arose here, for the father knew little about the younger generation in any detail and the mother had no links whatever with them. Thus an intermediary who knew both parties well was needed, so my wife was 'appointed' as the most readily available and trustworthy. Our visits to the Zeid partook of the nature of marriage-broking and we reported, to both sides, on available young men and girls, their exact matrilateral links, their characters, reputation and other attributes. Nothing came of these opening moves, at least not yet, and further negotiations seem to be in abeyance rather than abandoned. The next proposals were of a similar, general nature. Most of the girl's brothers and sisters had, so far, married outside the Mu'abhil and one of the three generation 'ibn amms' felt it was time for a reinforcing marriage in this generation. Unfortunately, the girl, who had known them all personally from childhood, didn't like any of them (and they were, it must be admitted, a rather unprepossessing lot). The negotiations, if the discussions can be dignified with such a title, took the form of generalised wishful thinking, references to the past 'when we always married our *ibn amm*' and rather clumsy teasing about *siyag*. This teasing about marriage is a frequent way of opening negotiations and serves to elucidate the prospects without any commitment. The girl was, however, adamant and her father, who didn't think much of these young men anyway, refused to put pressure on her. The relationship between the two three-generation 'ibn amms' was rather cool at that time. While these rather desultory negotiations were going on another suitor appeared on the scene. He came from the Frejje tribal section. On the face of it the whole idea was implausible, for the Mu'abhil are from the Murath tribal section and it is difficult to think of two groups that could be further away from each other and both still be Rwala. However, owing to a marriage made by the girl's father, her half-brother's mother was a full sister to a prominent Frejje's mother. So the girl's half brother was a matrilateral parallel cousin to the suitor's f.b.s. The suitor's f.b.s. was also married to the girl's full-sister. So genealogy and existing relationship produced no difficulty. Furthermore the girl's half-brother was under an obligation to the suitor, who provided a large sum of money to enable the half-brother to complete payment of compensation on behalf of his son, who killed someone in a car accident. The negotiations were conducted by the girl's half-brother, the *siyag* was arranged and a feast organised to announce the betrothal. Unfortunately the half-brother (a rather insensitive man) had failed to consult the girl, who turned the suitor down flat on the grounds that he was middle-aged, already married and had daughters nearly as old as herself. While these grounds are not really sufficient to prevent a marriage the father was not particularly keen on the match and refused to give his consent if the girl did not want to marry the man. The half-brother and the suitor were much discomfited and, by this error of judgement, both lost face in a ridiculous and public manner.

When we last heard, there were two more possible suitors on the scene. One, whom the girl herself rather fancied, was a suitable young man from the Jabr Muwasserin. The Mu'abhil and the Jabr already intermarry and the young man's mother came from another Muwasserin 'ibn amm' who were genealogically closer to the Mu'abhil. The young man, who was fairly dashing, worked occasionally with another of the girl's half-brothers and his father enjoyed a high reputation. This reputation had recently been enhanced by the behaviour of the young man's sister, who left her husband when he allowed himself to be bulldozed into a second marriage by his mother. The girl objected to the marriage and the method of arranging it and everyone felt that she had behaved correctly, in that she never publicly

wept or complained about her lot but put a good face on it. Formal negotiations had not yet started but the young man had become a frequent visitor, albeit informally, at the girl's tent, though only to the men's side,
naturally. The other current possibility was a young man from the Nuwasira five-generation 'ibn amm'. There was no close link but there was a
series of complex second-hand links through other 'ibn amms'. The young
man's father had a very high reputation, particularly as a mediator, and
was married into the Zuwaiyyid Nseir, who were, until recently, very close
neighbours. For reasons that never became clear the young man and his
father used to visit the girl's mother when the girl was elsewhere. (One of
the reasons was that the young man's father would bring messages from
the girl's mother's brother with whom he had fairly frequent contact – and
his son did the same.) The girl's mother rather encouraged the suit, for the
young man was bright and ambitious and was on the point of moving into
a larger-scale entrepreneurship, which he had developed through his own
unaided efforts. According to all the criteria governing marriage choice
either of these two suitors seemed eminently suitable, but when we left
negotiations hadn't yet begun.

In all these suits the girl's attitude was taken into account – she was in
no particular hurry to get married just for the sake of it, nor did she
urgently desire the degree of independence that marriage brings. Like
many of her contemporaries she saw marriage as a lasting partnership rather
than as a political gambit, although she was fully aware, and approved, of
the political and economic aspects of marriage as far as the groups involved
were concerned. It is difficult to measure but my impression is that personal feelings are given equal weight nowadays with other considerations.
This may have been true for ordinary tribesmen in the past but the evidence is lacking. For the Sha'alan, all the evidence points to highly politi-
cised marriages in the past with personal feelings coming nowhere. This is
now changing, as we shall see, and the two rather different sets of Sha'alan
and ordinary tribesmen are moving closer together in their attitude towards
this matter.

There are two factors that have constantly cropped up in the foregoing
discussion – political assets and economic assets. Both are important in
arranging marriages but their inter-relationship with each other and with
reputation is complex and is better reviewed in detail in other chapters.

6 The Position and Importance of Women

It must be emphasised that in structural terms, if not in theoretical ones, women are equal partners: men can get nowhere without a woman and women cannot be anyone without a man. The apparent inequality is due to the differing nature of the two faces of society, public and private.

Women are confined to the private sector and are therefore not seen, both literally and figuratively. While this might look like unfair discrimination and the relegation of women to a second-class status, it is, in fact, a measure of their extreme importance to society as a whole: they are simply too valuable and important to be allowed to embroil themselves publicly in the maelstrom of politics and feud.

In the formal genealogical structure, which is largely a political statement about relationships between groups, women do not exist at all. As jural identity and responsiblity are defined in terms of this genealogical structure, it follows that women can have no jural identity or responsibility either. However they are not left in limbo, they are socially incorporated into their natal group and take their personal identity from that group throughout their life. A woman is known as 'so-and-so daughter of so-and-so (male)' and this is her true identity; she never takes her identity from her husband as 'so-and-so's wife' nor is the title 'mother of so-and-so' more than a courtesy, for she and her husband or son may belong to totally different jural groups or even different tribes. So women, although they have no jural identity, are the jural responsibility of their father, brothers or other male relatives in the male line; i.e. sons are not necessarily jurally responsible for their mothers. As women have no jural identity except through men, it follows that men control them absolutely and can dispose of them in marriage at will and reap the benefits of their labour. In return for this subjection (but remember we're talking about theory, not reality), women receive total and complete protection, maintenance and freedom from responsibility. A woman's identifying group stretches and contracts according to context, just like a man's. She can be the daughter of so-and-so or, at the same time, be 'from the Nseir' or 'from the Rwala'. In like manner her protecting and maintaining group expands according to need, so there is no necessity for a close male relation to be present to afford her protection or to provide her with shelter or food – in the absence of anyone more closely related any male Bedu is duty-bound to look after her. In a society where feuds, raids and warfare were endemic and any strange male was treated with the utmost suspicion and reserve, this was a very real benefit. Even in the most heated battle women were inviolable and whatever happened to her menfolk, a woman was entitled, as of right, to a milking camel for sustenance and transport to her relatives. Except in the last stages of the Ikhwan revolt this right was never, as far as I know, ignored. There is even visual evidence of the reality of this protection and freedom from responsibility, frown-lines, worry-lines and grey hair are strikingly absent among Rwala women and, at rest, they project an almost physical aura of self-assurance and repose.

This runs throughout the society, from the 'senior' women of the Sha'alan to the most poverty-stricken tribesman's wife. This is scarcely surprising for, as all women take their identities from men and as all men are equal, so all women are equal; all are equally inviolable and equally due protection and succor. But just as men's reputations vary so do the reputations of women, although their reputations are, like their persons, private and little known in the public domain.

Women are controlled by those jurally responsible for them, i.e. their fathers, brothers and other male relatives, and it is these men who use the women to define the direction of the generative genealogy. If women were politically recognised, they would have to appear on the real political genealogy and this could not then be manipulated to fit political reality. Thus the non-identity of women is essential to the workings of the generative system. In effect, women are negotiable surrogates for men, for men can never co-operate with others from a different group without justification – friendship is not enough. If the woman is 'given' to another group, the giver can then quite legitimately involve himself with them, for co-operation with your sister's husband is permissible because you are simply ensuring her well-being, which is, of course, your jural responsibility. Responsibility for the children is the husband's, but by this time a link has been established that can, in the future, be used to incorporate both groups into one – something that is impossible by any other process. Exactly how this process works has been shown with reference to the Zuwaiyyid Nseir and it can readily be seen that had women a jural identity of their own such a process could not possibly work.

This analysis in theoretical terms looks appallingly cold-blooded, as though women, if not ciphers, were at best pawns. This is far from being the case, although in theory, at least, it is true. What the politico-genealogical theory fails to take into account is that women (and men) are flesh and blood, with feelings, prejudices, affections and personalities. While an insensitive man might insist upon a purely political or economic marriage against the wishes of the woman, such marriages rarely last long and there are mechanisms whereby they can be avoided or negated. If the marriage is motivated by purely selfish ends, i.e. does not benefit the group as a whole, the woman's f.b.s. can forbid it, if necesssary by exercising his absolute and inalienable right to marry the girl himself. (The only unhappy marriages of long standing are those where the unwanted husband and the f.b.s. are one and the same person. All are in the past and were rare then.)

The Present System

If the men of the group approve of the marriage and refuse to allow the girl to leave her husband, she can seek protection from a man of another family. By remaining in the women's side of the tent she puts herself beyond the reach of her husband and her brothers (who are quite within their rights to kill her if they so wish) for any attempt by them to remove her by force is seen by her protector as an attack on his honour, even if she is not in the tent at the time. The protector is bound to try to effect a reconciliation, or failing this an amicable divorce, but if this cannot be done he continues to support the woman until another suitor appears. If this suitor is prepared to pay the original bride-price to the protector he can marry the girl and the protector sends the bride-price to the abandoned husband. The husband cannot refuse the arrangement nor can the girl's father interfere, for the protector has taken his place; she is, in effect, adopted. Needless to say much trouble can be caused by this mechanism and any girl who contemplates it must be sure to put herself under the protection of a powerful and influential family. It follows that is is not a mechanism that is open to girls from a powerful and influential family, at least in practice. Such cases are in any case, rare and I have only ever observed one which did not involve the Rwala except as protectors. For the men this mechanism has the disadvantage of making their dishonourable behaviour only too public and their reputation suffers accordingly; the vast majority prefer to avoid the possibility by making sure that the women approve of their husbands-to-be. In the vast majority of cases natural affection as well as political reality leads to amicable arrangements, as can be seen from the account I have given of actual marriage negotiations. Usually fathers and brothers are far too fond of their daughters and sisters to do other than concern themselves with their marital happiness and women are far too valuable an asset to be used in such a potentially unproductive manner.

Natural affection might, to European ears, sound rather a weak force, but among the Rwala it is very strong indeed. The whole upbringing of children is angled towards the twin ideas that girls serve their brothers and boys look after and protect their sisters. This is accompanied by intense physical affection; sisters act as substitute mothers from an early age and boys are frequently to be seen lugging their baby sisters about; older brothers make room for their little sisters inside their fur cloaks by the fire in winter and older girls are quite happy to cook a special meal for their younger brothers. This kind of care and affection is general within families but it is noticeably more marked between siblings. At a slightly older age brothers and sisters sit for hours late into the night quietly discussing their hopes and fears, exchanging gossip and planning their futures. In fact, brother and sister behave, in private, in rather the same manner that we would expect a decorous courting couple to behave in public. This is not as far-fetched as it sounds, for it has been admitted, on more than one occasion, that the ideal marriage would be between brother and sister - only then could one be certain of their reputations and of having an identiy of interest. It must be emphasised that this close and physical affection has no sexual overtones whatever – the failure of f.b.s. and f.b.d. marriages, and the Rwala dislike of such marriages, is often attributed to the parties being 'too like brother and sister' and such marriages, rare though they are, are often not consummated. This is despite the fact that patrilateral, parallel, first-cousin marriage is extolled as the ideal. As we have seen f.f.b.s.d. is the preferred marriage and it is claimed that they produce fewer sexual hang-ups because as children the couple have never had such physical proximity. Thus the simple facts of everyday family life work towards the treatment of women as people in defiance of the strict theory of patrilineality and jural identity.

Many facets fit in with this explication of the woman's position. One of the most striking features of Bedu life is the division into public and private spheres, symbolised by the division of the tent into the men's side, which is public, and the women's side, which is private. By and large, public life means life beyond the three-generation 'ibn amm' and, like public life anywhere, it demands a certain amount of posturing, stating of principles and positions and impression-management. In furtherance of these, preposterous claims may be made, self-importance inflated and honour (in its widest sense) invoked. Under these circumstances it is only too easy for the gauntlet to be thrown down and for violence to ensue. Violence very rarely breaks out immediately (except verbally), but that it is likely to do so is shown by the extreme care men take never to indulge in anything but the idlest and most generalised chat before coffee has been served. Coffee formally signifies that the visitors are guests, and guests are inviolate. Should a visitor, in times of tension, refuse coffee, an air of uneasiness and apprehension pervades the meeting, and men shift around, ease their holsters and make sure that their gun-arm is unrestricted. When public life can so easily erupt into violence and where men's reputation is partly based on a propensity to controlled violence, it seems sensible that women, who are the reproductive assets of the whole group, not only biologically but genealogically was well, should be kept out of public life altogether. The equation of public life with violence is balanced by the equation of private life with peace and quiet, and this is not a theoretical construct. Any manifestation of violence on the women's side of the tent is strongly deprecated; even arguing is frowned upon. When a male servant stabbed another the entire population of the encampment felt a sense of outrage because the stabbing had taken place in the *muharram*, literally the 'sacred place', which is the Rwala term for the women's side of the tent. Nobody cared one way or the other about the participants (they were non-Bedu), but it was felt that the *muharram* had, quite literally, been desecrated and the tent wasn't moved to a new spot only because it wasn't actually possible. For those living in an encampment the whole area takes on some of the attributes of the *muharram*. When my wife and I had a rather loud and acrimonious argument about an academic interpretation, we were reprimanded, in private, by the sheikh's mother. Fighting between members of the same encampment is deplored and heavily discouraged, for a collection of tents is considered to be made up of members of an 'ibn amm', even where this is quite contrary to reality. A goum is a genealogically hetero-geneous agglomeration but it partakes of the nature of an 'ibn amm' in that it has an identity of interest and the same peaceful and private con-siderations are expected to apply. Private matters are never discussed in public and this principle extends to the whole goum. If a stranger asks the whereabouts of so-and-so, the invariable answer is 'I don't know.' This is one of the earliest lessons a child learns – strangers are public and mean trouble and trouble within the encampment is to be avoided.

Thus the entire emphasis is on keeping violence and the threat of vio-lence away from the private side of life, i.e. the women. This is very generally interpreted and respected. When the smuggling was at its height the convoy that reached the encampment was safe. This had nothing to do with numbers or military considerations; the camp was 'home' and there-fore sacrosanct. If there was any suspicion that an overzealous customs officer was going to ignore this convention, the loaded trucks were driven straight into the *muharram* where they became, literally, untouchable. On the one occasion when this principle was violated there was an almighty political row and the offending officer was immediately posted elsewhere, for the intrusion of violence into the privacy of the *muharram* attacked the honour of the women and the family in general and, under these cir-cumstances, he was likely to be hunted down and killed.

The placing of women in the private, non-violent sphere of life is not sentimental nor is it motivated by any idea that women are the weaker sex. Bedu women are just as tough, mentally and emotionally, as their men and, by observation, often physically stronger. The reasoning behind their position is that they are the means of survival of the group, the 'ibn amm'. It has been shown how women are used to coalesce groups and how tensions between half-brothers give rise to factions and threats of dissolu-tion. If an 'ibn amm' had no women at its disposal the tensions only would apply and although in theory the 'ibn amm' would be unaffected, in prac-tice it would dissolve. With no *bint amm* (f.b.d.) to marry, the young men would almost certainly marry their *bint khal* (m.b.d.) or some girl from outside, and so the divisions between them would increase. A couple of generations of this and the group would soon divide into separate three-generation 'ibn amms' which would tend to become elided with their mothers' or wives' groups; the original 'ibn amm' would disappear. Obviously this can only be a logical inference for, in the unlikely event of demographic chance throwing up an all-male 'ibn amm', its disappearance would remove the evidence of its former existence.

Confining women to the private sphere means that they cannot have their own jural identity nor hold jural responsibility, for that is public and would, of necessity, involve the women in that violence from which they must be protected.

The whole argument is circular, for as soon as one factor changes the whole structure crumbles. And it is a structure, for there are plenty of examples of women apparently going against the principles of the system without destroying it. In the first place, women can act as men if the menfolk are not available. It has already been mentioned that women can entertain if the man is away and these examples only take the process one stage further. Two women, one married the other widowed, gave protection to a woman at immediate risk from her brothers, who felt that she had acted in an immoral manner and should therefore be killed. The girl was employed by the women and there were no men immediately available. In another example, the mother of one of the sheikhs runs the smuggling in his absence. Like any business smuggling often demands instant decisions and this woman is quite capable of acting as executive director should the need arise. There is always a slight tendency for elderly women to act as social men and Turkiyya did just that. After her husband's death she continued to maintain his tent as an autonomous unit, entertaining, handing out prestations and mediating.

There are even women who have entered the formal genealogy, although they get turned into men in the process. The 'ibn amm' of the Bneyya are said to be called after their female ancestor; according to this account Bneyya was a much stronger character than her rather colourless son, whose name is totally forgotten. The other woman is the ancestress of the Sabte. Originally the Sabte were two 'ibn amms' descended from two full brothers, Salim and Suleiman and they appear on the formal genealogy as such. However the two groups elided and the new composite group takes its name from the brothers' mother. This is widely known among the Sabte and is not in dispute, although being about a woman it is 'private' information and is not known to many outside the group.

All these instances, and there must be many more of a lesser degree, show quite clearly that it is not the fact of a woman's sex that debars her from public life: a woman is just as competent as a man and this is generally admitted in private. They are excluded from public life simply because it is public and the system dictates that women must remain private – it would collapse otherwise.

Other cases, where women apparently enter public life in its more violent manifestations, come into a different category altogether. The women who kill their husbands, the unhappily married women who seek protection, the women who commit suicide, are all examples of women taking violent and public action. Not unknown are women who beat off raiders with tent-poles or when bereft of transport by raiders, raid camels in their turn. These atypical and 'unnatural' acts have nothing to do with protest against the system or women's liberation (a concept with which they have scant sympathy); they are all essentially concerned with honour and reputation. The husbands who refuse divorce, the fathers who refuse sanctuary, the men who fail to protect from raiders, the raiders who fail to leave subsistence camels, all have behaved dishonourably and the women have taken violent and public action to draw attention to it.

This is the extreme of an important function of women. Not only do they advertise dishonourable behaviour of the grosser sort, not only do they play a major part in maintaining, increasing and disseminating men's reputations, but they also cut men down to size. We have seen how a man, in building a reputation, must entertain frequently. At any public feast food must be abundant, for numbers are never certain. Moreover, the women who do the cooking must be fed and also their neighbours, sisters, female visitors or any female helpers. As a general rule of thumb if under twenty men are expected, enough food for double the expected number must be provided. For larger numbers an extra 50% margin must be allowed; i.e. if sixty men are expected you allow for ninety. The quality of the food is not very important but usually sheep and rice is served, one sheep for every ten adult males (excluding servants). Young men and boys eat at the second sitting, so one sheep feeds about twenty. The remains are for the women with the addition of the ribs and neck, which are usually kept back. If the man, who always buys the food or slaughters the sheep, has miscalculated or if he is showing off (i.e. trying to increase his reputation for generosity above its real level), this is readily apparent – the food may be sufficient for the men (although the appearance of neck and ribs is indicative), but there will not be enough left for the women. And this cannot be concealed. A miscalculation happens to all from time to time, but if there is consistently too little to satisfy the women, the man's reputation for generosity and hospitality will diminish and this will rapidly spread along the women's social network, which is extensive. Public life demands that a man should indulge in some self-aggrandisement and

Plate 3. Women preparing food for a feast

impression-management; it is the women who see that no one in the en-campment believes it too implicitly. A brother reports some statement to his sister, a woman overhears a boast from the men's side of the tent, or a husband comments on some man's behaviour; immediately the woman starts to relate it to other reports and observations from her own private network. Clearly this does not apply to impression-management before strangers, which the women aid and abet; it is only if one of her imme-diate family is in danger of being taken in by such claims. Perhaps a man wishes, for private reasons, to give the impression of being a slick trader who consistently get better prices than his colleagues. If it is untrue it will be immediately apparent to the women. His feasts won't support his sup-posed wealth, nor will his wife's and daughter's clothes: the question immediately arises, is he mean, doesn't he care for his wife and daughter or is he simply a liar? Whatever the cause the women will know and they will tell their menfolk and the impostor's reputation will rapidly diminish. At one encampment there was a man who consistently gave the impression that it was he, and he alone, who badgered the bureaucracy into providing schools, arranged for the building of new houses and was the mainspring behind the development plans. This was a half-truth; he did do a lot but he was helped and backed up by other men whom he never mentioned. His pretensions were punctured by the women, who were in a position to compare the different private reports, and they took to referring to him as 'The Emir' as a gentle form of ridicule. He became a figure of fun to many, though I don't think that he ever realised. Women can similarly bolster their husband's reputation by letting private acts of generosity be known, by displaying the jewellery given them (though this has another function as well), by keeping the tent neat and clean and in good repair, by being generous themselves to female visitors or indigents or by disseminating the true facts of some action that man has modestly dissembled. In short, women bring a sense of reality to the posturings of men, posturings that are intended to impress outsiders but at the same time may be misleading to others; the public image is not down-graded but the private reputation within the group is made to conform to reality. The women play the major part in this mechanism for the very simple reason that men rarely have the opportunity to gossip together in private. Unless very closely related, they must meet in the public side of the tent and as soon as any man at a loose end sees them he will join them, thus destroying the privacy. And there are always men at a loose end, particularly old men who spend a lot of time looking for someone to chat to – the Bedu hate to be alone.

The very process of this two-way exchange of gossip presupposes a close liaison between men and women in private. The public and theoreti-cal position is that women are simply there to keep house and provide children. In reality husbands and wives consult each other and advise each other about mediation, politics and economics. Men and women have dif-ferent social networks and women are just as well-informed about the issues of the day as the men, in fact often better, for they do not have to filter out the public statements that have to be made. It has been shown that women play a vital part in arranging marriages and this can be extended to almost any sphere – few decisions are made without their advice. Obviously the value of a woman's advice varies according to her experience and intelligence and it is probably true to say that young men rely more on their mother's advice than their wives', but information from all is welcomed. Moreover a woman can influence the quality and reliability of advice that is received from other men, for she has, through the process examined above, a firmer grasp of the reality of the situation. The nature of public life demands, from the men, a certain degree of self-delusion and fantasising; the women's function is to counteract this and ensure that reality is taken into account.

Women are not only concerned with promoting their husband's reputation nor with assessing the reputation of others; they have their own reputation to consider as well. We have seen on what a woman's reputation is based; after marriage this can be augmented or decreased by the part she plays in her husband's success. She also indulges in a little impression-management of her own, demonstrating the regard in which she is held by her husband by displaying the clothing and jewellery that he gives her. Good clothes and jewellery show not only regard but also trust, especially the gold, for this is traditionally the family's bank balance. Once it has been given to the woman it is hers absolutely and the husband cannot reclaim it should she decide to leave him or if he divorces her. Thus it becomes not only a symbol of her husband's success and generosity but also a demonstration of his trust. A lack of jewellery can only imply a lack of cash or a lack of trust. The exact state of a family's finances are fairly generally known and poverty is nothing to be ashamed of, but a lack of trust for a wife leads one to suspect that her reputation is in some way at risk. She must be either disliked or incompetent and both reflect negatively on her reputation. The same applies to daughters. Nubile girls spend much time on their appearance and accoutrements, not so much from vanity, although this comes into it, but to demonstrate to their peers that their fathers and brothers have a high opinion of them. The girls invariably report back to their families about the dresses and jewellery of their friends, so good clothes and jewellery help to spread not only the girl's reputation but her natal family's reputation as well. There is an interaction between the reputations of husband and wife and this interaction (or rather the end results of their interaction) influences the future direction of the generative genealogy.

This comes about because women are largely responsible for the education of the children. By this is meant basic education in what is acceptable, laudable or unacceptable behaviour. It is not that the men are uninterested but that they are frequently away from the tent while children under seven or so, especially girls, rarely stray far. In a society where the accent is so heavily on gaining a good reputation it might reasonably be assumed that children were constantly guided, nagged or exhorted into socially acceptable behaviour. In fact the opposite is true. This arises because although reputation is extremely important, autonomy of the individual is even more important. The concept of equality extends to children and while parents will make clear what is and is not acceptable there is very little attempt to coerce the child into following guidance. This emphasis on autonomy starts at an extraordinarily early age; no baby is put to the breast until it yells; a one-year-old is expected to feed itself from the communal dish and no one will bother to see that it gets enough - it is up to the child itself. A three-year-old falls over a tent-rope and cuts its knee; its mother will show no sympathy and will, if it starts to cry, merely point out that crying is shameful. (In reality a child of three or four will already have stopped showing emotion at purely physical pain - crying with rage and frustration shows spirit and is tolerated up to a point.) By the age of about five a child will have learned which actions are commended and which shameful and he will be long past the stage at which physical coercion might be used. Physical coercion must be distinguished from physical punishment, which is very rare and then only reflects extreme irritation rather than formal punishment. The sort of physical coercion is that used commonly by grandparents or aunts to teach generosity. A two-year-old is asked for some object that is dear to him, a skull-cap that was a present or a sweet, and if it is not given straight away it is taken with every appearance of finality. It is shortly given back only to be asked for again, and again it is snatched away if not freely given. This is conducted with the utmost seriousness and savage teasing until the child is reduced to near hysteria. But the lesson is learned early - it is better to be generous than not. Obviously the lesson is reinforced later when the tactics are used to a younger sibling, but direct teaching stops when a child is five or six. After that he (or she) learns from direct experience that he is on his own and is, from now on, directly responsible for his own actions and future. A seven-year-old who won't share sweets, won't help around the tent when asked or grabs the best bits of meat when visitors are present is scarcely rebuked apart from a mild 'shameful' - his reputation is in his own hands and he is responsible. From now on he only learns from the example of others and the most frequent examples are his own family. The result is that children are a direct reflection of their family's reputation and can influence it for better or worse. This extremely rapid and, to us, savage educational system is necessary because children of seven, eight or nine have real responsibility. A seven-year-old girl is expected to be able to provide unexpected guests with tea, coffee and creature comforts before she goes to find someone older to cook a meal - her family's reputation depends on it. An eight-year-old boy is expected to avenge the killing of his father - if the opportunity offers and there is no one else available he must, for family honour is at stake. This is by no means only theoretical. The eight-year-old son of the Emir of the Rwala, armed with a penknife and helped by a few friends his own age, attempted to storm the central prison in Damascus to secure the release of his uncle. No one though his action comic or stupid -

it was generally regarded as absolutely correct and laudable, if somewhat misguided.

There is a mitigating factor in these heavy demands. The child who behaves badly or incorrectly can redeem itself by turning it into a joke. Verbal dexterity and wit are much prized and the child who can respond in this manner finds much forgiven. The witty allusion, the poetic turn of phrase, can transform momentary greed or thoughtlessness into an occasion for demonstrating intelligence and humour. The skilful child can even turn it into an occasion for teasing its elders about similar lapses on their own part. Provided they are witty about it (and there is some element of truth) they can exceed what would normally be regarded as the limits of propriety. Teasing is a potent weapon in the Rwala educational armoury. Its use is not confined to children but is widely used within the family to correct or point out faults. A very greedy woman is teased unmercifully about her failing, but in such a manner that she cannot take offence and is soon reduced to helpless laughter against herself. If you can't see the funny side and are unable to sit and take it, but react by losing your temper, all is lost, for you are displaying weakness and your reputation suffers accordingly. Teasing is usually used by women but I have been present when the men used it to reduce a peasant, who had contravened practically every convention, to a quivering, blubbering wreck. The extraordinary thing about this deliberately cruel performance was that it was conducted in such a manner as to be funny; no one was really laughing at the wretched peasant but at the puns and jokes and allusions used by the performer, which showed skill, timing and intelligence of a high order.

This general emphasis on words, which is so apparent in all the educational processes, is augmented by a wide range of stories and poems. These cover not only ideal behaviour under a variety of circumstances but history as well. Most of it is in the form of poetry, which employs an enormous vocabulary and makes extensive use of metaphor and allusion. It is very widely known and children are encouraged to learn poems and make up ones of their own. There can be few Rwala, male or female, who have never composed a poem, for extemporary verse is resorted to at the slightest excuse. This is especially true of the women, and girls singing traditional songs antiphonally at a wedding can keep up a stream of instant verse full of topical allusions, for hours on end. I was once present when an elderly, unknown man dropped in at a tent where there was no one (apart from myself) except a young married woman. Strictly speaking he shouldn't have been there, but the woman had an impeccable reputation, the visitor was very old, the sun was hot and there were no men at any of the nearby tents anyway. For a full half-hour the two of them kept up a flirtatious conversation loaded with double meanings, about the impropriety of his behaviour, entirely in verse. Unfortunately my command of Arabic at the time was not such that I could appreciate the finer points, but it was quite clear that the conversation was ribald if not worse – and they both thoroughly enjoyed themselves.

Nor is it just verbal dexterity that the children are encouraged to develop. Relationships, too, can be manipulated. Broadly speaking, relations on the father's side are treated with deference and a sense of obligation, while those on the mother's side are seen more affectionately. The difference is slight but significant and a choice can arise as to how to treat those who are related to you through both parents equally. Much depends on what you want out of them in that particular context and the clever child can manipulate the difference to its own advantage. The same sort of thing arises in computing degrees of 'closeness' and 'distance'; situations also occur when it is more honourable to swallow pride and accept compensation. All these sort of conflicts can be seen as children play around the camp. Sometimes they turn into reality as when boys are playing one of their lethal team games with slings and stones, or when little girls playing houses (or rather tents) squabble over whose turn it is to make the coffee. Such games are quickly broken up when violence sets in, as are the boys' dangerous games if someone really gets hurt, although games that involve a likelihood of bloodshed always take place well away from the encampment. All these games involve a concept of genealogical nearness or distance and the appropriate behaviour, and demand quickness of decision-making and the awareness of assets and options, albeit on a small scale. The important point about them is that they are never supervised by adults; the children learn to manipulate their assets on their own and to weigh the risks of sling-fights against the accusation of fearfulness. Only when someone is actually badly hurt or fighting takes place actually within the camp do adults interfere. Then sides are taken in accordance with relationship, irrespective of right or wrong, at least publicly.

This rather tough educational regime is compensated for by the absolute security that children enjoy. Whereas we tend to cuddle and fuss over a child who has hurt itself or is badly frightened the Rwala only do so when a child is not hurt or frightened. Thus children, especially small children, are cuddled, hugged and played with most of the time. This behaviour is not confined to the parents or siblings; uncles, aunts, step-relations, servants or just ordinary casual visitors all take part. Small boys, sticky with sweets and running noses, are warmly kissed; sodden, puking babies are dandled on expensively clad knees or pressed to velvet-covered bosoms. Nor is it only small children who enjoy close physical contact. Until puberty, the elderly and close relations hug and kiss and cuddle children, sitting by the fire in the evening, lying around chatting during the day or taking them into their beds at night. This total, unconditional security, which has nothing to do with good behaviour, gives the children a very great degree of self-confidence and sufficient assurance to take their autonomy very seriously. Because approval doesn't need to be sought, because support can be taken for granted, children make their own decisions without, as it were, having to look over their shoulders. Whatever may be the parents' attitude in private, in public the children know that they are fully supported, not because they are children but because they are related.

Frequently they are supported in their decisions in private as well. Seven-year-olds make the decision not to go to school after consultation with their siblings and their parents accept the decision. Thirteen-year-olds decide, on their own, to give up their job at a local garage and join the National Guard. In the past ten-year-old boys would make up a raiding-party entirely on their own initiative. Parents often are consulted, of course, but the decision is the children's own and no great effort is made to persuade them to change their minds. Such momentous decisions are made as a matter of course and can only arise from a well-founded self-assurance and belief in the autonomy of the individual. It is this aspect of upbringing that the whole system, moral, emotional and educational, emphasises and encourages. As the foundation of the attitudes is laid at a very early age and as the direct educational process is largely completed before the child is five, the women are responsible for the sucess of the children's upbringing. It is the success of the child in living up to the expected standard that brings reputation to the mother. The child who whines, who is indecisive, who relies on others, who is sly or underhand, who is ungenerous, who is idle, brings the mother no credit and both pay in terms of reputation. No wonder they're tough in those first, few formative years.

The toughness doesn't stem entirely from principle. Women are very hard-working and busy and, as a young wife with two or three small children, a woman just doesn't have a lot of spare time: the children have to look after themselves and each other. The woman runs the tent; she makes it, repairs it and adjusts it to the weather as well as putting it up and taking it down. She collects firewood, makes the bread, plans the meals and cooks them, washes up, collects the water, makes clothes, quilts, rugs and pillows and keeps them in repair. She looks after the children, doctors them and her husband and has to have a fairly extensive knowledge of herbal medicine, collecting the herbs in due season; she must be able to cope with broken limbs, knife- and bullet-wounds, and scorpion- and snake-bite. The preserving and storing of food is under her care, as is the butter- and cheese-making if the family has sheep; carding, spinning and weaving of wool are her concern, though not the shearing of the sheep. And she must be ready at any time to entertain her husband's guests and visitors or down tent and migrate. On top of this she may well be pregnant. Put like this, it is surprising that they can stick it, but running a tent is rarely carried out in its entirety by one woman. Sisters, sisters-in-law, cousins, neighbours, mothers-in-law, nieces and aunts are usually close at hand and many jobs turn into social occasions. As the children grow older they too help. From an early age they bring in wood and collect dried camel-dung for the fire; they fetch and carry and wash. Later they'll make the dough, clean the fireplace, sew the clothes, raise and lower tent-poles, put up the side walls of the tent and help to tighten the ropes. A well-trained daughter of fourteen or so can run a tent by herself with the aid of a younger sister, leaving the more skilled and time-consuming jobs, spinning

Plate 4. Girl carding wool

for instance, to her mother. A competent girl of this sort will, if she is also cheerful, have rightly gained a good reputation and this will be reflected in the clothes her father provides her. A marriageable girl with a good reputation, from a respectable and reasonably well-off family, will have accumulated twenty-five to thirty good-quality dresses (made by herself), three or four gold rings, five or six thin gold bracelets and a gold necklace or pendant. Dresses are not cheap, nor is gold and each dress-length of material will cost in the order of £35 and upwards – a best dress may well cost £75–£80 for the fabric alone (1978 prices). It isn't money wasted. After the dress has served its purpose it will be passed on as an everyday dress to a younger sister or niece, cut up later into clothes for a baby, used to make cushion covers or a patchwork dividing curtain and finally disappear thirty or more years later as a worn-out kettle-holder or rag for cleaning the lamp.

What does a woman get out of it in the end? The answer, apparently, is a good deal of satisfaction. She has maintained the honour and reputation of her family, played a major part in directing the generative genealogy and increased the assets and options of her sons and grandsons. In short she has been successful. Perhaps more important, she can be conscious of having helped to maintain the system as a whole, for she is well aware that she is complementary to the men and equal to them in private, if not publicly. She will never (or only rarely) have known acclaim, but she knows that without her the Bedu would have disappeared long ago. And she is proud to be Bedu.

7 Political Power and Authority

(a) The ordinary tribesman

As I have said, the Bedu system is based on the premises of equality, autonomy and the acquisition of reputation. Thus no man has power over another nor can his authority outstrip his reputation. Economic wealth and inherited family reputation are admittedly variable but neither confer more than a starting point for a personal reputation. Indeed, in some circumstances great wealth and high inherited reputation are a disadvantage, for more is expected of such a man and he has farther to fall. In the end personal reputation is the basis of political power as far as political power exists at all. In a system where every man is equally free to follow his own bent and where there is no mechanism for coercion, the only political power available is the ability to influence the decisions of others. This rests on four factors: good information, the ability to give good advice, a reputation for sound counsel and an audience to influence. All must be acquired.

The ability to act as mediator in this way is developed over time. The process of acquiring it starts early and initially consists of sorting out childish squabbles, deciding where to hunt jerbo'a (desert rats) and similar minor manifestations. It is very similar to that vague phrase beloved of schoolmasters – 'displaying qualities of leadership'. But this is only a prelude, for the audience is always very small and the information limited. As a child grows and his social horizons widen the audience increases, but it is not until he becomes a young man that his store of information is sufficient to have much value. In the past when the significant information concerned grazing, camels and the movement of people, the ability to predict and assess probabilities rested largely on past experience, and this a young man did not have. Nowadays the variety of information is much greater and a young man may well have specialist knowledge about bureaucratic procedures, for example, which is unknown to his elders. Despite this, a young man is only in the position of a specialist consultant, for he will not have the experience to evaluate and assess his information in wider terms. Like any skill, the ability to mediate demands long practice and, ultimately, a knowledge of how people will react under certain circumstances. This requires a fund of information concerning the actual individuals involved, their families, their genealogies, precedents and the value of these in each particular case. This sort of background information is not acquired quickly. There are also practical constraints for a young man; before his marriage he is always under an obligation to defer to his father in public. After marriage he will not usually have the time or money to engage in mediation to any great degree. Until his economic base is secure and he has children to whom he can delegate everyday chores, he is simply too busy. Much mediation takes place at mealtimes, but producing a meal for twenty or more at short notice is difficult for a woman to combine with looking after small children. (It is perfectly possible but not very popular.) Nor will the young man have the wherewithal to entertain widely until his economic assets have matured, for he has little surplus to entertain with. This doesn't diminish his reputation for hospitality or generosity, for the constraints are widely known and a man who is consistently overgenerous to the detriment of his family is just ridiculous. The first spreading of a reputation comes at marriage. Spouses are chosen, in part, because their economic assets complement one's own, so that the wife's brothers will often constitute a new audience that was previously beyond the young man's range, but the serious acquisition of a reputation for mediation must wait until early middle age. By this time the children will be old enough to be real assets in practical terms and some surplus should be available. The vast majority of men reach the point where they have sufficient time and money to start acquiring a serious reputation as a mediator. Subsequent development depends on skill and information. Both are limiting factors, but skill is partly determined by native intelligence, over which a man has no control. Information can be acquired but, as we have seen, the sort of information necessary takes a long time to collect – there is, however, a short cut. A man who has a mother or an elderly aunt living with him has not only extra domestic help but also a treasure-house of exactly the sort of information he needs. Not only will she be a fund of information but she will also, in all probability, be part of an extensive female network; her daughters will be married and she will see them more frequently than her son does and she will maintain communication with her sisters and their children. While every man has access to his mother, aunts and sisters, it will be limited to visits, but a man with his mother living with him is constantly exposed to information about marriages, cousins, step-relatives, affines and the like, because this is a major topic of conversation among the women. He is likely to be better informed about relationships and the real personality of individuals than even his full brother.

His use of such information depends on an audience. Once he can spend much of his time around the encampment he is able to come into more frequent contact with casual visitors who form, as it were, the vehicle for increasing his skill and spreading his reputation beyond the confines of his 'ibn amm'. Casual visitors (who are usually men) will always go first to a tent where the other men are visible. More often than not the men will be clustered at the tent of the goum leader, i.e. the most influential man in the encampment, so inevitably the majority of visitors end up there. This is not, of course, invariable; older men often meet at one tent while the younger men congregate at another or everyone may be at a particular tent for the evening meal. The evening meal tends to be communal and provided in rough rotation round the encampment, so a casual visitor may end up at any tent. Often though, visitors make their way to a particular tent. It is difficult to generalise about the reasons, for they are many and various. The commonest reasons are relationship (through any channel), a specific query, previous acquaintanceship elsewhere or simply because the visitor's car broke down nearby, or it was too hot to walk further. It is more informative to consider the types of queries that were taken to particular individuals at a particular camp. The visitors may not have gone to these tents initially or even at all; the queries can be put at any social gathering. Someone seeking genealogical information would go to the oldest member of the Mu'abhil. Once, for instance, a man from the Sba'a tribe of the Aneze was thinking about renewing an old marriage link with the Mashhur Sha'alan. The Mu'abhil man was the obvious source of information because his genealogical knowledge was extensive and he was personally friendly with many of the older members of the Mashhur. At the same time he was fairly impartial, for he had no close marriage links with the Mashhur himself. If advice concerning the state of the sheep-market and transporting business was needed, the first man to seek was one of the younger Mu'abhil, who was in the business himself. An enterprising man, he was much consulted about new business enterprises too, especially agricultural ones. If he wasn't available (for he was often away) there were one or two other young men who also transported sheep from Syria to Saudi and if one's query concerned the state of the roads, customs procedures (which vary considerably depending on who is on duty), availability of sheep or just news from the north, they were perfectly well able to supply it. For information and advice about joining the National Guard there was a well-respected man from the Nuwasira – he was also consulted for information about the south of Saudi Arabia, for he had been posted there for some years. If one wished for legal precedents in customary law there was a member of the Zuwaiyyid Nseir. His advice wasn't much sought but he possessed a repertoire of poems that was extensive even by local standards and most precedents appear somewhere in poetic form. Bureaucratic problems had to be sorted out by a young man in the next encampment, although his specialist skill was rather differently based and will be examined in the next section. Rainfall and grazing were subjects of perennial interest to all, and any visitor or recent arrival was expected to have up-to-date information, although those actively engaged in herding were more reliable. So a man with information in some specialist subject who has the time to spend around the encampment and the financial resources to entertain, has no lack of opportunity to practise mediating and to develop his skill. In other words, he is exerting influence over others. As his skill increases and his reputation widens he will become more influential. The substrate for this extension is a steady stream of visitors, for they not only provide the occasions for mediation but are the means of spreading reputation over a widening field. It might be thought that travellers would be few and far between in such an environment as the inner desert, but in fact it swarms with them. The splitting of Rwala territory between four sovereign states and the bureaucratisation of central government accounts for much of the increase but there are multifarious reasons for travel. Men travel to visit their sons in the army, to visit a married sister, to seek new grazing, to collect compensation, to avenge a killing, to register a truck, to buy sheep, to collect a pension and for many other reasons. Everyone knows more or less where it has rained and can therefore plan his journey to pass through the inhabited areas at any given season and at every encampment the travellers will say where they are going, why, where they have come from, whom they have stayed with *en route*, where they were, where they planned to move on to and similar information. Obviously a fairly permanent encampment will receive a disproportionate number of visitors, but herding-camps also have numerous travellers passing through.

This system of reputation and influence is about as far as political power goes. Even where there is a feud no one can stop it or force a resolution. The Mu'abhil have been involved in a single feud for fifteen to twenty years. It started with a row over a camel or a sheep, no one can now remember. Anyway, a Mu'abhil killed a Sabih. A settlement was arranged and the Mu'abhil paid about forty-five camels in compensation. This should have been the end of the story but the dead Sabih left a son aged about four who is now a grown man. He claims that he never received the compensation as it was taken by his f.b. Therefore he feels himself to be still at feud and entitled to forty-five camels. It is possible that for the sake of peace and quiet that the Mu'abhil might have paid this second claim but the price of camels has risen so colossally in the intervening years that the cost would be in the region of £20,000. They feel that this is unreasonable and decline to pay. They say that the young man must seek the compensation from his f.b. The f.b. says that the camels died in the drought of 1958–62, so it is nothing to do with him. And so it goes on. Negotiation and mediation still continue in a desultory fashion and the Mu'abhil still take precautions against revenge. The facts of the matter are clear and general opinion is that the Mu'abhil are in the clear and that the problem lies only within the Sabih. But the young man doesn't agree and there is absolutely no mechanism whereby he can be compelled to accept majority opinion: nobody has that sort of power.

The individual autonomy that this story illustrates is very general. With no centralised power of any sort, no form of coercion can be brought to bear. As I have pointed out before, all men are jurally equal and the only constraint is the desire to succeed within the system, which means being swayed by public opinion. If a man continues to flout public opinion for too long, his reputation suffers, his options are reduced and his assets devalued. Beyond this there is nothing. If a man behaves so badly that his own 'ibn amm' refuse to have anything to do with him, then he passes out of the system altogether. There is no formal procedure for this; indeed nobody has the right or the power to cast anyone out. What happens is that if a man's reputation becomes so appalling that no one will co-operate with him in any way, he has to move out of the system physically in order to survive at all. Evidence of this process is obviously difficult to come by because such a man ceases to exist socially and his very existence will be denied by his relations. On one occasion I heard a man deny the existence of his son, after they had just had a terrific row: the son is a ne'er-do-well and may well pass out of the system if he isn't killed first. How commonly people pass out of the system in this manner is hard to tell. There is a large village in southern Syria called Sheikh Miskin, which is said to be inhabited by the descendants of renegade Bedu (Rwala among them) who had to settle in order to survive. As *miskin* in dialect means 'those who have settled' and only secondarily means 'wretched' or 'poor', which is the usual, town-Arabic, translation, the assertion may well be true.

Just as the process of exclusion is consensual, so is the process of accretion. The prime example, of course, is the adding on of a weak three-generation 'ibn amm' to a stronger one. Both sides must consent for the process to work at all; even one person from within the group would ruin the coalescing, if he disagreed and refused to co-operate. There is more latitude in the accretion of larger groups, for the host group can easily split without destruction to allow for disagreement. When the Kwatzbe tribal section 'became' Rwala about 200 years ago, the tribe split temporarily into two parts, those in favour of acceptance and those against. Nobody could compel anyone else to accept or refuse; it was a personal choice, and even families were divided on the matter.

No individual has political power, no group has political power and no family has political power; power is restricted to the workings of public opinion. Even public opinion has no formal coercive power; co-operation can be withdrawn and that is all. In every case it is an individual choice influenced by family considerations, no one is expelled from the tribe; they leave of their own accord. All men are autonomous and equal and there is no mechanism whereby these principles can be overridden – the best that can be done is to exert influence through reputation.

(b) Al-Tsebir

Al-Tsebir simply means 'the big man' and is used to refer to the most influential man in an encampment, if his name is not known. It is neither a title nor a form of address: the leader of a large goum can be referred to as *al-tsebir*, but so can the elder of two brothers who camp side by side alone. It does not imply power, authority or dignity. It is thus unfortunate that the Rwala should nowadays also use this term to designate a government-appointed tribesman in Saudi Arabia, whose job it is to steer his fellows through the bureaucratic maze. It is doubly unfortunate that this person's official title is 'sheikh'. The Rwala only use 'sheikh' as a courtesy title for the most influential members of the Sha'alan. In practice this comes to mean some of the Emir's brothers and one or two of the leading members of each tribal section. (The Rwala have never had religious sheikhs.)

A tsebir is expected (or maybe just thinks he is expected) to act as agent for the government within his own encampment. A fairly typical case concerned a young man involved in a traffic accident. The young man (from the Nseir) was driving his lorry by night when he came to the police post by the turn-off for his destination. As he had no lights he failed to notice that the barrier was down. Before the policeman on duty could turn out, the young man reversed and drove off, leaving behind him a demolished barrier and a rather bent sentry box. His lorry was recognised as he drove off. The young man arrived at the encampment, dropped in at the tent where all the men happened to be gathered, told what had happened with a wealth of detail and much laughter, had supper and went off to his cousin's for the night. Next day the tsebir was asked to present himself with the young man at the police post. The tsebir, who knew that the lorry had no papers and the young man no driving-licence, went alone and told the police that the young man had left the encampment. This was perfectly true, they had left together – the tsebir to the police post and the young man to the nearby town by a cross-country route. That evening when both had returned to the encampment the tsebir explained what had occurred. He had denied all knowledge of the affair and said that the young man had nothing to do with him, and was only passing through. However, he was prepared to act as mediator as he knew the young man's father. The police knew that the tsebir was lying and he knew that they knew – both parties also knew that the young man's family relied on the truck to water their sheep and that he was the only one who could drive. In the end the tsebir persuaded the young man to pay for the damage to the police post and tried to persuade him to register the truck and get a driving-licence. As far as the tsebir understood the position, the police could have required him to produce the young man and applied sanctions if he didn't comply. He may have been incorrect in this but it worried him that he could be ordered to do something which was beyond his control; nobody has this sort of power within the Bedu system. Fortunately the police are mostly Bedu themselves and recognise the discrepancy between bureaucratic theory and the reality of life in the desert and most incidents of this nature are treated sympathetically and tactfully, so things run fairly smoothly.

The government-appointed 'sheikh' has a more difficult task. He is a paid, part-time civil servant who has the job of explaining bureaucratic procedures to his fellow-tribesmen and helping them to comply. In Saudi Arabia, where this system is extant, the bureaucracy is formidable and a guide of some sort essential. Probably the commonest problem that the 'sheikh' has to deal with is the provision of citizenship papers. Until recently, nomadic Bedu have needed no papers and have never registered anywhere, but nowadays some identification is essential for the issuing of driving-licences, a job in a company, military service, an air ticket to Riyadh or the collection of a subsidy. For the Rwala it is most profitable to be a Saudi citizen because all education is free, jobs are fairly readily available and subsidies are generous. However becoming a Saudi citizen is difficult. In theory any Rwala can become a Saudi citizen, but there are problems. In the first place identity must be proved. This is one of the main jobs of the government-appointed 'sheikh'. Even if he doesn't know the applicant personally there will always be someone around who does and a few days usually suffice for this to be established. It is now that problems really start to arise. Saudi bureaucracy, at least at local level, appears to be based on a patronage system, so the attitude of the bureaucrat faced with a Bedu applicant is not 'Is this man entitled to citizenship?' but 'Who will be offended if I grant (or don't grant) citizenship?' The civil servant is protected in his decision, *vis-à-vis* the Bedu, by the Byzantine complexity of the rules and regulations, which means, in effect, that the decision can be postponed indefinitely and the delay can always be justified. Thus to get anything done the 'sheikh' must have a detailed knowledge of the personalities within the civil service, their career prospects and their inter-relationships as well as a thorough grasp of bureaucratic procedures. He must also be literate, which means that only young men can be considered for the job. This puts a considerable strain on the 'sheikh', for the majority of Bedu who have need of him are elderly and find it difficult to accept that such a young man with no personal reputation (in the Bedu sense) can be in such a powerful (to them) position.

The relationship between the Rwala and the bureaucracy is not a happy one. Although Bedu and townsman have always had a symbiotic relationship, that relationship has always been confined to the towns themselves: in the desert the Rwala have never had to bother their heads much about the settlers. Now, of course, with modern transport and communications, the town, i.e. settler control as opposed to nomad control, has covered the country and the Bedu find themselves beset with documentation, regulations and what they see as unjustified interference. Independence, equality and self-help are all highly prized by the Rwala but bureaucracy is antagonistic to all three and nowhere is this more clearly seen than in the prosecution of a blood-feud. This is not the place to examine feud closely and it is sufficient to say that whereas formerly feud was dealt with by the parties concerned in a closely regulated and satisfactory manner, it is now bedevilled by bureaucracy. In the past the killer could seek protection where he thought best and anyone with sufficient reputation could act as mediator. Nowadays only the courts can act as mediators and only Ibn Saud can give protection. In practice this means that the killer is imprisoned until the case is sorted out and compensation paid. During this time, and it is usually months, the killer's family are at risk and he has no opportunity of raising the money for the compensation. This interference by the state in what is regarded as a family matter is much resented.

This problem is magnified because the Rwala have little concept of 'the state'. Their loyalties, outside the tribe, lie in a more personal direction to the family of Ibn Saud. They make a clear distinction between the state (*al-dawlat*) and Ibn Saud (*al-hukumat*) but the relationship between the two is misinterpreted. *Al-hukumat*, the concept of government, is very familiar to them; they themselves 'ruled' vast areas at various times, through their Emir and his appointed agents. The application was simple; the Emir or his agents acted as mediators with outside forces while internally any reputable man could act as mediator on anyone's behalf. The secret of any successful ruler was to get his ruling accepted by the majority; any individual who could not accept that ruling was free to move to another area beyond the immediate range of the ruler and remained free to pursue his life. But the state (*al-dawlat*) that can enforce a ruling within arbitrary boundaries is an alien idea. To the Rwala 'the state' simply means absolute obedience to incomprehensible written rules, an obedience that can be enforced. The face of the state with which most are familiar is the bureaucracy and not surprisingly there is a certain antagonism. The townsmen, who make up the bulk of the bureaucracy and who understand the nature of the relationship between *dawlat* and *hukumat*, interpret the Bedu attitude as antagonism toward Ibn Saud. To some extent this was foreseen by Ibn Saud, for the Bedu have direct access to the royal family and to the Emirs of the various provinces. This is becoming increasingly eroded as government becomes more and more complex and in any case decisions, even by princes, have to go through the correct bureaucratic procedures. The Rwala see this as *al-dawlat* taking over *al-hukumat*, a development viewed with misgivings. At local level there is virtually a gap between the two cultures and it is this gap that the government-appointed 'sheikh' has to try to bridge.

It must be stressed that this confusion arises at local level only, for neither the 'sheikh' nor the local bureaucracy are very highly educated and both are relatively unsophisticated. Both parties are feeling their way in a new and swiftly-changing situation. At higher levels there is more understanding of the problems, for the traditional sheikhs are extremely well-trained and knowledgeable about bureaucratic procedures and, in any case, they probably know their bureaucrat counterparts in a private capacity. The lower echelons of the civil service are very ignorant of the Bedu system, perhaps understandably, and much of the conflict stems from this; equally the Bedu have difficulty in compromising with the hierarchic nature of the bureaucracy and are impatient with what they see as bloody-mindedness. The government-appointed 'sheikh' has to cope with this system with little but his native wit to guide him. It is surprising that the relationship between the two systems isn't stormier.

(c) The Emir and the sheikhs

The Emir and the sheikhs are scarcely a particular case: they are the same case writ large. An ordinary tribesman mediates within his own three- or five-generation 'ibn amm' or, if he is well known, between other 'ibn

Plate 5. Litigants awaiting the sheikh

amms'. He can never mediate on a larger scale because his reputation range is limited and because there are no larger groups to mediate between until the level of tribe. This is the job of the sheikhly family as well as acting as mediators at 'ibn amm' level for themselves and others. The difference between sheikh and tribesman is not so much in reputation as in reputation range. The Emir and the sheikhs are mediators on behalf of the tribe with other tribes or with national governments. With other tribes they negotiate with the sheikhs not because they are hierarchical equals (they are equals anyway as 'free Bedu'), but because their counterparts in the other tribe have the same sort of reputation range as themselves. As for governments, the sheikhs negotiate with senior officials or the heads of government direct. In Saudi Arabia they deal with King Khalid, Prince Fahad or Prince Abdullah; in Jordan with King Hussein or Crown Prince Hassan; in Syria with President Assad or the minister of the department involved. Obviously this is only when the whole tribe is involved. In exactly the same manner the tsebir of the Doghman or the Murath will deal directly with the governor of the province and the tsebir of an 'ibn amm' or other small agglomeration will deal direct with the officer or sergeant in charge of the police post, not the constable. The tsebir of a three-generation 'ibn amm' can deal direct with the Provincial Governor or even the King, but he will usually have to go through the government-appointed 'sheikh'. This is not because he is at the bottom of a hierarchy but because these senior officials are outside his reputation range. There is no suggestion that the tsebir of the tribal section or the government-appointed 'sheikh' are 'higher' than he nor that their reputation is greater, but the tsebir or 'sheikh' will know the governor personally and can vouch for his companion's reputation. It is the equivalent, for those who can't write, of a letter of introduction. My own bureaucratic problems were met in the same way. Initially I visited the governor of Jauf district through the mediation of 'my' tribal-section 'sheikh'; in Riyadh I went through the Sha'alan representative, my 'brother'. Once the mediatory introduction had been made I was on my own, I explained the problem, I stated my needs – I was my own advocate. This all sounds hierarchical with egalitarian overtones, but that is illusory. One of the Mu'abhil had a bureaucratic problem that could not be solved locally, so he went to consult Prince Abdullah ibn Abdul Aziz Ibn Saud personally. The man was well known and highly respected within the tribe and within Jauf district but Riyadh and central government were beyond his reputation range. He gained audience with Prince Abdullah (who holds public audiences three times a week) because his reputation was known to one of the Prince's personal bodyguards, a Murathi. This guard vouched for him to an official of the audience chamber, who allowed him in. In the subsequent meeting there was little question of hierarchy; it was a matter of two equals discussing a problem. The Mu'abhil was in no sense a petitioner, he was simply seeking advice from the man best qualified to give it. The conduct of this man and others on this sort of occasion bears out this interpretation. Formality in the sense of special etiquette doesn't exist; common politeness such as can be seen in any tent between host and guest, is observed, with a few flowery phrases thrown in at the beginning. It is very much a man-to-man affair; nor does the man seeking advice behave, in Western eyes, particularly respectfully – he will argue, interrupt and contradict, often heatedly. The interchange finished, he will get up, be given his *congé* after the normal fashion and walk out. There is no 'thank you' nor any form of pleading or supplication – a discussion between equals has ended. Of course there is a certain formality on such occasions, but scarcely more than between Bedu strange to each other and any self-abasement or obsequiousness is markedly absent.

In the dealings between sheikhs and outsiders impression-management comes into play. This seems to be a fairly new departure, for Burckhardt, Lamartine, Lady Anne Blunt and Musil all mention specifically that it was difficult to identify the sheikh by appearance or behaviour. Presumably the sheikhs are imitating the behaviour of the Turkish Pashas with whom they started to come into close contact in the late 1870s. The impression they intend to convey is one of power and magnificence. My earliest contacts with the Rwala sheikhs were at feasts given for visiting officials and the scene was of almost nineteenth-century splendour – slaves and servants abounded and there was a continual stream of fruit, sweetmeats, kebabs and drinks. The main course was two, three or more whole sheep on mounds of rice sprinkled with pine-nuts and, sometimes, vegetables. The slightest whim of the guests was fulfilled, fruit was peeled for them, glasses were topped up, cigarettes lit, new brands of tobacco produced; the guests

Plate 6. A feast given for Emir Abdullah ibn Abdul Aziz ibn Saud. Hospitality enhances reputation.

needed to do nothing for themselves. All these services were performed by slaves and servants at a sign from the sheikh and every action was carried out promptly. One would have said that they went in fear of their lives if they disobeyed or were even careless. As soon as the visitors had left, it became apparent that the whole scene was a charade designed solely to impress. The slaves lolled in the recently vacated seats, the sheikhs poured their own tea, the servants ate up the titbits or simply left. Later on, when it became obvious that I wasn't worth impressing, I heard the same slaves, those paragons of domestic service, telling the sheikh that it was too hot to do what he had asked, he'd have to do it himself. How far anyone is taken in by these phoney displays of omnipotence is hard to say; presumably other Bedu aren't, but maybe government officials and other non-Bedu guests are, to some degree. I was certainly taken in initially and probably most foreigners are if their stay is not prolonged. Impression-management is not the only interpretation of these scenes. The Bedu would undoubtedly claim that they are only insuring that their guests are properly looked after and, of course, this is true. But as many public statements (and formal feasts are statements) are only too apparently impression-management, both interpretations are probably correct.

Another reason why sheikhly power is misunderstood is historical. Between 1904 and 1936 the Rwala were represented by the present Emir's f.f.f., Emir Nuri ibn Hazza' Sha'alan. Glubb Pasha reports of him (Glubb, 1960, pp. 40-1): 'At a scarcely perceptible gesture by the old man, his clerk rolled a cigarette and placed it between his fingers. A slave stepped quickly forward with a glowing ember in a tongs to light it.' And 'Al-Nuri was a tremendous personality who maintained despotic control over his tribe. His authority was notorious' (*ibid.*). Col T. E. Lawrence (1937, pp. 85-6) remarks: 'His [Nuri's] headship had been gained by sheer force of character. To gain it he had killed two of his brothers. Later he had added the Sherarat and others to the number of his followers, and in all the desert his word was absolute law . . . All feared and obeyed him: to use his roads we must have his countenance.' Later Glubb (*ibid.*) goes on to say 'The authority which Ibn Sha'alan wielded over the Ruwallah [*sic*] was probably unique among bedouins and was due to personal fear of this formidable old man.' The implication is that it was the degree of Nuri's authority that was unique, not the fact that he had any control at all. There is no reason to doubt these reports, though Nuri's control is probably exaggerated. What is never made clear is the concatenation of circumstances that gave rise to Nuri's unique eminence.

Around 1902 Abdul Hamid, Sultan of the Ottoman Empire, made an effort to tie the great sheikhs closer to the bureaucracy. This was to be achieved by granting agricultural land to them. In return for this and dignities such as the title of Emir, they were expected to gather taxes from their tribesmen. Thus for the first time the sheikhs had an assured income that was independent of their raiding abilities and gave them the wherewithal to maintain slaves in large numbers to gather the taxes. Nuri inherited this from his predecessor and built up a veritable police force to coerce dissident tribesmen. This was a totally new development and did not last long. It seems to have reached its apogee in the early 1920s, when Ibn Sha'alan were not only large landowners but had increased their fortunes by the judicious acceptance of subsidies from both sides during the First World War. It was during this period that an elderly Damascene, whose family have been privileged traders with the Sha'alan for some generations, witnessed the spectacle of Nuri's entourage leaving for the desert. Apart from ninety camels carrying Nuri's immediate family and belongings, there were forty slave families in attendance with their accoutrements, a caravan that totalled some four hundred camels. The whole economic base of the Bedu changed with the introduction of the motor car and the decline in Nuri's power seems to have coincided with it, but political factors were also involved. The grip of the British and French mandate forces, coupled with the establishment of Ibn Saud in what is now northern Saudi Arabia, hemmed Nuri in on all sides. His freedom of action was restricted, especially as the desert was increasingly well policed from 1921 onwards. The emancipation of slaves during this period may well have had some effect although Nuri seems to have been well aware of the dangers of a Janissary corps.

Visitors do not seem to have recognised Nuri for the exception he was and, combined with the rise of Ibn Saud, first on the back of religious enthusiasm and then on oil wealth, this seems to have given rise to the opinion that sheikhs and emirs, in general, had real power. When it is realised that the vast majority of Westerners have only met sheikhs on public occasions, when the play-acting is at its height, the growth of the misconception can be readily understood.

A sheikh's authority is, like any other Bedu's, based on his reputation, especially in mediation, and this ability will have been acquired in exactly the same way as any other man's; the difference is one of degree. He will have learned his skills in his father's tent, just like anyone else, by observing his father entertaining and mediating with visiting sheikhs and high government officials. As a young man he will have started by acting as his father's deputy, dispensing hospitality to minor officials and thus starting to build up his own information network. This information network is of dual value, for not only does it represent information coming in, but it is also the manner in which reputation is spread: it is the medium for reputation range. First he will have his reputation within the family and his three- or five-generation 'ibn amm'. This is very similar to that of any Bedu's, small-scale decision-making, advice and influence. Further out will be his reputation among the tribe in general. This is based not only on his small-scale reputation but also on his successful participation in larger issues in the course of daily life in his father's tent. Mediation is not a one-man pursuit: everyone present can and does join in. For the ordinary tribesman, those present are usually limited to his three-generation 'ibn amm' and any visitors who happen to be around. For the sheikhs the audience is always wider, because their reputation and whereabouts are known to more people already. So a young man of a sheikhly family can begin to be known on a tribal basis in a way that is impossible for an ordinary tribesman of the same age. His inter-tribal reputation will be spread in the same manner but perhaps more important are his links with other sheikhly families through marriage, for this will constitute a major portion of his information network, along which reputation spreads. Examples of this are the matrilateral links between the Sha'alan and the Mheid, the sheikhly family of the Fed'an tribe. Turkiyya bint Jed'an Mheid was married to Emir Sattam ibn Hamad Sha'alan in 1877, according to Lady Anne Blunt (1879). This was the first Sha'alan–Mheid marriage, for Jed'an had only recently come to prominence following what appears to have been a split in the Fed'an tribe. Since then seven Mheid women have married Sha'alan men and nine Sha'alan women have married Mheid men. This is only for the Nayyif five-generation 'ibn amm' of the Sha'alan and only represents known marriages; there may have been other childless marriages that have now been forgotten. Although sixteen marriages may not sound very many it represents four per generation (allowing four generations per century). These raw figures are not the whole story; they conceal an extremely complex intermeshing of the two families and their further ramifications spread well beyond the two tribes.

Turkiyya bint Jed'an Mheid was married to Sattam ibn Hamad Sha'alan in 1877: she bore Khalid, Mamdurh, Misha'il (f) and Sita (f). Mamdurh was killed on a raid in 1911 and left no children. Khalid married from the sheikhly family of the Sardiyya tribe and had Sultana (f) and Tamam (f). He then married Nauf bint Mijhim ibn Turki Mheid (m.b.s.d.) and had several children including Minwar and Anoud (f). He then married a woman from the Rothan Sha'alan and had Lebiba (f). Misha'il married first Mohammad ibn Hazza' Sha'alan (f.f.b.s.) and had Mijhim and Tarifa (f). After Mohammad died in 1906 Misha'il married Nawaf ibn Nuri Sha'alan (f.f.b.s.s.) and had Fawaz and Fauza (f). Sita married Nuri ibn Hazza' Sha'alan (f.f.b.s.) in 1909 but had no children and, after his death, married Mijhim ibn Turki Mheid (m.b.s.). Sultana bint Khalid Sha'alan married Mijhim ibn Mohammad Sha'alan and only her daughter Tathi concerns us here. Tarifa bint Mohammad Sha'alan married Mijhim ibn Turki Mheid (m.m.b.s.) and had Turki and Jed'an. Tathi bint Mijhim Sha'alan married Turki ibn Mijhim Mheid (f.z.s. and other relationships) – she died in childbirth.

Jed'an Mheid was succeeded in the sheikhdom by his son Turki, who was succeeded by his half-brother Hatzim, who was, in turn succeeded by Turki's son Mijhim. One of Hatzim's daughters married Trad ibn Sattam Sha'alan, another married Fawaz ibn Nawaf ibn Nuri Sha'alan. Fauza bint Nawaf Sha'alan (Fawaz's full sister), after marrying Saud ibn Abdul Aziz Ibn Saud, married Mijhim ibn Turki Mheid and after his death his son and successor to the Sheikhdom, Nuri ibn Mijhim Mheid. Her daughters by Nuri married into the Haddal, sheikhs of the Amarat, and Abdullah ibn Abdul Aziz Ibn Saud.

Tamam bint Khalid Sha'alan, having first married her f.b.s., married Jed'an ibn Mijhim Mheid (f.m.b.s.s., f.m.d.s. and other relationships) She had Tarifa (f), Fawaz, Nayyifa (f) and Trad. Tarifa married Anwar ibn Fawaz Sha'alan (f.m.z.s.). Having divorced Tamam, Jed'an ibn Mijhim Mheid married Nura bint Fawaz Sha'alan. She had previously been married to Mish'al ibn Abdul Aziz Ibn Saud. Two of Nura's daughters by Jed'an are married: one to Nasr ibn Abdul Aziz Ibn Saud and the other to the sheikh of the Thulaim tribe of Iraq.

Khalid ibn Sattam Sha'alan had two other daughters who concern us: Anoud, whose mother is Nauf bint Turki Mheid, first married Abdullah ibn Abdul Aziz Ibn Saud, then Thamir ibn Nuri Mheid (m.b.s., also b.w.b.). She is divorced but Thamir ibn Nuri married her half-sister, Lebiba. Khalid's son, Minwar, married Gutna bint Nuri Mheid, Thamir's full sister.

It is probably unnecessary to go into the Sha'alan–Mheid marriages in any further detail – the point should by now have been made. This complex intermeshing promotes frequent contact, which increases the reputation range of the men involved. Every aspiring member of the Sha'alan should be able to spread his reputation among the Mheid, just as every aspiring Mheid should be able to spread his reputation among the Sha'alan. The Rwala and the Fed'an are, or were, the two most powerful tribes in the Syrian desert and each is from a different part of the Aneze confederation – the Rwala from the Jlas, the Fed'an from the Dhana Bishr. They used to be almost constantly 'at war', i.e. raiding and counter-raiding. The sheikhly families, although tribally enemies, were personal friends and the frequent marriages kept open the channels of communication so essential to the preservation of the proprieties of raiding.

The Sha'alan marry with many other sheikhly families although not so extensively, and so do the Mheid, so between them they cover practically every sheikhly family of every tribe of importance to them, from Aleppo to Riyadh and from Amman to Kuwait.

However, this process of spreading reputation doesn't really explain how a sheikh becomes a sheikh. An ordinary tribesman does not have the resources to become a sheikh in the normal course of events. In the past it must have been easier when raiding was the major way of building a reputation, although the 'ruling' sheikh would, unless very inefficient or unlucky, always have had a head start – his reputation would be further ranging and his information network more extensive, and he would attract a larger goum. Sha'alan, the patronymic ancestor of the Sha'alan, took over the sheikhdom of the Jlas, as the tribe then was, from the previous sheikh (from the Ga'ga' five-generation 'ibn amm' of the Ga'adza'a tribal section) by being a more successful mediator. The Jlas (or the Rwala as a tribal section of the Jlas) were at loggerheads with the inhabitants of an oasis, probably Khaibar. The Ga'ga' was unable or unwilling to resolve the dispute, so Sha'alan, an employed herdsman, opened negotiations with the oasis dwellers and achieved the desired results. From then on the tribe looked to him to deal with the outside world and he became sheikh. In other words Sha'alan was a better mediator and more in tune with what the tribe wanted. This is the common feature of most sheikhly takeovers. It indicates that the sheikh's prime task is mediation and negotiation. The sheikh's function as a mediator will be examined in the second section; here we are concerned with the sheikh's authority to act as mediator with the outside. At its crudest the sheikh has no authority to treat on the tribe's behalf, for there is no legal framework nor coercive force available to him. All the sheikh can do is represent the tribe and bank on knowing what the tribe want in any particular circumstance. He then has to persuade the tribe to accept the results of his negotiation. This is where the importance of the sheikh's acquired reputation and reputation range comes in. Unless he has a good reputation he will not have the reputation range necessary for the acquisition of information needed to decide on a course of action. He may well find himself limited by the fact that what the tribe want is unwise or dangerous, but unless he can persuade them to accept his alternative he must present their case or back down altogether. The sheikh is never a free agent, he can only act as the mouthpiece of tribal or group consensus. The consensus aspect is vital and real, as was shown, in a minor way, during an incident on the Saudi-Jordanian border. It took place at the time when the Jordanian authorities were beginning to clamp down on the passage of duty-free goods to Syria. A cigarette convoy was intercepted by a Jordanian customs patrol. As the convoy heavily outnumbered and outgunned the customs it was allowed on its way after a few transparent lies had been told about the contents. Quarter of an hour later the convoy stopped and there was a discussion as to what should be done.

Nobody had noticed whether the customs patrol had had a wireless or not, so reinforcements were a possibility. This put paid to the suggestion that the customs men should simply be killed. A suggestion that the convoy should return to Saudi Arabia and try again later was rejected as pusillanimous. Various other plans were mooted and argued about. The sheikh who led the party had not taken much part in the discussion but he scrupulously asked every person for their opinion – including even myself, who had no experience whatever nor financial interest. This wasn't just politeness, as others with as little to offer were also consulted, as were the servants and others with no direct financial stake. Only after this did the sheikh make his own suggestion, which was really an amalgam of several others – we should proceed, cautiously, until within striking distance of the dangerous section, the crossing of the Baghdad road, then hide while he scouted ahead for customs activity. Before this plan was carried out every single person was asked, individually, if he assented to it; the majority did, but one or two dissidents had to be persuaded so that a complete consensus could be achieved. Only then was the plan put into action.

The achievement of consensus is far more difficult when larger numbers are involved. For some time the burning issue in Jordan was the registration of cars and lorries belonging to members of the tribe. Many of the vehicles were not registered anywhere, had no number plates and no papers. Those that were registered had been sold and bought many times so that the names on the documents bore no relation to the name of the owner. No one worried about this too much as most were for desert transport and rarely used made-up roads. An ambitious local government official, however, decided to regularise the matter according to strict law. As Jordanian import duty at the time was 130% of the original value of the vehicle, such a move was not popular. The sheikh went over the local official's head straight to the minister involved. After two years or so an agreement was thrashed out. This agreement was reached after a long-drawn-out squence of private meetings and public feasts for local government officials, the area governor, junior ministers, the army commander, the police commandant and other interested parties. Every argument as to why all vehicles should be registered was countered by arguments as to why they shouldn't be. After each feast, which attracted up to 250 tribesmen, and after the officials had left, the men settled down to a long and often acrimonious post-mortem. Other sheikhs who had similar problems were consulted (and advised in turn) and again all the men present went through every suggestion in (to me) tedious detail. These post-mortems were supplemented by the daily meetings in the sheikh's tent, where new suggestions were put forward and discussed and the sheikh explained the government constraints that he was under. Eventually a broad consensus was achieved. The tribesmen were persuaded to realise that some concessions had to be made to the government and the sheikh gathered information about how much he could safely concede. Gradually the desirable was edged towards the possible and a compromise was reached. Registration wasn't necessary provided the vehicles remained in the desert and only visited the border town; trips to other towns could only be made in a vehicle that was properly registered somewhere and with proper papers. This simply restored the former *status quo*, but it became, as it were, official. Obviously the government could not straightaway accept special status for the Bedu, nor could the Rwala accept government dictation without public loss of face and the sheikh was the only person with the information, reputation and reputation range to bridge the gulf between the two sides. It also had to be a consensus decision, for neither side really had the ability to impose a settlement. The Rwala didn't have the power and the Jordanians didn't have the mobility to enforce compliance, for tribesmen can cross boundaries freely while government troops can't. The sheikh was well aware of this and had to achieve an agreement that didn't need enforcing, for he had no coercive powers over either party. If he failed he might find himself supplanted by another member of his family; it was consensus or nothing.

The case of vehicle registration demonstrates not only the importance of consensus but also how the Sha'alan carry on, under modern conditions, their traditional role as mediators with the outside. One aspect of this role was (and still is) to ensure that the tribe had access to markets while guaranteeing that the market was safe from extortion or predation. Under the Treaty of Hadda in 1924 the Rwala were guaranteed freedom of access to their traditional markets and grazing irrespective of political boundaries. In theory this still holds good but the Treaty had not foreseen import duty, nationality or currency regulations, all of which the Rwala feel entitled to ignore. Nobody in their right minds would attempt to transport goods by camel, for few towns, let alone customs posts, have facilities for them, but the rules and regulations concerning trucks, drivers, registration, etc. make even ordinary trade for nomads very difficult unless they settle. It is the sheikh's job to bend the rules, persuade officials to turn a blind eye and try to ensure that the tribe co-operates. In one way this widening of the arena has strengthened sheikhly families. It is now far more difficult for another family to take over because the necessary reputation range is now so enormous that it would take more than a generation to build up. However, there is still competition, for the principle of heredity is not linear, i.e. a man is not succeeded by his son; any member of the family can become Emir provided he can do the job. The family is large and their collective reputation high, so most tribesmen are content. As long as the Emir is from the Sha'alan it doesn't matter which individual it is as long as he is competent.

As the parameters of their world have widened, sheikhs have taken on a more ambassadorial role. This is not an anthropologist's construct but what they say themselves. Because the tribe still ranges over the territories of four sovereign states it remains, in some ways, semi-autonomous and it is the sheikh's job to maintain this. They rarely lose an opportunity to demonstrate their independence. This may be as dramatic as the sheikh's arrival at the royal palace in Jordan during the civil war at the head of

Plate 7. Sheikh Nuri Sha'alan with official guests

1100 armed tribesmen. Or it may be private. Emir Abdullah ibn Abdul Aziz Ibn Saud is a devout man; all members of his entourage are expected to pray regularly and he is said to have a little black book in which defections are recorded. A party of the Sha'alan visited him while he was hunting in Syria, but refused to join the prayer line at sunset – 'We are Rwala, we do not pray.' This can have been nothing but an assertion of independence for, although not markedly devout, all are practising Moslems and several of them do pray with fair regularity. The assumption of ambassadorial status is simply another facet of this independence. The justification of it is historical and it is by no means confined to the Sha'alan. Sheikhs of important tribes are frequently at airports to greet visiting diplomats or heads of state and they are frequently included at official receptions and hold such receptions in their turn. They feel that they have a right to maintain independent relations with heads of state and they take this right very seriously. When King Faysal ibn Abdul Aziz Ibn Saud paid an official visit to Jordan there was no time for the usual round of receptions. Rather than forego their opportunity to demonstrate independence the Sha'alan and the sheikhs of two other tribes reverted to an old custom and held a public reception in the street. Despite the protests of the police and the invocation of numerous by-laws and health regulations, eleven camels were slaughtered in the main street of Amman and the meat distributed to the poor.

The ambassadorial function is not all grand grestures and conspicuous display. It is serious work for the Emir, several of his brothers and his paternal uncle. The Sha'alan have few, if any, coercive powers nowadays –

they can no longer threaten to sack a town for instance – so their diplomacy is a delicate mixture of personalities, ambitions, political half-promises and the like. Not surprisingly I was rarely privy to these negotiations, which take place, unofficially, over coffee or at the dinner table. I never cared to delve too deeply into the shadowy world of political wheeling and dealing. What is quite clear is that it takes up a lot of time, much entertaining and many prestations. In consequence it is extremely expensive. Until the Sha'alan lost most of their agricultural holdings under the Ba'ath regime in the early 1960s, this didn't matter too much as they were extremely rich. Latterly they have started to recoup their lost wealth and their bargaining position has improved.

At this level the line between mediator and negotiator becomes blurred: as far as the tribe is concerned the sheikh is a mediator because he mediates between them and the outside and they dictate what he can and cannot concede. From the outside point of view the sheikh is a negotiator because he is part of the tribe, acts as their spokesman and is nominally their leader. I will stick with the word 'mediator', for the sheikh can never make a binding decision on either side, he can only hope that the tribe will follow his recommendations. Any belief by outsiders that he is a leader in any but a charismatic sense is wholly erroneous and can only lead to misunderstanding. Whatever the sheikh's exact semantic position, he must have something to offer the outside authorities in exchange for concessions; there must be a *quid pro quo*. For the tribe it is sufficient that the Sha'alan can offer them the best chance of maintaining the status quo and freedom from too much bureaucratic interference – but what can the Sha'alan offer the various governments in return? The answer seems to be, peace and quiet. The Bedu are well aware that governments are stronger than they, politically, economically and militarily. Any government could crush the tribes in their territory at any time but they don't, because the tribe's cause could only too easily be taken up by an unfriendly neighbour with unpredictable results. However weak the practical nature of segmentary solidarity may be in fostering inter-tribal co-operation, it is sufficiently strong for it to be a distinct threat; moreover many armies are made up largely of Bedu. The Rwala play a large part in this game of bluff and counter-bluff for they are very numerous and can cross borders freely and legitimately. The inter-state squabbles, which are the norm in the area at the moment, can be exploited by them fairly easily. Thus the affront to the Sha'alan, which affected the tribe as well, when their land was confiscated, was countered by a retreat into Jordan, which was hardly on speaking terms with Syria at the time. From there they waged economic warfare on the Ba'athists in terms of smuggling. This had certain economic effects, for the quantities of U.S. cigarettes smuggled into Syria were so enormous that the government was forced to start making U.S. cigarettes under licence. And the quantities really were enormous – at one time I calculated that the number of cigarettes passing through one encampment alone, if kept at that level, was sufficient to supply the entire population of Saudi

Arabia, man, woman and child, with two packets a day. Nor was this all the cost, for the Syrian government was forced to deploy troops in the area, complete with arms, trucks, light A.A. guns, tanks and helicopters to try to contain the smuggling. This is an example of nuisance, but there are positive benefits that the Rwala can offer too. Jordan, which had given the Rwala sanctuary, found her northern border effectively policed for free. At the time of the civil war this had the effect of denying the Fedayeen access to the loyalist flank and prevented infiltration. Moreover the presence of the Rwala across the supply- and retreat-lines of the Iraqi army is said to have been a major reason for their decision not to support the Syrian tank-thrust into north Jordan.

The Rwala can offer similar policing actions to any of four governments in return for being left alone. At the first sign of interference this facility can be withdrawn, which, in most cases, leaves the border wide open for smugglers, political dissidents and illegal immigrants. Further provocation can cause the Rwala to retreat across a border and become an expensive nuisance and a political sore point. This is never a concerted action, for there is no corporation or chain of command, in fact no power to change attitudes – the sheikh relies on his reputation and his example to persuade the tribe to follow him. Timing is essential; to move too soon leaves those behind open to reprisals, to move too late leaves the way open for a rival to usurp his position: in either case the outcome is likely to be a diminution of reputation and loss of influence. The commonest example of nuisance is smuggling. This is an activity that the tribesmen understand and enjoy (they quite specifically see smuggling as a substitute for raiding) and it can be very profitable. The negotiations with officialdom are in the hands of the sheikhs. They ensure that the central government of the host country is not going to object and they negotiate with local officials the turning of a blind eye and the making of recompense. In return they ensure that tribesmen only smuggle in the right direction. This is carried out by normal business methods; those who don't fall in line find that their supply of goods is curtailed, for the sheikh, as the biggest customer, can make sure that the supplier is careful to whom he sells. Often it is even easier than this, as the sheikh acts as guarantor of credit facilities, which he can withdraw at will. In short the sheikh is given the franchise to smuggle in return for peace and services rendered. The setting-up of such nuisance operations is fairly easy, but closing them down is far more difficult. Relations between states change and there is a constant risk that the tribe's activities will become an embarrassment to the host country. For this reason the sheikh must keep his eye on the wider political arena so that he can redeploy his assets with a minimum of disruption. This is an area where a sheikh's reputation range is a vital asset, for it is the major means of obtaining information on current political thinking, the groundswell of popular opinion both inside and outside the tribe and the likelihood of political moves and *volte-faces*. As soon as a hint filters through of a change in government policy the sheikh must reorganise his dispositions and start to inform the tribe of changes. As he is still bound by consensus decisions he must balance the likely behaviour of the government against the inertia of the tribe. To initiate change too slowly lays the tribe open to the risk of reprisals for which he will bear the blame; to try to change course too quickly brings the risk of losing touch with the tribe and being accused of being subservient. In either case he lays himself open to the risk of losing his influence and damaging, maybe fatally, his personal reputation. By some means he must present new options for the tribesmen and at the same time keep the host government happy while he is working the changeover. A rearguard action of this sort demands diplomatic skills of a high order, especially as there is the everpresent danger of a more reckless rival from within the family ready to supplant him in influence.

In a political system of this sort, where the 'leader' has no coercive powers at all, his best means of justifying and maintaining his position is by being better informed than anyone else. Thus the sheikh has to ensure that information pours in from all quarters. This isn't as difficult as it sounds; it is just very expensive, which is not to say that information is bought but that the sheikh must keep open house (or rather tent) for all comers. A smuggling encampment is an obvious focus for opponents to a regime. Political dissidents, as such, rarely appear but clandestine contacts are maintained. This is largely an insurance policy, for the Rwala are not very interested in political ideology but are aware that, in the volatile political atmosphere of the Arab world, today's dissident may easily be tomorrow's prime minister. The majority of those who come to stay are either out of work or wanted by the police. These latter are not common criminals (for whom the Rwala have no sympathy whatever) but those who have killed in defence of family honour – the man who murdered his wife and her lover, the soldier who murdered his sister for prostitution. Such protection-seekers are common and to give protection and act as mediator has always been one of the functions of a man of influence. The desirability of these incomers lies in their ability to enlarge reputation range and to bring in information, as well as to promote creature comforts, as they frequently work as servants. Occasionally such men bring in financial benefits because they come from groups not normally in contact with the Rwala and thus promote links into Turkey or Kurdistan, for instance.

This catalogue of illegality must be seen in perspective. The purpose of smuggling is not primarily to make money (though that is not ignored) but to make a political statement. Its aim is not to destroy a society but to embarrass an unfriendly government and to assert tribal rights and independence. For this reason, as well as moral ones, only 'legitimate' goods are handled, i.e. cigarettes, cloth, electrical goods etc. Narcotics, liquor and illegal immigrants are handled only by a few and then in a strictly private capacity – narcotics, in particular, are despised and those who deal in them (other than hashish) suffer a severe diminution of reputation.

All these tribesmen, protection-seekers, servants and hangers-on have to be carefully vetted, not only to minimise the risk of embarrassing the host country but also to ensure that none of them are agents of an unfriendly government. For a man who comes from the Turkish border this may take months because of the number of intermediaries necessary to determine his bona fides. The mention of agents may sound melodramatic, but they certainly exist and every new arrival is treated with reserve until his provenance is established. This is not peculiar to smuggling communities, which only make up a very small proportion of the tribe, for in the raiding past any stranger was suspect. Even today, at any encampment, the inquisitive stranger will be met by a blank wall of 'Don't know' until his identity is certain. All these visitors are augmented by large numbers of straight unemployed, itinerants, peddlers, gypsies and just plain beggars. This is the other face of a large reputation range. Few of these people have any tribal affiliation; they are mostly peasants or townsmen who have heard of the generosity of the Sha'alan and have come for help. They are courteously greeted, listened to, fed, clothed and sent on their way with a cash gift or other hand-out. In effect the sheikhs run an alternative welfare benefit system for those who don't fit into any official category – the man whose house and family were wiped out by a stray Israeli shell, the widow with three children who fails to qualify for a state pension, the man collecting money to pay compensation for a fatal car smash, young men seeking support for university education, the pilgrim to Mecca who had run out of money. All had heard of Sha'alan generosity and all had come for help. They come from far and wide, Syria, Iraq, Jordan, Turkey, even Afghanistan. Quite apart from this the sheikhs (or indeed any man of influence) run what amounts to a complete welfare system for the tribe. They can say, with justification: 'There are no poor Rwala, they come to us.' Widows, orphans, the old, crippled or mentally-handicapped, anyone who has no one to turn to, can call on the sheikhs for support. This generosity, which is common to all Bedu, is not just to fulfil religious obligations, but is, in itself, a political statement of autonomy and a means of spreading reputa- and gathering information. Naturally all those who are entitled to state benefits collect them, but the many who are outside them can be certain of sustenance and protection.

All these gifts, jobs and financial support that the sheikhs provide are personal, individual matters. The degree of generosity depends on the individual concerned and goes to increase his personal reputation. Nor is it entirely confined to the sheikhs; few in need are turned away from any tent completely empty-handed. Obviously the Sha'alan bear the brunt of it because their reputation range is the widest and their whereabouts known to many people, but any Rwala will give according to his means. For total outsiders the personal aspect doesn't come into it; for them it is just 'Ibn Sha'alan are generous' and they do not distinguish between individuals who are only known to them by the family cognomen. There is no direct reciprocity for this generosity: this was emphasised over and over again, at all levels. The sole repayment is the increase and spreading of reputation and even this is verbally deprecated. Any form of thanks is always brushed aside with 'God is generous.' Again the Sha'alan are no different from any other tribesman in this respect, it is simply that they are known more widely and are rather richer than others so that more people come to them for help; they work on a larger scale. It would however, be wrong to imply that this generosity is wholly disinterested. Quite apart from increasing and spreading reputation, it is also an insurance policy. As will be shown in the chapter on economics, wealth can be uncertain and unpredictable: the emphasis on generosity, while it may confer political influence, also ensures future subsistence if things go wrong – tomorrow's beggar might be you.

Recapitulation

Political power and authority, in their normal usage, have little relevance to Rwala society. Political power implies socially legitimised right, while authority implies a moral right, to exercise coercion. Neither of these rights exist among the Rwala. Even where a right might exist, as in *lex talionis*, it would be more accurate to say that avengers have an obligation to avenge their loss rather than a right to do so. This may sound like semantic quibbling, but in a society where the largest corporate group is, in theory, the five-generation 'ibn amm' but for practical purposes is the smaller three-generation 'ibn amm', the fulfilling of obligations towards one's group is far more important and productive than insisting upon one's rights. It seems pointless to talk of rights when there is no form of coercion available to obtain them, other than diffuse public opinion; all that can be said is that all have their obligations. Failure to fulfil obligations lowers reputation and reduces the honour of the group and this, as we have seen, has effects on the options available, security, political influence, marriage partners and the generative genealogy. This principle applies to the Emir as well as to the poorest tribesman. The Emir has no right to negotiate on behalf of the tribe but, being the most influential man in a position to negotiate, he has an obligation to do so. If he fails to fulfil this obligation he is no longer Emir, although he may hang on to the empty title. He won't be deposed, for no such mechanism exists, but individuals and groups will no longer trust him or seek his advice – they will turn to someone else. Similarly the meanest tribesman cannot insist, as of right, that his adult son should co-operate with him: his son undoubtedly has an obligation to do so, but there could be circumstances where non-fulfilment could be a better option, e.g. if the father has an appalling reputation. Thus self-interest seems to be the mainspring, not self-interest in the sense of selfishness, but self-interest in the sense of the desire to succeed within the system. Any man is free to leave the system altogether if he so wishes, but if he wants to stay within the system he must fulfil his obligations. Success within the system is based on reputation and any man with a good reputation is a *rajul tayyib* – a good man. Anyone who becomes a good man is able to pursue political ambitions, which can only mean political influence. Obviously political options are not the only ones open to a man of good reputation nor need such a man actively pursue political ambition. In fact the majority of men reach a sort of plateau of reputation where some degree of activity is needed in order to continue further. Those who remain on the plateau tend to intermarry, as ambition doesn't lead them to do otherwise, and the more ambitious individuals see them as a poor option in their upward climb. Some groups and individuals seem to refrain deliberately from pursuing the political path as an option in itself. Their reasons may be demographic, i.e. they are too small a group to achieve a wider reputation range, or they may simply see other options, such as wealth or personal comfort, as more attractive. Nobody despises them for this nor do they necessarily lose reputation; they, like all other members of the tribe are free to exploit their assets as they wish and to concentrate on whichever option they deem the most worthwhile. There is some evidence that this is a factor in the manner in which groups split into smaller units, but as the process takes a generation or two it is difficult to be categorical. Most men never leave the plateau; they have a good reputation among their five-generation 'ibn amm' and a degree of influence within that group. Wider influence is mostly confined to some tsebirs of tribal sections and the active members of the Sha'alan. The principles are the same but through inheritance their reputation range is wider and their economic base is larger and, in some degree, more secure. The political influence of the sheikhs is undoubtedly maintained, in part, by their wealth, but that wealth, which enables them to entertain on a scale commensurate with their influence, cannot be used to coerce. Any attempt at enforcing a decision would simply result in the fading of influence for it would imply a lack of equality and consensus. Decision by consensus and public opinion are the only 'rule' that free Bedu will tolerate.

Emir Sattam ibn Hamad Sha'alan met the Blunts in 1878. He is quoted as saying: 'I can only do what my people wish' (Blunt, 1879, p. 140). He spoke no less than the truth, for although he thought that what the tribe wanted was mistaken, in this instance, there was nothing he could do about it. The Blunts took him to be weak, but had he tried to coerce he would have been deserted. The fundamental principle remains the same today, leadership by consensus. Political power does not exist.

8 Economics

This chapter is not about accounts and cash flows but about what economic options are open to the Rwala. While an analysis of family incomes has a certain fascination and usefulness (and I do have a few figures) the varying rates of inflation and the restlessness of exchange rates makes it very difficult to elucidate. Beyond these objections there is another far more serious. The Rwala don't think in these sort of terms anyway and to explain their economy in Western terms would give a lopsided and essentially unfaithful view. Very few could give a profit-and-loss account or a breakdown of income and expenditure; they just don't think in that way. Money comes in and money goes out; if you have money you spend it or lend it to relatives, if money doesn't come in you go without or borrow from relatives. One of the sheikhs, through whose hands tens of thousands of pounds sterling passed annually, was frequently strapped for cash and used to borrow £50 off me to pay for repairs to a truck. On the other hand, when money was available he would hand out hundreds with gay abandon or buy another new car (which would be given away in a few weeks). This insouciant attitude is very attractive but it makes it almost impossible to maintain accounts. Consequently I make no attempt to do so.

This carefree attitude to money is in part genuine and in part impression-management and it is, I think, confined to surplus money, i.e. cash over and above the needs of the immediate family. The women, who are equally generous, keep household accounts fairly carefully and are keen on value for money. They could often tell one with no difficulty whether sugar at 35 Syrian pounds a rotl was cheaper or more expensive than sugar at 42 Saudi riyals a kilo, and at last week's exchange rate as well. All this could have been worked out with the aid of a calculator and a figure arrived at for average family expenditure, but the problem is complicated by other factors. Visitors and relations are always laden with presents – dates from Jauf, sheep-fat from Iraq, cheese from Aleppo, rice from Riyadh, olives from Lebanon, coffee-beans, spices, flour, wool, cloth, ammunition, honey, yoghourt, biscuits, chocolate, jewellery, tent-cloth, in fact practically anything. This wouldn't be too difficult to take into account but what do you do about flour from the peasants who now own the land confiscated from you fifteen years ago? Or dates from the slaves who now farm those groves that belonged to your grandfather but have

Plate 8. Abu Satwe (in skull-cap). Third generation of a Syrian family that has a special trading relationship with the Rwala.

since been abandoned by the family? I'm not talking about small quantities but about six months supply or more. There is no standard 'shopping-basket' for comparison. If you have nothing but broad beans and rice for two months you eat broad beans and rice for two months. A herding family once asked me to a lunch that consisted of coffee and camel's milk – they had nothing else and hadn't had anything else for over three months. They didn't feel hard-done-by or poor, nor were they particularly short of cash; they could quite easily have gone to the nearest market (about two hours' drive) and bought food and new clothes, but they didn't. This wasn't meanness or laziness or apathy, they found camel's milk and coffee quite adequate for the time being and that was all. With such a markedly different attitude to money and goods how can one produce accounts that have even the smallest meaning? Another problem is that debts are rarely paid and credit can be of indefinite duration and inheritable. I know traders who haven't seen a penny in cash from certain families in eleven years or more, yet they still extend credit. Some of the debt was certainly paid but in the form of a quiet word to the immigration official not to worry about proper papers or to the customs and excise concerning the import of goods without tax payment. How do you put these in an account? Like debts, compensation and the payment of bride-price can be dragged out for years, over twenty years in some cases. Obviously in many cases the on-going relationship was of greater importance than the cash, but how do you put it on a balance sheet?

There was nothing tidy about Rwala economics in our sense of the word and I abandoned any attempt to make Western sense of it.

(a) The economic options of the ordinary tribesman

The economic situation of the Rwala has changed rapidly in the last fifty years or so. The main concern in this chapter is what the Rwala do for a living now; the events that lead up to it are considered in greater detail in Part II. Before the First World War the primary economic activities were raiding and selling camels, but when mechanised transport became available the bottom dropped out of the camel-market. This not only removed the value of the Rwala's main marketable asset (they, unlike other tribes, had few horses), but also the whole point of raiding. The demand for camels as meat could not hope to fill the gap, so the ordinary Rwala moved, for a short time, into what was virtually a subsistence economy. This was a totally new departure, for whereas formerly they had lived symbiotically with the townspeople, providing transport, meat, protection and desert products, they now had little to offer in exchange for dates, metal goods, grain and cloth. About fifteen or twenty camels are reckoned necessary for the survival of a family of six and the Rwala had far in excess of this, but this excess wasn't readily convertible any longer. This situation seems to have obtained, more or less, until 1958, when a

severe drought occurred over the whole Middle East. This drought continued, as far as the Rwala were concerned, until 1962. (According to official Saudi figures the drought lasted from 1956 to 1972, but the Rwala
of course could exploit rainfall in Syria and Iraq.) The toll in camels was
enormous: the Rwala claim to have lost about 85% of their herds. Such
figures as I have been able to collect indicate a death-rate nearer 70%, but
even so it was very severe. While it is possible that, on average, fifteen
camels per nuclear family survived, the effects were uneven and the
remaining camels gave a greatly reduced yield in terms of both quantity
and quality of milk. (It is interesting to note that while we heard many
tales of hardship and illness dating from this time, scurvy being the commonest symptom, on no occasion did anyone claim that any person or
child died as a result.)

The upshot of the drought was a large number of Rwala who desperately needed an alternative source of livelihood. Fortunately the oil boom
in Saudi Arabia was just getting into full swing and many tribesmen found
work there, but it was not sufficient for all. The other major opportunity
was the National Guard. This private army of Ibn Saud's was greatly
expanded at this time in response to the Bedu need and many thousands
flocked to join it. Other armies, the Jordanian and Kuweiti in particular,
also attracted large numbers of tribesmen. The opportunities in industry in
the early 1960s would have been greater but for the fact that the majority
of the Rwala were illiterate. This confined them to seeking jobs as un-
skilled labourers, drivers or guards in the oil companies or the lower non-
commissioned ranks in the armed services.

Today the situation has changed. The herds are slowly being built up,
many men were educated in the companies or armies (and their children
were educated as well) and with increasing skills at their disposal new
options have become available. The attraction of the oil companies has
declined, even for those with a trade skill like welding, and the majority of
employed men are in the National Guard, Reserve National Guard or some
other armed service. Those who are herding seem to be turning increasingly
to sheep - the reasons are examined later. In the absence of any official
statistics it is difficult to compute even the proportions of those employed
and those herding, but from figures I have obtained from the Rwala (figures
compiled from lists of individuals in various five-generation 'ibn amms') it
would appear that about half the adult males, mainly the younger ones,
are employed, while the other half are engaged in herding of some sort.
There is also a small number doing something else.

Whatever the proportions, they are not, from the anthropological point
of view, very important because in no sense is the tribe split into different
blocks. As with almost every other aspect of life the situation is very fluid,
nor are the two categories of employed and herders at all distinct. The
practical group for economic activities is the three-generation 'ibn amm',
which usually includes a whole range of age groups. So while the younger
men may mostly be employed, the herds (be they sheep or camel) are

looked after by the older men. Although there is a clear concept of private ownership, the three-generation 'ibn amm' is thought of as essentially corporate, or at least co-operative, so a young man who owns some camels is able to leave them with his father, brother, uncle or some other near relative. The money he earns is his absolutely but owing to the prevailing ethic of generosity and for the sake of his own reputation, it is usually available for the use of anyone in his three-generation 'ibn amm'. The majority of those who are wage-earners use their savings to increase their herds by purchase: in fact nearly all those who used to be engaged in smuggling have retired, having invested their capital in sheep. Very recently there is evidence that more money is being invested in other areas such as trading, contracting or services, but this is not yet marked.

As far as herding is concerned there has been a major change since 1920. Until then only the Frejje tribal section had sheep in any number; the others were almost exclusively camel-herders. The type of sheep which the Frejje owned were the Turkish or fat-tailed sheep. This breed does not do well in the south but whether the Frejje stayed north because of their sheep or took to sheep-herding because they moved north is not clear. Camels do not do very well in Syria owing to the cold in winter, which is when they calve – the death-rate among young camels was unacceptably high. Recently, since about 1970, other sections of the tribe have turned increasingly to sheep. The reasons are twofold. Sheep breed faster than camels and are more easily marketable, and by using trucked water grazing can be exploited that was not previously available to sheep. In addition the outlay required for a subsistence number of sheep is far smaller than that for

Plate 9. Sheep belonging to the Zeid 'ibn amm' being watered by tanker

an economically comparable number of camels. In 1976 a flock of sheep sufficient for survival plus a truck for water would have cost around £2000: a comparable camel-herd would have cost double that. When it is realised that sheep will more or less cover their purchase price after one year while a camel will take at least three, it is hardly surprising that sheep are the more attractive option. In fact about half those Rwala who herded actively had sheep in 1976; now, in 1978, the proportion is higher. Herding sheep has other advantages, for the herder if not the environment; as sheep need water daily the encampment must be either near water or within daily driving distance. For much of the year this means that a town or other permanent settlement must be regularly visited. This gives the herder the opportunity of maintaining frequent contact with his children while they are being educated. This is more difficult for camel-herders, who can camp further from water and need to visit settlements far less frequently. The Rwala are well aware of the advantages of literacy; they were seriously disadvantaged in the years after the drought. However they are not blind to the inadequacies of the educational systems in which they find themselves. It is probably inevitable, in the Arab world as elsewhere, that the least socially desirable schools get the least competent teachers. What is less excusable is that all education is town-orientated, frequently Western town-orientated, and that everything is geared to laud town life and deride peasant, and particularly nomadic, values and practices. This tendency is probably unconscious, but the Rwala resent it and see education (in their more despondent moments) as being deliberately designed to settle their children and turn them into townsmen. Unfortunately, education as it is organised at present

Plate 10. Murath camel-herd at a rainpool on the Syrian–Jordanian border

is incompatible with camel-herding and camel-herders are presented with an either/or choice, for ever. This is because camel-herding demands a very long training in terms of environment, rainfall, ecology, grazing, nutrition of camels, micro-climates and many other factors that are all inter-related; this can only be learned by doing. Education prevents the building-up of this kind of essential information and the Bedu are the loser – so, in the long run, are the states involved. By 1979 there seemed to be a swing against formal education in schools. Many boys were only going to school to become basically literate and numerate; they then left and continued their education in an army or the National Guard, where the training is of a more practical nature. Girls, especially in Saudi Arabia, are beginning to refuse to go to school at all as they see it as pointless. Why become literate when there are no jobs for women afterwards? (Adult education for women is a different matter: it is enormously popular as it is an opportunity to meet other people.) It must be pointed out that this is the view of the children themselves. Personal autonomy is so highly prized that such decisions are made by the child, although the parents will advise.

If the present and future economic advantages of sheep seem to be so overwhelming, why do so many Rwala stick to camels? In the first place they like camels and don't much like sheep: this is emotional and has no economic basis. Secondly, and more importantly, camels have the great advantage that it is possible to subsist on them for long periods of time with little or no reference to any outside body. The Rwala see this as independence and as an insurance policy. With camels, if the economic climate turns sour or if oil runs out (both possibilities to which they are alive), they can survive; with sheep they cannot. For many Rwala this is their stated reason for maintaining marginally economic camel-herds. At a more abstract level, the Emir and others see camels as essential to the long-term future of the tribe and the maintenance of their identity. So strongly do they hold to this view that the majority of 'ibn amm' (in 1978) had both sheep and camels, thus keeping both options open. The sheep produce the main income while the camels provide subsistence for those who herd them and an insurance policy for the group. This splitting of assets leads to fewer complications than might be expected. Sheep and camels have different requirements and are best herded separately, but the division of personnel that this entails is more apparent than real. Five- or three-generation 'ibn amms' have rarely, if ever, lived and worked as a single residential unit, but rather as several subunits exploiting different areas or options. Thus the children of camel-herders can be educated with their sheep-herding cousins, while extra members of the group can herd camels or sheep as necessary. It is a very elastic system, which ensures that the group maintains cohesion by the constant, informal swapping of personnel, even though the different herds may be far apart. By 1979 there were some indications that this was breaking down. More and more individuals, families and groups seemed to be giving up camels to go into farming, contracting or entrepreneurial activities. How widespread or permanent this development may be is not yet clear as the entrepreneurial/trading scene is wide open for exploitation and agriculture has its attractions at the present; it may well be only a temporary phenomenon reflecting present conditions. In 1979 all the camels were in Iraq (for which I could get no visa) so I only saw those who had already made the decision to take up new options.

The same fluidity seems to permeate the other major option open to the Rwala – paid employment. Most men (and this option applies almost exclusively to men) who are employed work for the National Guard, Reserve National Guard, a non-Saudi armed service or an oil company. There are a few bureaucrats, customs officers, teachers, drivers, school janitors, mechanics and the like, but they make up a very small minority, though it will probably increase as the first generation to have full-time education grows up. Far and away the most popular option is the Saudi National Guard. Not only is the pay good but the duties are not very arduous and as they are essentially martial, without much parade-ground militarism, it fits well into the Bedu ethos. There are also ample opportunities and encouragement for basic and further education and the acquisition of trade skills. The number of Rwala who belong to the National Guard is not publicly known but it is very large and they say that they make up the largest single tribal group within it. Some men make a definite full-time career of it and achieve high rank and commensurate responsibility, but the majority see it as a method of acquiring a skill and saving enough money to invest in another enterprise. Thus the major proportion of the Rwala in the National Guard are under thirty-five or so and intend leaving when they judge that the time is ripe. Many of those who leave join the Reserve National Guard, a lower-paid body of men who can be called up in an emergency. As far as the Rwala understand it the duties of the Reserve National Guard are rather vague and, apart from appearing at the local headquarters, complete with rifle, every six months or so, it appears to entail little. It doesn't seem to prevent those on the payroll from helping out with herding, engaging in trading ventures or, indeed, any other activity. It doesn't even seem to prevent members from crossing international boundaries, although special permission may be necessary for this. A job with an oil company is a less popular option. Apart from a few career administrators most of the Rwala who work for a company are skilled craftsmen, drivers, mechanics or guards. One of the reasons for the lack of popularity is that most of the openings are in Dhahran or Hasa, areas well outside the normal range of the Rwala and therefore unfamiliar. With no relations in the area, a rather depressing compound environment and a humid climate, the attractions for the Rwala are not great. The small number who do go are only there temporarily, usually doing a course in electronics, welding, English or some other skill. Very different is the case of T.A.P.-line, which runs along the northern border of Saudi Arabia. The western end, up as far as Turayf, runs through traditional Rwala territory and the majority of employees are Rwala. The few small villages that cluster round the pumping-stations are almost 100% Rwala and are mostly the families of men working for the company. However, many are now leaving and not encouraging their children to take up employment in it. Since the Lebanese civil war and the destruction of the pipe's outlet at Sidon the line is only used to supply Jordan and it is generally acknowledged that it would be more economic to close T.A.P.-line and truck in Jordan's requirements. The pipeline is kept open for social rather than economic reasons and the employees feel that they have an uncertain future, so many are leaving. Again no figures are available. Conversations with former employees suggest either that they use the money saved and the training acquired to set themselves up as traders, building contractors, mechanics or in some similar self-employment or that they use the money to buy sheep or to enlarge existing herds.

Thus the major economic options are sheep-herding or employment, with camel-herding as an insurance. There is, however, a significant difference between the two. Sheep-herding is largely a family or three-generation 'ibn amm' affair while employment only involves the individual. As gaining employment is still largely a family affair in any field the divisive tendency in the move from co-operation to personal income is still masked, but the Rwala are aware of the danger and guard against it as far as they are able. Most three-generation 'ibn amms' get the best of both worlds by combining both options: the older men, helped by some of the young men, herd the sheep or camels, while a high proportion of the young men seek paid employment for a varying number of years. Some three-generation 'ibn amm' herd exclusively or have no herds at all, but most spread their assets as widely as possible and have fingers in many pies. Size is obviously a limiting factor, but any 'ibn amm' that is too large or too small is only temporarily so; the generative genealogy and the essential balance of the segmentary system soon rectifies it. So within the tribe as a whole there is no division between herders and non-herders; indeed no such division is apparent among tribal sections or smaller groups. Within groups, individuals move freely from herding to employment and back again, so most groups have a pool of experience upon which they can draw to take up new options.

While these are the main options there are a host of minor ones (minor in the sense that few take them up), which run the gamut of livelihoods. As education becomes more usual the range will undoubtedly spread to include more people. Of these opportunities the most important are local government bureaucracy; teaching and the professions; agriculture; and smuggling/trading. So far, lack of education has kept Rwala participation in local government and the professions to the minimum. Of the Rwala I have met (who make up only a small proportion of the tribe) there have been one *Qadi* ('lawyer/judge'), four or five teachers (including one woman) and several employed in the Post Office, municipal offices and the local offices of government departments. As the educated generation comes of age this section will probably increase but there are disadvantages to these sorts of jobs in Rwala eyes. Although the jobs give access to some low-level information they never give rise to the financial means to exploit that information. The jobs are secure and the pay comfortable but it is never (or rarely) possible to build up enough capital to acquire economic independence. And this is what most Rwala want, to be independent and self-employed. Against this is the fact that families, groups, sections and the tribe can benefit by having a strong presence in local government. The Rwala made a late start in this field and have found that much aid and many grants and government funds are steered towards others who have more functionaries (and of longer standing) in local bureaucracy. This, at least, is their interpretation of it and it seems likely enough, for controllers of funds are bound to be swayed by the advice of their own colleagues. Rwala ambivalence toward local government jobs in particular, is a reflection of their awareness that involvement necessarily means some loss of independence. This is a dilemma that they have not yet solved.

Agriculture in Saudi is in a period of change, experiment and frantic expansion. Formerly no Rwala practised agriculture except as a landowner or date-grove owner employing share-croppers. However, the prospects, especially in the form of grants and soft loans, are now so attractive that increasing numbers are trying it out. The Bedu may despise the behaviour of peasants but not the peasants themselves nor their skills, which the Rwala have not yet acquired. It is difficult to portray the absolutely total ignorance of the ordinary Rwala in agricultural matters – the fact that plants grow in the ground, have seeds and need water seems to be the sum of their knowledge. And they freely admit it. They have not yet been able to utilise their extensive knowledge of the eco-system in terms of straight agricultural production; it will come in time. So however willing they may be to learn, their lack of expertise hampers them from the start. So far their efforts have met with little success. This is scarcely due to any failure on their part. Starting from scratch on marginal land they are virtually confined to the easier crops like barley, tomatoes, melons, radishes, spring onions etc. Unfortunately all these can be grown perfectly well in and around the towns, so they end up with a low-quality crop when there is already a glut. They are also forced by their lack of skill to employ peasant labour from Syria, which pushes their costs so high in Saudi (the main market) that imported produce from Jordan or Syria still undercuts them. Many do not pay labourers direct but work a share-cropping system. The arrangements vary but for most small plots the profits are split fifty–fifty with the peasants doing the marketing. The peasants also get their keep during the planting and growing season, but this comes out of their share later. The whole agricultural system has other drawbacks. Syrian or Iraqi peasants have detailed knowledge of irrigation farming in their own environments, but this is not wholly suited to conditions in northern Saudi Arabia. Water, even with the new wells, is limited and saline: the high rate of evaporation from channel or flood irrigation not only wastes water but leaves a heavy deposit of salt on the surface. On one typical farm the salt

Plate 11. Iraqi expert supervising fig-pruning in a new garden at Sweir

glistens in the sun and is clearly visible as a white crust over the soil: this plot is only three years old. Some of these problems could be overcome by techniques such as trickle irrigation, but the peasants employed don't know about it and no experts have got as far as Rwala territory yet. Another drawback is that share-croppers only contract to work for a year at a time. If, as is usual, the returns are far below what they have been led to expect, they are reluctant to return the next year. So the Rwala land-owner has to find another share-cropper, complete the paperwork for his entry and residence permits and start all over again, usually rather late in the seasons. The sad cycle begins again, if it is not abandoned.

The earliest serious attempt at farming that I know of was undertaken by a Rwala some twenty or more years ago. A man from the Ga'adza'a tribal section made a definite decision that the old days were over for ever and that the future lay in agriculture. Despite opposition from his family, ridicule from his friends and official refusal to take an interest he managed to obtain the title deeds for a piece of land near a well that traditionally belonged to the Ga'adza'a. By scrimping and saving, wheedling loans from sceptical officials and sheer hard work he managed to survive. He acquired more land, invested in pumps and irrigation equipment, bought machinery and now appears to be a prosperous landowner. The little settlement has grown to about forty houses (all from the Ga'adza'a) and boasts a primary and intermediate school, a clinic, a police post and a mosque. From appearances one would say that it was a success. Economically it is not. The crops provide subsistence and the surplus just covers costs. The public buildings, which the pioneer built himself with government grants, are now leased back to the state and these rents form his sole spendable income. His fellow-villagers are in the same position except that their spendable income comes from sons and brothers in employment. As the pioneer says himself, he might just as well have kept his camels and saved himself a lot of trouble.

There are a few traditional landowners among the Rwala. They inherited date-groves in Jauf, Khaibar and round Kaf in the Wadi Sirhan. These were cultivated by slaves or peasants on a share-cropping basis and brought in supplies, if not cash. At some point, probably in the 1920s though nobody is clear, the owners gradually stopped visiting these groves. Notwithstanding the fact that after the 1920s the Rwala economy was in a poor way, it seems that the owners found that it was scarcely worth their while to bother collecting their dates. The reasons may have been political in part. By 1956, when slaves were freed in Saudi, few people still maintained contact with their date-groves and the subsequent labour costs made any revival uneconomic. I only know of one member of the tribe who has a date-grove as a going concern, although there may be a few more. The groves in Kaf are decayed and the village deserted. It is possible that this sort of farming was more widespread in the past, but the evidence is sketchy and families have forgotten about it. It is also complicated by semantic problems; 'ruling', 'owning' and *khuwa* ('protection money') all merge into one another without legal classification. As it scarcely affects the present economy of the Rwala, it is a subject better left for Part II, where change and the Rwala response to it are considered.

To return to modern agriculture, a growing number of Rwala are trying their luck as farmers following the example of the Ga'adza'i. The main motivation seems to be that interest-free loans and grants are readily available and it is a way of making ends meet while children are being educated and while camel-herding is so depressed economically. One man I know has had a garden for over three years and still hasn't achieved subsistence. He is paying off his loan from his salary as a Reserve National Guardsman, his eldest son's wage as a Post Office employee and the payment he obtains from herders for supplying water (though he only charges non-Rwala). Only in his most euphoric moments does he expect to make a profit in the future. His father, aged seventy-five or so, started a more ambitious garden/ farm in 1977. He never expects to get more than subsistence – as he says: 'I can always live on my pension.'

In 1978 the pace increased. The Saudi government, more in an attempt to share the national wealth with the relatively impoverished Bedu than to induce them to settle, handed out grants of up to 300,000 Saudi Riyals (£47,000) to each head of household to enable them to build houses. As a result the desert around Turayf, Ar-Ar, Sakaka and Jauf is dotted with imposing villas in varying stages of completion. Many have embryo farms attached and the lesser bungalows of those who took up smaller sums from the government. The Rwala were never clear as to the terms of the grants and many find themselves bound to remain in residence for up to thirty years unless they pay the grant back. This was not understood by them initially and has produced a certain resentment. One result has been the proliferation of schools and clinics. Any settlement with a determined number of children is entitled to a local school and with suitable buildings available some settlements are desperately trying to attract inhabitants so that the rents can be used to pay back their grants. While the elderly with a safe pension are often happy to settle down for a while, the young have little intention of doing so permanently (as they admit in private) and it is difficult to see what they would do if they did. The agricultural aspects of these new settlements seem doomed to failure and it is to be feared that some will develop into totally pointless communities living on the wages paid to them to administrate themselves and taking in each other's washing. This is not impossible or even unlikely. I know of at least two settlements that 'work' in exactly this way. It is possible that this settlement will encourage camel-herding in that there is a fairly fixed focal point where some members of the wider family are always in residence to look after the children at school while the rest carry on herding. It hasn't developed this way yet, but it is still unknown how many Rwala have taken up the housing option at all.

Far more important in terms of income is trading. By this I mean the transporting of goods as well as buying and selling. The Rwala have always been traders to a certain extent. The practice of consensus politics with its necessary give and take has made them expert bargainers and this expertise has been easily transferred to trading. The negotiating of *khuwa*, marketing arrangements etc. has never been confined to the sheikhs, so there are many Rwala with a background of bargaining with townsmen and villagers. Although straight trading was never widespread in the past, they were never in a seller's market for their camels and their widespread information networks must gave given them some ideas about where best to sell camels or, at least, the price they ought to obtain from the middle-man. Camel-trading was an option that some took up, for Nayyif ibn Abdullah Sha'alan (f.f.f.f.f. of the present Emir) is said to have died in Egypt while engaged in camel-trading. Be that as it may, trading in all its manifestations is an option that many Rwala take up nowadays. Mostly it is on a small-scale, part-time basis. A man in Turayf hears that tyres are in short supply in Riyadh owing to shipping problems, so he buys up a truckload in Turayf and sells them at a profit in Riyadh. *Tibbin* (chopped straw for fodder) is profitably bought in Syria and sold in Saudi. Colour televisions are bought in Saudi and run up to Syria, where they are a banned luxury. Turkish sheep are bought profitably in Syria and transported to the market in Ar-Ar or Hafr-al-Batin. Some of this is strictly illegal but it is trade nonetheless. Nor is trade confined to the Arab world. Several Rwala travel to Turkey to buy sheep direct and cut out the Syrian middle-man, while more recently Rwala buyers have been going to Thailand to buy Japanese television sets, thus avoiding the enormous mark-ups of Saudi merchants, which make the Syrian trade scarcely profitable. The most recent inter-

Plate 12. Sheep-market at Hafr-al-Batin

national development has been the importing of complete factories from Europe for the local manufacture of light-switches, cloth and similar consumer goods. While this is mostly in the hands of big business houses in Jiddah or Riyadh, at least one ordinary Rwala tribesman is doing the same thing by using contacts he made in Leeds while on a technical course. More widespread is the trade in second-hand cars and lorries. Groups of tribesmen fly up to Munich where they buy second-hand Mercedes from an Arab-run depot; they then drive them back, either to the free-trade zone in Damascus or direct to Saudi Arabia. Participation is not confined to the Rwala, though many take advantage of it. A new trading-venture is developing that combines agriculture and sheep-herding as well. Sheep are trucked in from Syria or Turkey, herded and folded onto fodder crops and then sold at a favourable market. It is slightly intermittent at the moment owing to the disorganisation of the fodder-growing and it is more or less confined to the periods before the big religious festivals, when the demand for sheep for slaughter is at its highest. It is a trade that will probably grow. There must be very few areas of trade that some members of the tribe are not involved in – some of the richer ones with access to a telephone even play the international currency market, with apparent success.

Few, however, trade as a full-time occupation. More typical is the herder's son who uses the family lorry to transport an occasional load for a fee, the man who hires his truck to a Syrian sheep merchant or cashes in on a temporary shortage. Even the smuggling is a short-term occupation for most of those who engage in it. It is seen as a quick, though risky, way of accumulating capital for a less sensitive enterprise. It cannot, however, be carried out on a casual part-time basis like other trading-ventures owing to the need for intimate, up-to-the minute information if disaster is to be avoided.

There are two other sources of income that do not fit conveniently into any other category. The first is pensions. These apply to Saudi in the main, although Jordan and Syria also have pension schemes. In Saudi there are a whole host of pensions, old-age pensions, widow's pensions, disability pensions, military pensions and others not clearly specified. These only apply to Saudi nationals, which in theory should mean that all Rwala can collect them if in the right category. However, the complexities of the bureaucracy are such that obtaining the right papers may take years. Some pensions are mysterious. Why, for instance, should a few elderly men travel to Hail to collect their pensions? Hail was, in their youth, a stronghold of Ibn Rashid, Ibn Saud's major rival and a rival to the Rwala Emirs as well. Is there any significance in the fact that the men involved were once members of the now-banned Ikhwan, or at least fellow-travellers? This is still a tricky subject to approach and nobody was prepared to enlarge upon it. Most of the Rwala are not terribly clear as to which pensions they are entitled to; the normal practice is to apply for anything that, by a stretch of the imagination, they might be eligible for.

If pensions are a category that is a bit hazy in the details, the second

source of income is even more nebulous. It consists of a variety of payments for advising local government officials. These might be fairly well-
defined, as in the case of an adviser on tribal affairs to the district governor, but they tail off into payments to shadowy 'advisers' and 'guides' to
the local police chief. Whether these latter groups are paid out of the
governor's privy purse, or by central or local government funds or by the
individual official concerned I could never make out.

While the majority of these payments are straightforward pensions,
paid employment or payment for being prayer-leader at a small settlement,
for example, some are very hard to categorise. They could be payments,
gifts, hand-outs or bribes, according to one's point of view. Whatever their
origin they probably contribute significantly but, like so many areas of
tribal life, it is impossible to put a figure, or even an estimate, on their
contribution.

(b) Sheikhly economic options

The sheikhly family and their close collaterals are in a rather different
position from the ordinary tribesman. Educated, wealthy and sophisticated, their economic problems did not come to a head until 1958. Before
that they had a large income, collectively and individually, derived from
agricultural properties, real estate and *khuwa*. None of the opportunities
were denied tribesmen, but their scale of operations was so small that the
income, in terms of share-cropped dates and *khuwa* from tiny hamlets or
sections of weaker tribes, was only a minor portion of that brought in
by other economic activities. In 1958 the Ba'ath party came to power,
abolished tribal law, 'freed' the tribesmen and finally did away with *khuwa*.
Later legislation nationalised much of the sheikhs' agricultural holding, so
that by 1962 they felt so persecuted (several were under house arrest) that
they fled from Syria. In so doing they effectively cut themselves off from
what income remained to them, for they had no land in Jordan or Saudi
at this date. They became virtually destitute. Showing a resilience and
hardihood that surprised even themselves, they set about recouping their
fortunes. That they received the support of the tribesmen is a tribute to
tribal loyalty and the charisma of the family, for the relationship with
members of the tribe had been neglected for some years and this, it is said
by some, contributed to their downfall.

The family camped in north-east Jordan and started up the smuggling.
Tribesmen who had lost their camels in the drought flocked to them and
the enterprise was a success. The sheikhs saw smuggling not only as a means
of making large sums of money quickly but also, as previously explained,
as a form of economic warfare against the Syrian government, which, they
felt, had treated them unfairly. Quite apart from this, the danger involved
appealed to them and they (and many others) regarded smuggling as a
surrogate for raiding. It gave them the opportunity, denied them for some
thirty years, of displaying traditional Bedu virtues of bravery and resource-

fulness and it provided the money necessary for their casual generosity. The initial capital for this venture, i.e. for buying trucks, goods and arms, came almost entirely from the women, who sold their jewellery. Traditionally jewellery has always been a bank account and that of sheikhly women was no exception. Bracelets, necklaces, medallions and head-dresses, mostly of solid gold, were ruthlessly broken up and sold, the proceeds being put at the disposal of husbands, sons and brothers. As well as providing capital, it financed the family until money started to come in. The Jordanian authorities, ideologically opposed to the Ba'ath, tactfully looked the other way and the Syrian authorities were in no wise prepared for a major policing action. For about ten years the Sha'alan had things more or less their own way. During this time the younger members of the family recouped some of the family fortune and refurbished its reputation among the tribe, while elder members entered into prolonged and delicate negotiations with the Syrian government. As capital became available for other investments and as the Syrian border guards became more active and better armed, members of the Sha'alan began to drop smuggling in favour of other options.

Some close collateral branches moved their money into sheep and the bulk of their income began to come from herds, although some of the young men continued to smuggle. Other three-generation 'ibn amms' followed a wide variety of options: trading (legitimate), liaison jobs in oil companies, the professional army, local government (as tribal advisers) and the like. These options were taken up by the non-Emiral lines of the Sha'alan. This branch has capitalised on its wide reputation range, prestige and political connections and has moved (or some of them have) into entrepreneurship. In so doing they have widened their scope considerably and act as brokers between rich individuals and the European finance houses. The initial contact between the Western institutions and these Bedu brokers may have been mediated by Ibn Saud when the major entre-preneurs of Beirut were in disarray. (Or they may have been cultivated by other means; it isn't clear.) However it may have started, they are now in constant touch with businesses, finance houses and merchant banks in West Germany, Switzerland, Spain and Italy, to name only those that I know of. And naturally they maintain their links with merchants and traders throughout the Arab world. Their entrepreneurship is not just local. A personal friendship with the ruling family of one of the Gulf states resulted in their being offered the marketing rights for the oil. This scheme, which I never fully understood, is said to have been vetoed by American interests. The friendship, however, has continued and has been ratified by a marriage between the two families and one of the Sha'alan is now an accredited diplomat with the embassy in an Arab capital.

The vicissitudes of Arab politics and these newly-developed opportunities have not led the Emiral line into abandoning their old options. After many years of negotiation, some of their former land in Syria has been restored to them. Whether by chance or by design, the restored portion has been earmarked for industrial development and has now been profitably sold and the money invested elsewhere, some of it certainly in land, some in real estate. Nor has the tribe been neglected. Not only do some members of the family negotiate or mediate with governments on the tribe's behalf, but one of them keeps open the smuggling-routes, with increasing difficulty. He freely admits that he enjoys the risks and the opportunity to maintain traditional virtues, but more importantly he feels it his duty to make the opportunity available for any member of the tribe who might wish to partake. In this he does not have the full backing of the rest of the family as his activities make negotiations with governments more difficult, but no effort is made to stop him beyond arguments, and opposition is pragmatic rather than moral.

The range of options open to the main Emiral branch of the Sha'alan (roughly the Hazza') is enormous and very varied. No one directs individual choice and there is no central organised plan, but through each following his bent the range of careers covers most aspects of the modern Middle East. Although the professions are poorly represented as yet, this gap should soon be filled by sons and nephews (and girls in Syria) who are currently at university. One gets the feeling (and it can be no more, as numbers are so small) that the Sha'alan are using this period of flux and change to explore as many options as possible. Which of these will prove to be the most fruitful, in a tribal context, is still very uncertain.

There is one notable exception in the range of economic activities in which the sheikhly family engage, and that is camel-herding. With the exception of a prestige herd maintained by a rich cousin of the Emir, a herd that has absolutely no economic significance, camel-herding is no longer a sheikhly option. This is not a very recent development as the late Emir sold the remaining herd in the early 1950s. The reason for this was strictly economic. A primarily town-based sheikh cannot look after, or even supervise, a herd himself and it was becoming increasingly difficult to find competent professional herders. This difficulty has become almost insuperable in the last few years and the sheikhly economic position has not allowed for a luxury herd. It is possible that this may change. The Emir and others are becoming more worried than ever about the present dependence of the tribe on the oil wealth of Saudi Arabia – wealth, moreover, that only enters the northern province at second-hand, as it were. This area of Arabia, which is where the Rwala are concentrated now, makes virtually no contribution to the state; it simply administrates itself and provides a pathway for imports flowing south. Should oil fail or serious political upheaval take place, the Rwala will be left with very few options at all. For this reason, insurance, the Emir is considering the long-term advantages of camel-herding and he may find it worth his while to maintain a herd simply to encourage others to do the same.

Sheikhly economic options must fulfil three conditions. First, they must generate sufficient income to maintain a high level of generosity and and impressive 'front'; secondly, they must enable the operator to be independent, i.e. he must be his own boss: thirdly, they must not be so time-consuming as to interfere with the sheikhly role of mediator. The first condition is not too difficult to achieve in the present boom conditions, given the connections that the Sha'alan already have. The second condition is essentially negative; it simply means that being an employee is out. The third condition is the most difficult.

Owning land cultivated by share-croppers fulfilled all three conditions admirably. Unfortunately, as the Sha'alan discovered, it is only too easily disrupted by outside agencies and, in any case, it is not politically respectable in the present climate. But it does generate a large income with minimum supervision. Trading and sheep-herding fulfil conditions one and two but they both demand a high degree of personal supervision and mobility, which is difficult for a sheikh who is politically involved and consequently largely town-based. Entrepreneurship almost succeeds in fulfilling all three conditions but a really successful entrepreneur must maintain a flow of customers and cannot rely on a few lucky breaks. To some degree the

Plate 13. In the courtyard of the Emir's house in Damascus

wheeling and dealing can be combined with carrying out the sheikhly function of mediation, but those who practise it find it an enormous strain. Ironically, smuggling is probably the best option. A great deal of money can be made, the sheikh is totally independent and because smuggling tends to come in great bursts of frantic activity followed by long periods of comparative idleness, it leaves plenty of time for mediation. It has the additional advantage of forcing close liaison with the tribe and giving the opportunity to demonstrate traditional virtues. The main drawback is the political complications that it can engender, complications that might be to the detriment of the tribe as a whole, even though it is, of itself, a statement of tribal autonomy.

At the present the Emiral line works more or less as a unit, a system that largely overcomes the disadvantages of any single occupation. The Emir owns some agricultural land and spends most of his time in Damascus on sheikhly business; one brother is a successful entrepreneur in Saudi Arabia, which provides cash and access to ministerial and royal circles; another brother is a successful entrepreneur in Jordan; a fourth is an accredited diplomat in Jordan; while a fifth continues to smuggle and thus maintains a closer contact with the tribe in general. This doesn't mean that most of the tribe smuggle; but that by being out in the desert he has more opportunity for keeping in touch and being available to herding tribesmen. Between them they fulfil all the necessary conditions and by supporting each other with information and, if necessary, with cash, they manage to carry out the sheikhly function over an enormous area and several national states, with a fair degree of success.

Part II Change and Adaptation

Introduction

Bedu society is unlikely ever to have been static. Camel nomadism only has a history of some 4000 years and it is improbable that it sprang into being fully-fledged. The basis of Bedu society is jural equality but this is cut across by reputation, which depends essentially on the successful exploitation of assets and options. As political conditions, technology and economics have changed, so have the assets and options of the Bedu and those successful within the system have had to adapt in order to maintain their success. If camel pastoralism had never been more than a subsistence economy this need for adaptation would never have arisen. The Rwala, at least, have never lived in a self-sufficient environment and have always had to react to change in the other systems that make up part of their world. This they continue to do, albeit at a more accelerated pace in the last hundred years or so.

In Part I I have considered how the Rwala survive today, politically and economically, with little discussion of what they developed from or by what processes they have arrived at their present position. Part II focuses on this.

Before I embark on this there is a point that needs to be cleared up. Much of Part I and even more of Part II may appear to be in direct conflict with what other visitors have reported. This is particularly true of reported statements. What visitors seem never to have realised is that much of what they saw and heard was designed to be reported – it was impression-management. One of the problems for any investigator dealing with a segmentary society is that he is always outside that society by definition and therefore in opposition to it. Thus dealings with him are part and parcel of impression-management. In a sense the outsider sees himself, for how the members inside a society react to an outsider is largely determined by how outsiders behaved towards them in the past. Thus Philby and Glubb found the Sha'alan proud and overbearing to the point of offensiveness. As both represented governmental agencies, the behaviour of the Sha'alan was a reflection of how governmental agencies had, in the past, behaved toward them; in this case it was probably the Ottoman imperial government rather than the Mandate administration. What should be borne in mind is that much overt behaviour towards the outside has little relation to reality; it is a political statement and it must be recognised and analysed as such.

9 History

It is possible to construct an amalgamated history of the Rwala but, at the moment, it would be very brief and uninformative. This comes about because outside sources, i.e. European travellers, were usually in the area for only a short time. So the events of which they heard were always heard of at second or third hand and they were not in a position to interpret even these reports in the light of their knowledge of the working of the social system and of the bias of their informants. Much the same provisos go for Rwala tradition. Different informants give different accounts of the same event depending on who they are and what their motive is. For instance, there is a tradition that the Rwala originated as an act of political will through the binding-together of disparate elements in the environs of Baghdad. An alternative version states that the tribe started around Wejh in the Hedjaz, spread across Arabia, having helped the Prophet take Khaibar, and then, in the last 300 years, gradually moved northwards into Syria. The first version stresses the autonomy and political independence of the tribe, the second the symbiotic nature of nomad/settler relationships. Neither need be true; both are simply political statements. Essentially history is viewed by the Rwala in much the same way as a genealogy, that is, as a justification of present conditions. For instance, the second origin version may well be the 'official' history, which justifies the inclusion of Hedjaz in Saudi Arabia, because Ibn Saud are from the Aneze confederation and it was as part of that that the Rwala left Wejh. Naturally, as conditions change so too does history. It is therefore more fruitful to construct a model that conforms with Rwala ideas and includes actual events known to Western historians. The necessity for a model only became clear to us after several years of fieldwork and endless conversations around the same events. There was no generally accepted 'history' in our sense; everyone was really putting forward a point of view and because the tribe is so large and has never worked as a unit every person shed a different light on any event. This approach may not tell us a lot about the physical movement of men nor about the progression of significant events, but it does tell us a lot about the things that the Rwala regard as important, such as autonomy, equality or symbiosis. Even my interpretation of their history is biased for I was mostly with tribesmen from the Murath tribal section and have not taken into account Doghman or Frejje versions. On the whole the ordinary tribesmen are more interested in mundane matters like access to markets, while the sheikhs will stress independence and political activism.

It is as well, before misunderstanding sets in, to consider what 'rule' means in the Bedu. It is a word that crops up frequently and like many concepts it varies in meaning according to the context. Perhaps the best way to think about it is to make it synonymous with the word 'dominate'. It does not have any necessary connection with the word 'govern', though on occasion to rule and to govern may be the same. The Rwala make a sharp distinction between the two. For instance, Ibn Saud rules but the *dawlat* governs; which is in control is unclear to the Rwala. The same contextual considerations apply to the concept of ownership. A man will talk about his grandfather 'ruling' or 'owning' the area between Sakaka and a certain wadi 300 or 400 km to the east. What does it mean? There is nothing in the area except four wells 'owned' by tribal sections, seasonal grazing and wild animals; there is no town, no village, no agriculture, no date-groves, nothing but gravelly desert. In practical terms it means that the 'owner' or 'ruler' is the dominant personality, the man who has the best reputation in the area and a prior claim of usufruct (a claim not a right). He is usually in a position to negotiate *khuwa* with other weaker tribes who use the same area. He may also be able to demand payment from caravans passing through. The point really is that he only rules it when he is there and he only owns it under the same circumstances. As with the ownership of wells, he only has a prior claim to it: it is available to anyone else at other times. The same considerations apply to tribal territory. The Rwala are popularly said to 'own' the greater part of the Syrian desert and it is sometimes so marked on maps. They only 'own' it by right of dominance and have no exclusive right to it at all. As they cannot possibly cover the whole area the whole year round other tribes use parts when the Rwala are not there or, by custom, when they are. In the past when the Rwala were fully nomadic there was frequently more grazing than they could consume, owing to the vastness of the area. It did not matter to them if another tribe grazed in the north while they were in the south, provided the two did not meet. In most cases it didn't matter much if they did meet, for most of these other tribes were small ones who paid *khuwa* in return for grazing, but this wasn't necessary if they used the area at different times of year.

This brings us to a consideration of *khuwa*, which is in many ways fundamental to an understanding of the symbiotic relationship between Rwala and townsfolk as well as to a fuller comprehension of the meaning of ownership. It is easier to explain first what *khuwa* is not. It is not extortion, it is not 'protection' money (although for ease I've used this word previously), it is not a tax, it is not bribery. It is (or rather was) the payment of a negotiable sum of money or goods to opt out of the economy of raiding. As will be shown later, raiding was the mainstay of the Rwala economy, so those who did not wish to take part paid 'brotherhood' to those most likely to raid them. It is rather as if farmers in Europe paid a sum of money or goods to the largest manufacturers in their area rather than allow the workers to ravage their fields at will in search of food. It was a method of distributing surplus and providing services without the intervention of a central government. Thus ownership of a village or area meant that the 'owner' was influential enough to arrange protection from others in return for supplies. The supplier disposed of some of his surplus dates or grain or sheep and didn't have to worry about being raided by anybody. If he were raided the 'owner' was obliged to restore the stolen property or pay the compensation. In other words for the payment of a fairly moderate sum the *khuwa*-payer had the territory fully policed with compensation for those who suffered from breaches of the peace. This is the crux of the matter – the 'owner' of a territory, be it large or small, be the 'owner' an individual or a group, guaranteed the peace in that area and the orderly conduct of trade. So when the Prophet Muhammad 'gave' Khaibar to the Rwala he was handing over to them the responsibility of the town and its environs, the responsibility of guaranteeing order and protection, in return for which the Rwala acquired part of the surplus produce for their own use. One of the features of *khuwa* that is frequently misunderstood is that it was transferable by both parties. It was never, for the Rwala, a sheikhly monopoly, though they probably took the lion's share, nor did the sheikhs 'own' a village as a group. The responsibility was always individually apportioned. Thus a man called Sagr ibn Mishhin Sha'alan 'owned' a portion of the village of Qaryatain in Syria and collected *khuwa* from it. (He also owned, in our sense, agricultural land there.) The five-generation 'ibn amm' of the Nuwasira 'owned' the oasis of Gara in Juba, although in this case it is not clear whether the leading member collected the *khuwa* and distributed it or whether the village was divided up among individuals. In both these instances the source of *khuwa* was sold. To whom Sagr sold Qaryatain I don't know, but the Nuwasira sold Gara to the Doghman tribal section, probably in the 1830s, in return for horses. 'Ownership' of a source of *khuwa* was thus an asset like anything else. The Nuwasira, in reckoning up their assets and options, chose horses as a better asset than an assured source of dates, grain and water. What prompted their decision time conceals from us; it may have been a whim of the leading member, a bid for more political influence (for horses were a prestige possession and increased raiding success) or it may simply have been that the Nuwasira had decided to move northwards towards Syria and so assets in Juba had become redundant. In the long run the Nuwasira seem to have chosen the wrong option, as Gara is now one of the few thriving agricultural communities that still belongs to the Doghman, although *khuwa* has been abolished. Towns and villages, also, could change to an alternative 'owner'. In 1909 the power of Ibn Rashid, the ruler of Hail and the Nefud, had declined to such an extent that the inhabitants of Jauf decided to switch allegiance from Ibn Rashid to the Sha'alan, who had, it is said, ruled Jauf until 1865 or thereabouts. In other words, Ibn Rashid could no longer guarantee the peace *vis-à-vis* the Rwala just as earlier the Sha'alan could not guarantee the peace *vis-à-vis* Ibn Rashid. Jauf changed sides peacefully in 1909; they stopped paying *khuwa* to Ibn Rashid and paid the Sha'alan instead. Sakaka did not. They opted for Ibn Rashid but he was unable to protect them and the Sha'alan defeated their forces and from then until about 1926 ruled Sakaka as well. The same thing happened in the mid-1920s. In the face of the Ikhwan, Emir Abdullah of Transjordan and Ibn Saud, the Sha'alan could no longer protect the area and so they gave it to Ibn Saud after defeating the Ikhwan army at Minwa. At least, they say they gave it; Ibn Saud claims to have conquered it. In actual fact the Sha'alan probably ceased to demand *khuwa* (or the inhabitants refused to pay it) and Ibn Saud took over the payment and became guarantor of the peace. (It is really rather more complicated than this as the Mashhur Sha'alan were Ikhwan who supported Ibn Saud at the time for reasons of internal family politics – but this needn't concern us here.)

Khuwa was essentially the same when it was a client tribe (or part of a tribe) paying one of the Rwala. The payment guaranteed the peace, but instead of regulating the market, it regulated grazing. Any tribe could graze in Rwala territory, but either ran the risk of being raided or had to pay *khuwa*. This was not a payment for grazing, for the Rwala never felt that they owned the grass or water. Again and again they emphasise the fact that grass and rain come from God and is free to all. The payment represented the withdrawal from the primary economy of the desert, raiding, and had nothing to do with utilising a scarce resource. Obviously the *khuwa* system regulated grazing, for the return from grazing must exceed the amount of *khuwa* to be of economic benefit to the payer, so *khuwa* regulated the numbers grazing to the maximum that could benefit from it. Members of the Rwala quite clearly saw this, but it does not seem to have been the original intention of *khuwa* payment. So *khuwa* became a regulatory mechanism for an ecological balance.

Only two factors could change the system. Either *khuwa* is abolished, as has happened, and the desert is massively and visibly overgrazed with all its long-term implications, or the 'owning' tribe becomes so wealthy in animals that overgrazing, similarly, takes place. Both factors have affected the Syrian desert. There are reasons for believing that the Rwala became so wealthy, in terms of camels, that they overgrazed their own territory in the period 1930–58. Raiding had ceased with the Rwala well up at the top of the league, so to speak, and there was virtually no market for camels. Herds increased enormously (people speak of parts of a tribal section owning tens of thousands of camels) and the grazing suffered accordingly. If this assessment is correct it would explain why the drought of 1958–62 was so peculiarly disastrous – already under-nourished animals had no reserves and died like flies. Be that as it may, the Rwala clearly understood the regulatory nature of *khuwa*, as they pointed it out to me, rather bitterly, one year in Jordan when 90,000 head of sheep were trucked in from all parts of the Kingdom to take advantage of (and ruin) the grazing around Ar-Risha.

If looked at in this rather less emotive way *khuwa* can be seen for what it was – the necessary regulatory mechanism for symbiosis in a system where coercion was not possible. In the case of other tribes, it regulated the grazing; in the case of towns and villages it guaranteed the peace and encouraged trade. Nobody even made much profit out of it, directly. The taker of *khuwa* only got it if he could persuade his fellow-tribesmen to honour the agreement. As his influence was directly dependent on his generosity, his profits from the *khuwa* had to be dispersed. If he kept it for himself his influence declined, his fellows broke the peace and the townsmen found someone more effective to replace him. The towns depended on trade and trade depended on a modicum of security, so one can logically go one step further and say that the *khuwa* system of symbiosis maintained the autonomy and wealth of towns. The protecting tribe, by exacting levies from caravans from elsewhere, acted as a tariff barrier that favoured home production. Whether it actually happened this way is open to speculation, as no records appear to exist. In any case it is perfectly clear that *khuwa* was a mechanism for regulating relationships between town and nomad to their mutual advantage.

This is a far cry from the normal view of the Bedu preying on towns and villages. Only wealthy settlements were of any value to the Bedu as markets, so it was in the interest of the Bedu as much as the settlers to encourage peace and stability. The Bedu were reacting to existing trade patterns rather than forming or disrupting them. This can be seen in relation to the sophisticated towns of the Syrian littoral. According to Lewis (1951) handicrafts in Damascus and Aleppo were offering a better option to settlers than agriculture in the period 1800–40. Part of the reason was international trade cycles but a major one was the rapacity of the tax-gatherers, which made the anonymity of the towns more attractive. Thus 'the northernmost Arab tribes' (Aneze) were 'tempted to plunder' the outlying impoverished villages. This may well be true, for if the villages were paying Turkish taxes they were unable to pay *khuwa* and the Turks were unable or unwilling to protect them. But any plundering was incidental; the tribes were not taking advantage of weakness and they were moving into the marginal agricultural areas because they were empty. The Rwala are quite specific about this and complain that the reintroduction of peasants into the Golan in the 1930s was disturbing their traditional grazing-rights. In the 1840s and 1850s handicrafts and manufacture declined in the Middle East because of cheap imports from Europe, so once again agriculture became a more attractive proposition. But the desert fringe was controlled by the Rwala among others and Turkish forces had to intimidate them. Although the *khuwa* system reasserted itself in time, the increasing incursion of strong central government from the 1920s onwards finally destroyed it. It seems probable that once one side can enlarge its arena and thus dominate the partner the delicate symbiotic balance is inevitably destroyed.

The symbiotic balance is always in tension. It is easier to see the mechanism if we take a simple example of an oasis town surrounded by deserts impassable without Bedu help. If the town dominates the Bedu, the Bedu melt away and attack the town's lifelines, its caravans. The town loses its customers and its trade and so declines. The weakened town then has to pay *khuwa* to the tribe in order to survive at all and the symbiotic balance is restored. If the Bedu try to dominate by demanding more and more *khuwa* the town also declines, as its trading position is weakened. The Bedu are left with a much impoverished market, which can afford less and less *khuwa*, so the town gets little protection, is plundered, becomes weaker still and disappears.

This simple model breaks down as soon as outside factors come into play. A town important and strong enough to dominate the Bedu will not remain inviolate for long because it will get drawn into the orbit of a larger town or political unit. On the other hand the Bedu cannot really dominate for long because they cannot logistically remain in the area for long; they must move off to graze. What can happen is that an individual or family from the Bedu, usually the sheikh, moves in on the town, dominates it and settles down. Initially he has the support of the tribe, but no oasis town seems ever to have generated enough income for a ruler to have kept the townsmen and the Bedu happy. As soon as the ruler favours the townsmen his Bedu support slips away, for he is being ungenerous and therefore loses reputation and influence. If he favours the Bedu he's taking too much out of the system and trade declines. Exactly this happened to Ibn Rashid: by becoming a townsman he lost the support of the Shammar; and without the support of the tribe he could no longer rule Hail, for the tribe moved away and the prosperity of Hail declined. In the end Ibn Rashid and Hail were dominated by Ibn Saud and Riyadh. Very nearly the same thing happened to the latter in the 1920s. As a Bedu, Ibn Saud first dominated the towns and then as a townsman tried to dominate the Bedu. The Bedu, in the guise of the Ikhwan, rebelled (or rather withdrew their support) and it was only with difficulty that Ibn Saud survived. More recently, of course, cash from oil has enabled him to keep both townsmen and Bedu fairly happy, but real support for him is uncertain because the Bedu resent their loss of independence.

Rather more important than economic factors are the philosophical ones. A sheikh, however influential, remains an equal among equals for the tribesmen. A ruler, by definition, has power to coerce. Thus a ruler/sheikh must be schizophrenic, behaving as an equal to the tribesmen but as a ruler to the townsmen. This is impossible, for he has to treat between the two. The Bedu cease to regard him as sheikh and he becomes absorbed into the town. The symbiotic system then reasserts itself with a new sheikh treating with the townsmen through their ex-Bedu ruler. *A* Bedu may dominate a town, *the* Bedu can never do so. In other words, ruling a town may be an option open to an individual Bedu, but by doing so he loses equality and autonomy within the Bedu system, he has to enter the town system in order to dominate or succeed and the two systems are incompatible. In segmentary terms, town and nomad are opposed although complementary; and just as one man cannot belong to two tribal sections, so he cannot be townsman and nomad; it's an either/or choice.

Despite appearances, this is not a digression. It is essential to understand the nomad/settler symbiosis and the results of its imbalance if one is to understand much of Rwala history. The crucial period here is 1901 to 1930, for what happened then has had a marked effect on the tribe. In 1901 Emir Sattam Sha'alan died; he was succeeded by his b.s. Fahad ibn Hazza'. By the acceptance of land from Sultan Abdul Hamid, Sattam had had to collect taxes from the tribe. This was resented but understood, for without land Sattam could not negotiate successfully on behalf of the tribe with the government. However, Fahad increased the taxes and kept the extra for himself. As was to be expected, his influence among the tribesmen declined, he found taxes more and more difficult to collect and he became more and more unpopular. His brother, Nuri ibn Hazza', tried to reason with him and suggested that he, Fahad, should remain as *sheikh al-bab*, i.e. 'sheikh of the door', in charge of negotiation with the Turks, while Nuri became *sheik al-shedad*, i.e. 'sheikh of the camel-saddles', who kept in touch with the tribe. This would have entailed a diminution in Fahad's income that he was not prepared to accept. In 1904 Nuri found that his brother was intriguing with the Turks and had him killed. So Nuri became Emir *de jure* as well as *de facto*. Nuri maintained the support of the tribe by being a thorn in the flesh of the Turkish authorities (he was imprisoned at least once). In 1909, with the decline of Ibn Rashid, Nuri's son, Nawaf, made himself Emir of Jauf and Sakaka with his father's reluctant support. The castle at Jauf was rebuilt, the one at Sakaka repaired and a completely new stone one was built at Kaf. Revenues came in from general trade, the date-groves and the important salt trade from the Wadi Sirhan. Nawaf toyed with the idea of proclaiming himself the independent monarch of the Kingdom of Sha'alan Arabia, but he died in 1921 before anything could come of it. His son, Sultan, continued in his footsteps, but rather ineffectively as he was only eighteen years old. Nuri was still alive and remained bitterly opposed to his son's and grandson's ambitions and did all he could to thwart them. (Note that he couldn't forbid or prevent them, he had no power.) Sultan died in 1924 and Nuri handed Jauf over to Ibn Saud about two years later. His motives were probably mixed, for it was becoming more difficult to remain in control flanked by the British Mandate forces and Emir Abdullah of Transjordan on one side and Ibn Saud on the other, especially as the Ikhwan were getting out of control. This doesn't seem to have been the sole reason, however. Conversations with members of the Sha'alan, especially Faysal ibn Fawaz Sha'alan, have made it quite clear that the essential antagonism between sheikh and ruler is well known to them and that Nuri ibn Hazza' feared the consequences of the family becoming too involved in the rule (in our sense) of Jauf. He therefore retreated to Syria where he could negotiate with the various central governments without there being any possibility of dominating.

Plate 14. The Castle at Jauf. Now in ruins, it was repaired and used by Nawaf ibn Nuri Sha'alan before the First World War.

It is against this background of symbiotic balance that the function of the sheikh must be seen. The sheikh's job has changed over time, not really in content but in scope. It has been shown how political influence was, and is, acquired and, very briefly, how sheikhs came to play a prominent role. The earliest reference to the sheikhly role to be gained from the Rwala concerns the manner in which Sha'alan himself became sheikh. This was probably at some time in the middle of the seventeenth century. The Rwala, at this date, were still in the south of their present territory, for they don't appear to have started moving north for another 150 years. In any case the changeover from Ibn Ga'ga' of the Ga'adza'a to Sha'alan of the Murath took place at Taima or Khaibar, probably the latter. All the versions of this changeover vary somewhat except for the main theme, which is that Sha'alan was more successful in negotiating on behalf of the tribe with the townsfolk and 'so became sheikh'. It can be assumed that Sha'alan already had a good reputation as a mediator, for the townsmen insisted on dealing with him in preference to Ibn Ga'ga' and the fact that he became sheikh implies that his mediation was satisfactory to the tribe. It seems likely that the town was paying *khuwa* to the Rwala, as we are told that the tribe was encamped peacefully and that the trouble was caused by the straying of camels into the crops: it was against this sort of accidental depredation that the *khuwa* system operated, as well as against raiding. In most versions the camels were seized by the townsfolk in lieu of compensation or until compensation was paid. In no version is there any hint of aggression of any sort, so we are left with the strong implication

127

that Ibn Ga'ga' was unable to fulfil the normal obligations that he had accepted along with the *khuwa* payment. In other words, the sheikh's function, in this instance, was regulating nomad/settler relationships and keeping the peace. Where Ibn Ga'ga' failed, Sha'alan succeeded; this implies that the issue was of prime importance as Sha'alan displaced the former sheikh and there is no suggestion that Sha'alan was remarkable in any way; he wasn't a great warrior or war-leader. If anything he was the opposite, as we are told that he was a poor but honest tribesman employed by Ibn Ga'ga' as a herder. Whether Sha'alan re-negotiated the *khuwa* or simply fulfilled the already-existing obligations is not known, but the outcome must have been satisfactory to both parties in the long term, for the Sha'alan are still the sheikhs and Taima is still used in the summer by the descendents of Sha'alan's brother, Nasr (the Nuwasira). The same goes for Khaibar because, although it is no longer visited, it still contains date-groves belonging to individuals among the Sha'alan and used within living memory.

This version of Sha'alan's takeover is recorded by Musil in *Manners and Customs of the Rwala Bedouin* in much the same form. There is however, a totally different version also extant, which highlights, again, exactly the same facet of the sheikhly role. According to this story, Ibn Ga'ga' was too ready to capitulate to tax demands made by the Sherif of Mecca or, alternatively, the Turkish government. Sha'alan stepped in, made a more satisfactory arrangement and 'so became sheikh'. Again there is nothing warlike about it; it all concerns nomad/settler relationships and keeping the peace. In this case, however, the boot is on the other foot and it is the Rwala having to pay *khuwa* as it were rather than receiving it. A slightly different version says that Sha'alan told the Turks (or the Sherif) where to get off, paid nothing and returned to the desert with the tribe. In this version the emphasis is changed, for it concerns the other main function of the sheikh, which is preserving the tribe's autonomy. This was quite clearly the moral drawn from it by the Rwala today.

This insistence on autonomy comes up time and again as a motive for sheikhly action. In the very early 1800s attempts were made to dominate the Rwala by the Turks in Syria and by Ibn Saud in the south. It has been mentioned that Aleppo and Damascus were booming in the early part of the nineteenth century, and that the tax-collectors were very active. This activity stretched out into the desert for some distance and Sheikh Mehenna Milhim of the Hessene tribe of the Aneze negotiated with the Turks on behalf of the entire confederation and claimed the title of Emir of the confederation. (It was the same Mehenna who escorted Lady Hester Stanhope to Palmyra.) What reality this title had is unclear but when, on his death, his son took over the situation changed. The son, Mohammad, was more subservient to the Turks and when he tried to collect taxes from the Rwala he was ignominiously chased back to Damascus. The sheikh of the Rwala at the time was Adre'i ibn Mashhur Sha'alan who happened to be distant on this occasion, but sent word of his anger and of his intention to avenge the insult and the attack on the tribe's autonomy. His anger must have been real and his reputation formidable, for Mohammad, on his deathbed shortly before Adre'i returned, requested that he should be buried on the top of Mount Kasyoun above Damascus so that his body would be safe 'from the fury of Adre'i and his Rwala'. The tomb is still there, although it has now become part of a radar installation. Adre'i had been detained in the south by negotiations with Ibn Saud. At this date the Wahhabis, under Ibn Saud, were becoming very active. The Ibn Sha'alan had no objection to Wahhabism as a creed but refused to accept the political suzerainty of the Imam, Ibn Saud, which was an integral part of Wahhabism. So Adre'i had been resisting the incursions of the Ikhwan. In 1809 Adre'i was fighting somewhere outside Baghdad and had just defeated a Wahhabi army when a Turkish army appeared. Whether the Turks were really interested in Adre'i and the Rwala or whether they were in late pursuit of the Wahhabis is uncertain, but Adre'i attacked and defeated them and then 'laid waste the city'. (He probably did a bit of looting in the suburbs.) Whatever anyone's intentions may have been, Ibn Saud took Adre'i's action as a gesture of Bedu solidarity in the face of outside intervention and relieved the Rwala of having to acknowledge him as overlord if they became Wahhabi. Thus, at a stroke, Adre'i, intentionally or not, had asserted the tribe's independence of the Turkish Pasha in Baghdad and of Ibn Saud. As related above he returned to Damascus and asserted their independence of the Milhim and the Pasha there too.

The theme of independence comes up again with the ceding of Jauf and Wadi Sirhan to Ibn Saud. This was an additional reason for Emir Nuri's retreat to Syria – he could not be certain that he wouldn't become subservient to either of his larger neighbours if he became a town ruler rather than remaining purely nomadic.

Even today the Rwala never tire of asserting their independence of central governments. One of the reasons for the present Emir's remaining in Syria, when he could become very much richer by living in Saudi Arabia, is that by staying outside Ibn Saud's domains he is a freer agent to act on behalf of the tribe. Most important sheikhs in Saudi are now government officials but this has the same effect as the earlier policy of liquidation; by turning them into retainers the government is effectively muzzling them, because their personal interests and comforts are dependent on Ibn Saud and conflict with the interests of their tribe. The Rwala Emir is aware of this and remains a Syrian citizen living principally in Damascus. His brother, Sheikh Nuri, is similarly motivated but makes his political statement by maintaining traditional markets (smuggling) and continuing to run, at enormous expense, the independent social welfare system. While people may not agree with the manner of his making his point, saying it is old-fashioned and does more harm than good, nobody disagrees with his intentions.

The change, over the years, in the function of the sheikh is more apparent than real and is really a change in means rather than ends. Previously the sheikh was more concerned with maintaining markets and guaranteeing peace; foreign relations, so to speak, were largely confined to dealings with other tribes. (This latter, as we shall see, was conducted through intermarriage.) Central governments were fairly irrelevant to the Rwala, for they could always retreat into the inner desert and use different towns for their needs, Damascus, Homs, Aleppo, Baghdad, Karbala, Najaf, Jauf, Khaibar, Taima, Mafraq or Zerqa, depending on circumstances. The change in emphasis from maintaining markets to maintaining autonomy seems to have started in the 1870s when the Turks began to tighten their grip on the desert. One line of attack was the giving of agricultural land to the sheikhs, which was meant to give the Turks some sort of financial control over the sheikhs and, through them, the tribes; this seems to have been the theory, at least. In some degree it was a successful policy, for it gave sheikhs more to be generous with and enhanced their reputation. However, it soon changed its purpose, for displays of wealth have never impressed the Bedu, but they did impress the Turks. At the Turkish court wealth meant power: wealth to make gifts, wealth to bribe, power to corrupt, power to subvert and both to make trouble and to intrigue. While it is unlikely that such diplomatic practices were wholly unfamiliar to the sheikhs in the past, they now assumed a far greater importance. The gifts of land were not being used to suborn the tribes but to provide the necessary wealth for the Bedu sheikhs to enter a new and larger political arena. Previously they seem to have been a nuisance but now they were a new factor in domestic politics. While the emphasis had changed the function hadn't, for the sheikhs were still concerned with keeping markets open and persuading the tribe that peaceful coexistence was the best way of achieving this, but they were increasingly concerned with keeping the central government at arms lengths. The means too had changed. Whereas previously much of the income from *khuwa* had gone as casual generosity to maintain reputation, an increasing amount of their new wealth went towards impression-management *vis-à-vis* the government. The Rwala had never been able to dominate Damascus, the seat of a powerful *pashalik*, as they had dominated oasis towns in the past, for there was no way that they could really affect the commercial life, but by entering the domestic political arena they could continue to make their presence felt. This demanded an increasingly ambassadorial function and an increasing emphasis on their political autonomy. As the twentieth century progressed it became less and less possible for the tribe to retreat into the fastnesses of the inner desert; raiding broke down as a comprehensive economic system for lack of a market for camels and finally ceased altogether and the Aneze tribes found co-operation and unity more profitable *vis-à-vis* central governments. So inter-tribal mediation, the control of markets and the maintenance of peace were all removed from the sheikhs by force of circumstances. The only major role left was foreign relations with central governments. In this the Sha'alan and the Rwala were perhaps lucky, for they had, and have, four central governments to treat with and could thus ring the changes. They can also still retreat, not into the inner desert, but across a political boundary, so that the sheikhs can negotiate from a position of moderate strength and with fewer fears of reprisals. Until all four governments agree on a policy and an ideology the Rwala can maintain a modicum of independence and their sheikhs know this. For many tribes the function of the sheikh has changed to negotiating jobs, subsidies and grants – a form of maintaining markets. To do this they have had to be patronised by the central government or, at least, be openly politically subservient. This the Sha'alan have refused to do. They seem to be reverting to the older pattern of economic independence in order to bolster their political autonomy. They know that as a tribe they can no longer compete with central governments in military or economic terms, but by keeping all their options open and by partaking as individuals in all the economic spheres open to them they can remain economically independent of any one government and therefore politically independent of them all in some degree. It is perhaps a state of mind that is being encouraged rather than a policy, an emphasising of the concept of self-help within a tribal context (the basis of the Bedu system) and trusting to natural good sense and the traditional mechanism of reputation and influence to maintain tribal cohesion.

Throughout their history the Rwala have been at pains to preserve individual freedom and tribal independence. Where the one interferes with the other the sheikhs and other men of influence have had to mediate, between individuals or tribes or social systems. Only the latter remains as a problem for it has overshadowed tribal divisions and welded the Bedu into a solidary unit – by no means an indivisible or united group, but far more so than at any time previously. Some of the Sha'alan feel that the end of the road has been reached and that, despite their best efforts, the tribe will break down and disappear in the face of modernisation; a few feel that before this happens it would be better to defy modernity militarily and vanish in a blaze of glory; yet others feel that it is nothing to do with them and simply get on with their own lives. However, the most respected and influential of the Sha'alan (and of the tribe as a whole) reckon that they are capable of further adaptation yet and are actively exploring the means of doing so.

10 Changing Marriage-Patterns

The variations in sheikhly function are reflected in the variations in their marriage-patterns and, to a lesser extent, changes in the marriage-patterns of ordinary tribesmen.

In chapter 7, 'Political Power and Authority', the manner in which reputation was spread was considered with outline reference to marriages between the Sha'alan and the Mheid of the Fed'an tribe. In the past, marriages were used to spread reputation and ensure personal access to those who were the main mediators of other tribes. This demanded, for the Sha'alan, a plethora of marriages, partly to keep open channels of communication and partly to counterbalance opposing 'ibn amm' within the family. The full extent of these marriages is no longer remembered, but Emir Sattam (died 1901) is known to have married twelve times; Emir Nuri (died 1936) is said to have married seventy times (and I have records of forty-two of his marriages); and Nawaf, Nuri's son, married at least six times although he was never Emir and died aged forty-one. (Musil, in *Arabia Deserta*, implies that Nawaf was married far more often than this.) The last exponent of this pattern was Al-Aurens ibn Trad Sha'alan who married eleven times – he died in 1976 and admitted to being old-fashioned in this matter. If this is compared with the present generation (and those still alive from the previous one) there is a marked contrast. Very few have been married four times and the norm is once or twice with polygamy almost totally absent. I am uncertain as to how extensive polygamy was in the past – the women certainly disliked it and it seems to have been confined to the most influential sheikhs. Emir Nuri must have had four wives at a time (the permitted maximum) simply to get through such a large number, although many of his marriages lasted only a few months or even less. The main feature, however, is not the simultaneous polygamy but the multiple sequential marriages.

It is at this point that analysing marriages as an institution becomes inadequate. People are individuals, in part, because of their parents, i.e. marriages in the previous generation; they grow up and marry, constrained in their choice of partner by existing political and economic considerations; they divorce and remarry constrained, again, by changing circumstances and, as we have seen earlier, by hopes for the future, as well as by their contemporaries' and rivals' marriages. Thus marriage is a continuous process and must be analysed as such; multiple sequential marriages and the generative genealogy make this abundantly clear.

Changing Marriage-Patterns

In the foregoing chapter it was shown that the emphasis of the sheikhly function changed from mediating with other tribes and semi-dependent settlements to negotiating with central governments. This change increased the sheikh's financial needs, for he became dependent on costly impression-management. One result of this was that the number of rivals was reduced, for while another man might have the necessary reputation range he was less likely to have the financial resources.

First let us see how mediating with other tribes affected marriage-patterns and couple this with the need for maintaining balance within the family. (We can ignore the relationship with *khuwa*-paying towns and villages, for they were complementary and not competing and very few marriages between the two systems took place.) Broadly speaking the Sha'alan needed to maintain close links with the sheikhly families of the Fed'an, the Hessene, the Beni Sakhr, the Sirhan, the Wald Ali and, formerly, one of the branches of the Shammar. The importance of these tribes (to the Rwala) varied over the years. For instance, the Shammar marriages were only of importance before the fall of Ibn Rashid. Similarly, the marriages with the Sirhan declined in importance and numbers when the Sha'alan gave up their 'rule' of northern Saudi Arabia (as it now is). For the others, they raided and counter-raided, opposed each other, briefly allied themselves and split up again. At each shift the relative importance of a marriage changed. When Nuri was struggling for the emirate an important ally was Ibn Gendal of the Swalme – so there were marriages between them. When he had consolidated his position the need came to an end and the marriages ceased. The purpose of these sorts of marriage was to increase reputation range and provide channels of communication direct to those with whom mediation was most necessary. The alliances were not military, for no family should interfere in the internal affairs of another – the alliances were so that you had the channels of communication rather than your internal family rival or to counteract those that he already had.

Segmentation continues down to individuals, especially where half-brothers are concerned – half-brothers who were frequently rivals. If they are rivals (and the descendants of f.½b. and f.f.½b. will also be rival groups) they will try to counteract your marriage with a marriage to the sister of your brother-in-law's rivals within his family. Just as competition between tribes changes over time so does competition between subgroups within the family, your own and others'. To keep up with this, marriages must be broken and remade constantly. This, of course, is likely to result in an increase in half-brothers, which keeps the whole complicated system going into the next generation.

The changeover from inter-tribal mediation to negotiation with a different system shifted the emphasis of the whole segmentary system from opposition to complementarity. The former rivalries became less imporant than co-operation. If we look at the lowest level of segmentation and follow it upwards we will see why the marriage-patterns changed. The

Change and Adaptation

financial resources necessary for impression-management were in the hands of the principal sheikh at the time of the changeover, for they were initially provided by central government. By the time potential rivals acquired the finance to oppose the principal sheikh, he had a virtual monopoly of information concerning the ins-and-outs, intrigues, rivalries and tensions within central government. So he was in an almost unassailable position. This took the steam out of internal family rivalry; the potential gains of supplanting the sheikh were far greater, but they were far less attainable. This political and financial pre-eminence of the principal sheikh gave him a certain amount of patronage to dispense to his erstwhile rivals; obviously those who were most trusted, i.e. had no intention of rivalling him, were the most likely to benefit from this. Internal family co-operation becomes the order of the day. All other sheikhly families are in the same boat, so that inter-tribal relations are no longer fraught with balancing splits and potential splits. These forces that promote harmony within families also foster co-operation between tribes, for they too follow the principle of segmentation and coalesce in the face of opposition from the outside world. So even at this level, the emphasis is on complementarity rather than opposition.

The cessation of jockeying for influence within sheikhly families means that each family no longer has to divorce wives who have become redundant in order to marry the sisters of the new man of influence. Because the man of influence within each family remains the same, the wives of other men of influence can remain the same; it is no longer necessary to try to catch up with every slight change of course, because the course stays predominantly the same. And the lack of rivals within the family means that, while the balancing act still continues, the equilibrium remains much the same. Without the constant pressure to change wives to reflect shifts in influence, divorce becomes rarer and marriage more stable. Marriages are arranged to repair splits not to exploit them, with the result that there are fewer groups descended from half-brothers who might become rivals. The children of descendants of half-brothers who intermarry with each other might just as well be the children of descendants of full brothers, for they will all be equally related to each other.

The whole sequence is more easily comprehended if we follow a simple model. (See Figure 8.) $A1$ marries $a1$, a girl from another tribe, R. He also marries $a2$, a girl from 'ibn amm' X of his own family. His son, $B1$, will probably marry from his mother's family (tribe R), while his second wife will probably be from 'ibn amm' Y, which is opposed to 'ibn amm' X. $B2$

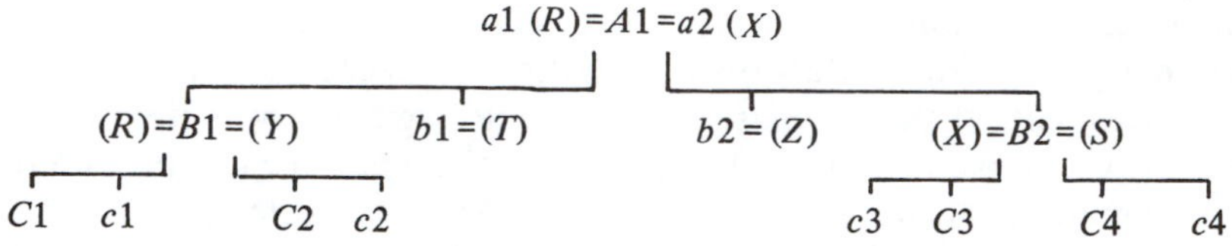

$$a1\ (R)=A1=a2\ (X)$$

$$(R)=B1=(Y) \qquad b1=(T) \qquad b2=(Z) \qquad (X)=B2=(S)$$

$$C1 \quad c1 \qquad C2 \quad c2 \qquad\qquad c3 \quad C3 \qquad C4 \quad c4$$

Figure 8. Model to demonstrate pathways of coalescing and splitting

134

will also marry from his mother's family ('ibn amm' X) and his second wife will probably be from another tribe, S. Thus $A1$ is nicely balanced for his daughters marry into tribe T and 'ibn amm' Z. $B1$ and $B2$ have children: $C1$ marries into tribe R, $C2$ marries into 'ibn amm' Y: $C3$ marries into 'ibn amm' X and $C4$ marries into tribe S. When $A1$ dies, who succeeds? $B1$ and $B2$ have nothing in common except a father and their children have nothing in common except a f.f. $B2$ probably has a slight advantage as his full sister, $b2$, draws another whole segment of the family into his orbit, but if, as is likely, her children are married into 'ibn amm' Y, the sheikhly family of tribe Z will be split anyway. Assume $B2$ becomes sheikh but soon dies and is succeeded by $B1$, who proves ineffective and soon dies as well. There is now not only competition between the descendants of $B1$ and $B2$, but also within each group: $C1$ competes with $C2$, while $C3$ competes with $C4$. Say that $C1$ marries $c3$ and a descendant from $b2$ from 'ibn amm' Z. He will be backed by tribe R (if they enter into it at all, and they probably will through similar marriage sequences), by 'ibn amm' X and by 'ibn amm' Z. But the permutations are endless and we've only had two generations with two wives each. In practice we're considering maybe four or five generations, groups of five or six brothers and every man marrying maybe six or seven times: every woman has, probably, three or more brothers and sisters, who are all partaking in the system, and she herself will probably have married three or four times and had children by each marriage. This is a very simple model.

Staying with our model, conditions change. $B2$, who became sheikh, was given agricultural land by the government and became rich. If he remains sheikh for some years, his son, $C3$, will in time have had more experience in deputising for his father and will have acquired land of his own by the judicious use of options. When $B2$ dies, $B1$ will succeed but is old, not very rich and sheikh in name only – $C3$ is really the sheikh and will become such when $B1$ dies. When this happens, $C3$ has no real rival: the best that $C1$, $C2$ and $C4$ can do is coalesce and arrange their marriages and children's marriages so that the closest cohesion possible takes place. Not only do they become associated with $C3$'s success, but all their children partake as well. And by reducing the number of their marriages they contribute further to reducing tensions and potential splits. By harking back to marriages with tribes R, S and T and 'ibn amms' X, Y and Z the whole family and federation can be welded into a unity to oppose central government. The extraordinary thing is that $A1$ could have said the same thing – by arranging his children's marriages as he did, he could claim to be welding the family and confederation together, when in actual practice his intention had been the exact opposite. Of course, $A1$ would be justified if, by weakening all potential rivals, he made himself 'paramount' sheikh of the confederation. He could then negotiate with central government from a position of strength and, to the outside at least, the whole confederation would be united in opposition to central government. But $A1$ would have to be very lucky and exceptional to manage it, because the sheikhs of tribes *R*, *S* and *T*, as well as the most influential men in 'ibn amms' *X*, *Y* and *Z*, would be trying to do the same thing. And, of course, the sheikhs of tribes *R*, *S* and *T* also have rivals from their own 'ibn amms'.

At the risk of straying from the subject of changing marriage-patterns, there is a further point that all this raises. It is quite clear from the hypothetical *A*1's claim that context is all-important. In the total Bedu context and from the viewpoint of a weak tribe, *A*1 was doing good and should be encouraged: in the context of the family and from the viewpoint of his nearly equal rival, the 'leader' of 'ibn amm' *X*, *A*1 is being fatally divisive and overbearing and should be removed. *A*1 knows that both viewpoints, contrary though they are, are valid and will present now one, now the other depending on his audience. All Bedu statements seem to partake of this dual character and it stems from the basic premises of equality and personal autonomy. Every man is an island and is responsible for his own affairs, thus his context is always shifting depending on his audience and on his intentions. Segmentation produces paradox: a brother is also a rival, so is a cousin, a three-generation 'ibn amm', a five-generation 'ibn amm', a tribal section and a tribe. What is true at one level at one time is a lie at another level at the same time, a lie at the same level at another time, yet true at another level at another time. It is extremely difficult for the outsider (and this means anyone in opposition) to disentangle truth from falsehood, fact from fabrication. A man can marry a girl from 'ibn amm' *X* and say he is trying to draw the two groups together – true: at the same time, at a different level, he is trying to counteract the close connection between 'ibn amms' *X* and *Y*; at the same time he is intending to counteract his half-brother's marriage, also into 'ibn amm' *X*, and doing down his other half-brother, who is married into 'ibn amm' *Y*. The official explanation is that he is marrying his m.f.z.d. who is also his f.f.b.s.d. He says he is marrying for love. Pontius Pilate had a point when he asked: 'What is truth?'

The reason for this digression is to make it quite clear that although 'explanations' given for marriages may be true, they are only partially true for that particular time. The Bedu are aware of this, but never analyse it. Even my analysis is still only partially true. Outside political events give rise to changes in sheikhly functions, which make multiple sequential marriages redundant or even potentially dangerous; but the very fact that marriage is now more stable is also potentially dangerous, for it reduces, over time, those cross-cutting ties that can be used to heal splits and divisions: it reduces the options. The earlier analysis of the opposition between the two goums at Ar-Risha (pp. 15–18) demonstrate this. The two full brothers who opposed the rest have married, apparently outside the family. One has married into the Mheid family, the other into the Ibn Saud. The girl from the Mheid can, by emphasising her maternal links, be drawn into the Sha'alan very closely (three of her four grandparents are Sha'alan), but equally she can be pushed further away by stressing her Mheid origin. The Ibn Saud girl is more of an outsider, although her family are from the

Aneze confederation. It is probably perfectly possible to trace connections through her mother, who came from the Ebde Shammar; for the Ebde Shammar were opposed to the Jirba Shammar with whom the Sha'alan used to marry. I am morally certain that the Ebde and the Jirba intermarry and that a link could quite easily be found if necessary; in fact it has probably already been done. The marriage to the Mheid girl can be used to pull both brothers back into the family through her Sha'alan links (as is being done), while the Ibn Saud marriage opens up new options for the whole family. Equally the girl's Mheid father can be emphasised and the two brothers distance themselves from the rest, while keeping their Ibn Saud option open and personal to them. Thus the context and intention is important. The fact of fewer marriages doesn't mean that the family is necessarily more unified, but it makes it appear so, for that is the intention. It is also desirable in the context of the family in the present political arena. If the intention is to compete and split up, it can just as easily be done.

The usual explanation for the change in marriage patterns is now said to be economic. Very few men are rich enough, under modern conditions, to maintain more than one wife or the offspring from three or four sequential wives. Nowadays, sheikhly children must be educated, preferably to university standard (even, increasingly, the girls), they must be well dressed to maintain family dignity, they must travel to learn a foreign language. All this is expensive, for a good education demands a house in a city, which is in itself increasingly costly to buy and to maintain. The Sha'alan are no longer very rich or very powerful, so their options are slightly limited and their children will have to earn their own living; consequently they need to be educated. In the past this was not so. The Sha'alan were enormously rich and extremely powerful and the young men did not need to earn a living but a reputation. This was extremely competitive, but it didn't demand much cash. The price of failure was not destitution and being supported by the rest of the family, but death. Thus in the past sequential marriages were a positive asset; the cost involved was not high and anyway implied success, and a sequence of children, especially sons, was essential because the death-rate was so high. Emir Nuri Sha'alan with his seventy-odd marriages produced some thirty-nine sons and an unknown number of daughters. Thirty-seven of the sons died, mostly in raids, before they married: one married but was killed before he had children and the remaining one had four sons and died aged forty-one. This alone could be given as a valid reason for multiple sequential marriage – it was essential to improve the chances of a line surviving.

At the time of these multiple sequential marriages the Sha'alan were rich, powerful and warlike. The economy was booming, the inner desert was still inviolate and raiding and warfare extremely bloody. It is quite possible that this was an interim period and that the marriage-pattern reflected it. The evidence of earlier practices is slight, but there seems to be a tendency towards fewer wives. For instance, Mneif ibn Gherir (*c.*

1750) only had remembered sons from two or maybe three wives; Abdullah ibn Mneif only had sons from two wives; Nayyif ibn Abdullah had sons from three known wives. Previous to the mid-nineteenth century raiding was far less lethal, so deaths in battle must have been rarer. Burckhardt mentions that a full-scale war only resulted in about eighty deaths over a year. In fact, Nayyif ibn Abdullah is always associated with the fact that all his seven sons were killed in battle, as if it were exceptional. Even Hazza' ibn Nayyif, Nuri's father, only had three known wives and five sons with no hint of others now forgotten. I would be surprised if the death-rate from natural causes was exceptionally high, for the herding Bedu today are extremely healthy and live on the traditional diet of fresh milk, dates and bread – monotonous but more than adequate and scarcely a recipe for malnutrition. So what evidence there is tends to indicate that multiple sequential marriages started with Hamad and Nuri Ibn Hazza' and was a practice that only lasted about eighty years. It was a response to a particular set of political and economic circumstances and was confined to the sheikhly family. If this is so, then the present pattern is just a reversion to the earlier norm with present political circumstances, by suppressing internal family rivalries, reducing still further inter-tribal marriages.

It must be remembered that throughout all the changing functions, pressures and marriage-patterns the fundamental basis of marriage remained – the generative genealogy. Every marriage, unless it was occasioned by sheer lubricity, must have been measured by the advantages and disadvantages it brought to the family and the children, just as marriages are considered now. So political gain had to be seen as a better option in spite of the danger of splitting in the next generation. While the Sha'alan were powerful (roughly 1860–1940) they could ignore, to a large extent, the divisive tendencies that arose through the production of many half-brothers. It could be seen as a mechanism for further domination by relying on family solidarity always to counteract any outside threat. And outside threats were not many, for no one was powerful enough to exploit the potential divisions. Prior to 1860 the Sha'alan were not powerful enough, politically or economically, to take such risks, nor are they now. No other family within the tribe shows, as far as I know, the same pattern; it seems to be confined to the Sha'alan. It reflects the political and economic arena in which they found themselves at one particular moment. It was a response, within the framework of the generative genealogy, to a particular set of assets and options.

11 Economic Development and Technology

Political changes were not the only ones to have their effect on the Rwala. Economic and technological parameters have varied over time and the Rwala have responded to these as well. Politics and economics become entangled so there is some overlap with political events, which might appear better placed in another chapter, but this is inevitable. Equally, technology is closely bound up with policy and economics, especially as far as the Rwala are concerned, for modern technology came to them from the outside.

As mentioned elsewhere, the Rwala economy was based on camels. Most food, and all transport and wealth, came from camels. Wealth is what we are interested in here. However, wealth, although based on camels, was never dependent on the numbers of camels owned; camels were only the means of acquring wealth, which was measured in terms of reputation. The first necessity is to clear the mind of preconceptions about wealth, most importantly that wealth is necessarily tangible – among the Rwala it was not and is not. There are very good reasons for this. Fifteen to twenty

Plate 15. Zuwaiyyid Nseir herding-encampment on the edge of Al-Labbah

camels will provide basic subsistence for a family of six very adequately, so anything over twenty camels is surplus. What on earth can you gain from them? It would be difficult to increase milk consumption much and camel's milk can only be converted into preservable dairy products to a limited extent. You can't eat your surplus, for camels are too large for a family to consume; you can't even sell them for much of the year, as there is no market nearby. So, you decide to keep them; but one man can only look after fifty camels, so as your herd increases you have to employ someone to herd them, and then another and another. However, raiding is a popular pastime, so you have to guard your camels as well. This adds a whole new layer of employees, for herders are herders and not guards. But employed men have to be paid – and you only have camels so you pay them in those. As each employee acquires fifteen or so camels he can become independent and you're back where you started, with too many camels for comfort. In other words, camels as a direct measure of wealth are a non-starter. It just doesn't work.

So camels must be converted. What into? Gold? Your relations will borrow it and it will be a standing temptation to others. Fine clothes? All clothes look much the same after six weeks' hard wear in the desert. More grain and dates? Possibly, but they've got to be carried about and there is a limit to your appetite. Weapons? A sword or spear or club of gold covered with gems and with an ivory handle is probably not as efficient as an iron one and, like gold, is a temptation. Horses? These are certainly a possibility, but very expensive to keep and a favourite target of raiders. There are an infinite number of possibilities but useful wealth in the desert must be highly mobile, easily preservable and non-stealable – in other words non-material, like reputation. So the acquisition of camels is only a stage in obtaining wealth – you're not measured by how many camels you own, but by how many pass through your hands and what happens to them. To lose camels to raiders is not a very glorious way of shedding surplus, so you give them away. Your reputation is increased, but where do you get more camels? Obviously you raid others for them. So the basis of wealth is generosity and success in raiding. If an economic system is measured in wealth and wealth is measured in generosity and success in raiding, then the raiding of the substrate is the capital that keeps the economy going. Just as land or coal or factories are valueless assets unless used, so are camels: just as work makes land and coal and factories valuable, so raiding makes camels valuable. The only difference is that work converts things into money, while raiding converts camels into reputation. Once it is absolutely clear that wealth means good reputation and not mere material riches, the purpose of raiding and the whole economic system becomes comprehensible. You acquire camels to give them away to build up reputation: to maintain that reputation you need more camels so you go raiding again. Once this basic cycle is established it can be elaborated.

Raiding can take various forms. It can be one or two men cutting out a few straying beasts and making off with them or, at the other end of the scale, it can be a large number of men making off with a complete herd. Both extremes have disadvantages as far as reputation is concerned. Rounding up three or four straying animals is far from difficult (so there is little glory attached to it – it doesn't make a good story), while for a large body of men a herd comes down, in the end, to only two or three camels each – not a lot to be generous with. The ideal is a small number of men raiding a large number of camels and succeeding by daring and strategy. Each man then has a sufficient number of surplus animals to make a significant show with, while his success enhances his reputation for daring and resource. Clearly too much daring and resource have their drawbacks; your career, though glorious, is likely to be short, a factor noticeable in the death-rate among sheikh's sons between whom competition in raiding was keenest. Quite apart from raiding, daring and resource have their uses in the preventive field: raiding was a two-way process and daring and resource were equally necessary to preserve your own basic herd – an important feature for those who might entrust their daughter or sister to you as a wife.

It is difficult to get across the full flavour of raiding. It is often said to have been almost a sport and there is certainly some element of truth in this for it was governed by fairly strict rules that made it more difficult. For instance, it was dishonourable to attack a sleeping enemy, any defender who submitted must be spared, women were inviolate even if they counter-attacked, herdsmen (as opposed to guards) were never involved in fighting, sufficient camels must be left for the family to reach relatives etc. Raiding was more than just an economic activity ensuring the circulation of surplus camels to be exchanged for reputation; it was a code of conduct as well. A man not only had to be successful but had to be successful within the rules, or his reputation suffered. This, at least, was the theory of it. Nobody can remember those halcyon days, for the nature of raiding changed during the second half of the nineteenth century. Indeed it is improbable that the golden age of raiding ever really existed, except for a very short time. Burckhardt (1831, pp. 133ff.) indicates that the rules were somewhat different at that date and actions were allowed that would be thought of as dishonourable nowadays.

Until the middle of the nineteenth century camels had been, as it were, bearer bonds that could be 'traded' for reputation. However, the growing outside economy and the change in the relationship between the sheikhs and central government brought the tribe much closer to a money economy. Money, of course, had never been wholly absent, for the trading of camels for meat or transport had always contributed to the Bedu economy, but it had remained a fairly minor part because of the difficulty of conversion into useful commodities. Of far greater importance was the introduction of firearms, which took place at about the same time. I am not talking about muskets, which the Bedu had had for some time. Muskets are only really useful in set-piece battles with volleys, and are only marginally useful in guerilla skirmishes owing to the time they take to be reloaded. The repeating rifle was a different matter. One of the conventions of raiding was that bloodshed was avoided as far as possible. This had a strong foundation in commonsense. Swords, spears and maces are all close-quarters weapons, so who kills whom can be fairly easily determined and this involves the killer in a feud. In all killings outside formal warfare *lex talionis* applied (and still applies) and the sorting-out of the identity of the killer was one of the major mediating roles of the sheikh or goum leader. However gloriously the killer's deed might have been accomplished there were, not unnaturally, members of his family who resented being involved. This had little to do with the sanctity of human life, which has never ranked very high among the Bedu, but was occasioned by the fact that every male of the five-generation 'ibn amm' was at risk. It is hardly surprising that those on the fringe of the group avoided involvement if possible, for they had least to gain from the raid in question but just as much to lose. So strong was this resentment that killings on raids were deprecated and tended to diminish, rather than enhance, reputation. The avoidance of bloodshed was so general a desire that the Bedu gained a reputation for cowardice (Burckhardt, 1831). More realistically, it was a question of discretion being the better part of valour. The weaker party usually saw retreat and the loss of camels as a better option; they could always recover them later.

The advent of the rifle changed all this. To start with, the numerically weaker group might be more heavily armed, but, more important, the rifle made killing anonymous – the attackers could pick off the guards from cover and their identity need never be revealed. This might not have conferred advantage as far as honour and reputation went, but the booming economy had increased the demand for meat and transport and camels could now be exchanged for modern arms, particularly rifles. Rifles made success more certain but they required ammunition, so more camels were needed to buy that. In short, rifles became the durable useful commodity that fitted in with nomadic life but had been absent before. The rifle might not have had such a devastating effect if there had been no other change in conditions, but at precisely the same time the sheikhs needed money for impression-management in their dealings with central government. While the display that this exercise required does not seem to have filtered down to the ordinary Bedu till much later, the political aspects of it did. The sheikhs became victims of their own propaganda. By implying that they controlled their tribes they had to do so in reality, to some extent at least. But they did not have the power to do so. How do you most easily persuade someone to do something? You give him a present. What does he want? Rifles for himself and/or his goum. The desert arms race was on. While *A* is more heavily armed he can raid *B* quite easily, but *B* acquires arms and can defend himself; so *A* gets more or better arms, and so on. The killings that arose out of these new raiding techniques inflamed passions, because the killer could only rarely be positively identified. The category for legitimate revenge became larger, not in formal terms but in practice. The attitude developed that if a group of Fed'an (or Beni Sakhr or Sba'a) raid us and kill our guards, we are entitled to do the same to them. Such uncontrolled revenge under the guise of raiding soon developed into virtual warfare, with retaliation being taken for damaged prestige as much as for booty.

The early part of this process cannot be documented; there is a gap from 1877 to *c*. 1904 and the change in raiding has been reconstructed from informants and what is known of conditions in the area at the time. What is perfectly clear is that by the early 1900s the raiding system was in danger of total collapse. All around, raiding was becoming inextricably entangled with political ambitions – Ibn Saud, Ibn Sabah of Kuweit, Ibn Rashid, the Sherif of Mecca, the Turks and their clients in Damascus, Baghdad and elsewhere, the British in Kuweit and the Gulf, all were involved and the participants, not least the Bedu participants, were seeking something more than a few camels. Straightforward raids (if such existed by now) acquired political overtones. Things went from bad to worse. First the revival of Wahhabism, as a deliberate weapon of policy, reduced raiding to almost complete anarchy. The Wahhabis formed themselves into bands of brethren, the Ikhwan, and looted and plundered all who disagreed with them either politically or in matters of faith. As Wahhabism included the political supremacy of Ibn Saud, all those not with Ibn Saud were against him and fair game. The Ikhwan raids were 'jihads', 'holy wars', by definition and thus not subject to the rules of raiding. It would be unfair to suspect all the Ikhwan of opportunism rather than pure faith, but equally it would be naive to assume that all were solely motivated by religion. Frequently both aspects could be combined, as with the Mashhur of the Sha'alan, some of whom joined genuine religious conviction with straight political ambition and remained Ikhwan till the end. But whether the Ikhwan were individually motivated by belief or by greed, the result was the same. For the Ikhwan, non-Wahhabis could be plundered and slaughtered with perfect propriety; for the non-Wahhabis, the Ikhwan could be treated in like manner. The behaviour of the Ikhwan seems to have given the final push to the degeneration of raiding into straight pillage, although in all fairness they may have been a symptom of change rather than a contributory cause.

It is possible that raiding, as an economic system, might have reasserted itself if the outside world had retreated again, but it didn't. The result was that other items of Western technology, notably the motor vehicle, changed the whole way of life irrevocably. It wasn't so much the motor car as such, that did this, for the Sha'alan had a fleet of Fords, Panhards and Buicks with mounted machine guns by the early 1920s, but the fact that improved transport enabled central government forces to interfere in the inner desert with far greater ease and effectiveness than hitherto. Also, mechanised transport killed, to all intents and purposes, the market for camels. By the 1930s, raiding had ceased to be an economic option. Not only was it frowned-on and increasingly suppressed by central authorities, but also the returns were negligible. What did you do with your surplus camels? You couldn't exchange them on the market for nobody wanted camels, yet you couldn't give them away, as formerly, because everyone had more than enough. From about 1920 onwards the Rwala were pretty well supreme in the Syrian desert; few ventured to attack them or even raid them, while they were usually successful in their own raiding activites. The only area where they might have expended camels was in the south (where they were the only means of transport and therefore saleable), but by largely avoiding the dynastic and religious quarrels of Ibn Saud and the Ikhwan, they simply grew richer, in terms of camels at any rate. Fairly small tribal sections, or more probably parts thereof, are reported by outside observers as having tens of thousands of camels and men still living, who have never had any claim to great reputation or wealth, had camel-herds measured in hundreds – 200 or 300 head was commonplace.

Raiding, in any sense, ended by 1935, for the majority of the Rwala. According to the Sha'alan, the sheikhs of the Aneze met and agreed formally to forbid raiding between their tribesmen. If such a conference ever took place it was redundant: not only had raiding died a natural death, even if it had been alive the sheikhs would have had no means at their disposal to ban it effectively. The last raid, that I know of, took place near Sakaka in 1951 or 1952 and was of a punitive rather than acquisitive nature, and it was soon suppressed by the authorities.

I cannot pretend that I have all the detailed evidence to sustain this developmental argument, for the evidence is lacking unless it is tucked away in forgotten archives in the Middle East. The outlines, however, are plain. Raiding was the primary economic activity, but for reputation rather than for wealth as such. Surplus camels were given away to increase reputation. Firearms enabled raiders to ignore the conventions and avoid feud retribution at a time when general prosperity came to the area so that camels could be exchanged for arms (and, for the sheikhs, political display). Exacerbation of this development by the Ikhwan created near-anarchy. The bottom dropped out of the camel-market with the introduction of motor vehicles, which also enabled central governments to extend direct control over the tribes. Raiding ceased.

Between 1935 or thereabouts and 1958, the Rwala apparently just herded their camels. The meat market for camels still existed and the Sha'alan had the main Damascus camel-trade under their control. The value of camels had declined but there was still sufficient demand to enable the ordinary tribesman to buy the necessities of grain, dates, cloth and metal utensils. Extra cash came in from outside employment, particularly in the Arab Legion and the Syrian equivalent, the Méharistes. During the war years the Rwala favoured the Free French and the British and were employed in transporting goods across the desert. How extensive this was I have not been able to determine. Whether their reticence about the recent past is a result of possible political repercussions or whether there was really very little activity cannot be determined with precision. The latter seems more likely. With their vast herds of camels they had plenty for subsistence and plenty to sell, even if the price was low. Most families could afford to sell sufficient beasts for other products without endangering their subsistence. In farming terms they were herding extensively rather than intensively.

The Sha'alan involved themselves in local politics and farming, while the rest of the tribe seem to have lived their own lives, using men of influence to sort out feuds and advise on compensation. Having plenty of camels they were under little pressure for change; reputations grew through generosity, and mediation and skill as a herder seems to have developed into a reputation-maker in place of skill as a raider. But this development died in infancy owing to the drought of 1958–62.

The drastic curtailment of herding occasioned by this drought forced the economy to change. With basic subsistence removed, the Rwala had to turn to other jobs simply to survive. As mentioned in chapter 8, 'Economics', the oil companies and the National Guard in Saudi Arabia filled the gap. Since then the Rwala have diversified considerably.

Clearly there is a conflict here. In the span of one lifetime the Rwala have moved from an economy that was essentially non-monetary to an ordinary economy where wealth is measured in financial terms. To put it another way, the Rwala have moved from a community where wealth was measured in moral terms towards inclusion into a society where wealth is more materially based. The switch is not quite as drastic as it might appear at first glance for in both cases wealth (moral or material) is acquired, not inherited: moral wealth is determined by personal behaviour while material wealth hasn't yet been going long enough to have become entrenched in any particular branch. (The wealth of the Sha'alan can be ignored for they were seen, by the tribe, in traditional terms. Their wealth (financial) was irrelevant; what mattered was their personal and collective reputations.) Nevertheless, the switch poses problems for the Rwala and has given rise to tensions, especially between age groups. In 1976 the dilemma was becoming increasingly apparent. Young men employed as guards, drivers, mechanics etc. made a decent living but never had a surplus with which to build a traditional reputation. Their elders were loud in their condemnation of the younger generation until they realised that one cannot be generous in the old way under the new economy. Later the realities of life were understood by all and attitudes changed. That is to say that the young men started to change their attitudes. Having initially welcomed the new options offered them by education and diversification, they are now far from sure about them. In particular, the young men are becoming disenchanted with the steady job that does not allow for capital accumulation and they are beginning to realise that agriculture comes into this category as well. More favoured are trading and entrepreneurial activities that increase the possibility of lucrative windfalls. Office and bureaucratic jobs, which once they lamented that they were insufficiently educated for, are now well down everyone's list of priorities, for exactly the same reasons.

At the same time the elderly approve of this new emphasis. This is not to say that the Rwala spurn office jobs or agriculture; they don't, but they see these sorts of jobs as stop-gaps, not as long-term options.

It is interesting to note that it is the more go-ahead of the young men who are taking up the options that make windfalls possible; it is the more docile who farm, take jobs in the bureaucracy and stay on at school. This is obviously a subjective evaluation, for no measurable results are yet in, but from observation it seems clear that those most committed to Bedu ethics are the same ones who take up the riskiest options. And it is these same young men who have the best reputations. I must draw together several strands here. The dynamic become entrepreneurs etc., who 'raid' the capitalist economy; the less dynamic take safe jobs; the family spreads its assets with a view to maximising its options; the old approve of these developments. One thing is quite certain: this adaptation to the new economy has not been imposed by the elderly, even though they approve. The Bedu have no reverence for age as such; great age does not improve reputation. While the old will be listened to deferentially and even consulted, the deference is only for public consumption (it is how the young should behave toward their elders); the advice will be accepted or rejected purely on its merits. The experience and reputation of the adviser will be taken into account, but his age is immaterial. For the family to spread its assets is obviously sensible, as it means survival for all if the risk-takers fail. But why should the most traditional and those with the highest reputations be the risk-takers (including those who smuggle)? The majority of families have a more-than-adequate income; they live very comfortably and they are as secure as they ever have been. Why do they approve of adventurers? Part of the reason is that the risk-takers replace the resourceful raiders of the past, but far more important is the fact that the Rwala haven't adapted to the new economy at all; they have adapted the new economy to fit their own requirements.

The direct evidence for this interpretation is slight but telling. In the past, how many camels you had was fairly irrelevant; what mattered was how you acquired them and what you did with the surplus. The same applies now, not to camels, but to money. The risk-takers gain reputation by the manner in which they make their living and the way in which they distribute their gains around the camp or among their 'ibn amm'. The money may be used to help a cousin get married or set up house, or it may be distributed as presents – clothes, feasts, toys or by buying a new truck or colour television set that is available to all. Whatever they do with it is not very important provided they don't keep it or invest it in something private. Just as with camels, the surplus should be given away (after the family commitments are honoured) and it is notable that those who do retain the private usufruct of their surplus earnings have rather poor reputations. As is frequently the case, those who do not conform are more visible and so point up the conformity of the majority. I only know of two private investors who are also entrepreneurs. They are both very successful financially but their reputations are poor, for they reinvest their money simply to make more for themselves and their immediate families. Both are credited with meanness and both worry about it, but cannot see how to escape from the vicious circle of their own making.

This explains the reduction in tension since about 1976; the essential morality is beginning to reassert itself after a total change in economics. An economy based on moral wealth came into conflict with an economy based on material wealth; after a brief, muddled and unhappy flirtation with the Western importation, the old standards have re-established themselves and materialism, in its grosser manifestations, has been decisively rejected by the majority.

We now start to get into deeper water, for the moral economy is closely tied not only to how one makes a living (and spends the proceeds) but to Rwala values and beliefs. The distance between their attitudes and ours is most apparent in the matter of security. Personal security comes very low on the scale of values. This is implicit in the generosity ethic, which is, among other things, an insurance policy. It is also implicit in the family's spreading of assets to maximise options. Whatever happens to various individuals the group can survive a multitude of hazards. (This is probably one of the reasons why 'ibn amm' groups of all sizes never worked together, why tribal sections spread themselves around and why the tribe never attempted to work as a unit. If one part came to grief, economically or militarily, the rest would survive to carry on.) The distinction must be emphasised between personal security and the survival of the collective – again we are working on at least two levels. The generous man, in the past as well as nowadays, must take risks to obtain the wherewithall to be generous with. His success increases his reputation and that of his immediate group and should he be killed or grow too old, his past generosity will ensure that others will, in turn, be generous to him and/or his group, if they are in real need. Thus the risk-takers, be they raiders, speculators or entrepreneurs, by setting aside personal security, ensure the long-term security of the group. The whole system of the generative genealogy, asset-spreading and personal autonomy can be seen in the same light. Careful marriage choices increase the options open to the offspring, asset-spreading increases the options open to individuals, personal autonomy gives each individual the right to choose which option he will take up. The risky option of raiding could, if succcessfully carried out, increase political influence and provide the group with greater collective security by increasing marriage choices, thus widening future options. More recently, smuggling played the same role by increasing personal reputation, which in turn enhanced marriage choice and, by providing the money to buy sheep, or whatever, increasing the options of others within the group. This provision of options, although it may look like reinvestment, was never private; it always opened up other options for others in the group. Even in the days of raiding, those who benefited materially were nephews, sons or cousins who could then set up their own goum: but then as now much of the generosity was of a purely casual nature. Many former smugglers are now traders, for smuggling is only trading under special conditions; the same skills apply, so smuggling can be seen as a way of exploring new options and acquiring those skills that will make it an option for others. The same holds good for agriculture. The Ga'adza'i who first settled to agriculture did so before the drought and before officialdom in Saudi Arabia had given much thought to turning the Bedu in the north into farmers. He was taking a risk. It didn't pay off for him particularly, but it paved the way for others to do the same – his risk provided security for the group, for farming is now a safe and steady, if unglamorous, job. Those who first went into the oil companies and the armies were taking a personal risk, for they could not know how it would turn out and they were new options of no proven worth. However, nepotism being the normal method of recruitment, these new options opened up whole new areas for the risk-takers' families. And, at the same time, the new jobs provided cash to be generous with, for most others were almost destitute after the drought. The area the Rwala missed was local government and the civil service. A very few entered at the advisory level in various provincial governors' entourages, but this has not led anywhere very much. The ordinary tribesman has only recently been sufficiently educated to enter at all and then only at the lowest levels. Whether it would have been a suitable risk leading to greater group security is difficult to determine now. It probably would have, as more aid, grants and loans could have been channelled towards the Rwala as a whole. The tribe certainly feels that it has been discriminated against in this field, but whether this is true or not I have no way of knowing. Even sheep-herding was initially risky. The limited area that could be exploited, the shortage of watering points and the small scale of the market made the acquisition of sheep on a commercial scale a definite risk. It has, in practice, paid off handsomely, for more wells have been drilled, the population of the towns expanded and the quality of trucks improved, making more distant grazing practicable; it is now a fairly safe and lucrative occupation. While trade and general entrepreneurial activities seem good for new risky ventures, the long-term security seems to lie, paradoxically, with the camel. Camel-herding has been in sharp decline, for while it still supplies basic subsistence it does nothing more; it couldn't be called even a modestly lucrative option. However, some of the more dynamic young men are beginning to look at it with renewed interest. By injecting capital in the form of modest technology and a technological infrastructure of slaughter-houses, processing-plants, cold stores etc. camel-herding could be made fairly profitable. And it would undoubtedly be risky. At the moment it is probably too high a risk to take but it has an added attraction – it makes one as independent as is possible nowadays. This is not all. The Rwala have long seen that they are living in a false economy. If oil runs out or Ibn Saud goes, their whole economy will collapse, for the north of the kingdom is completely dependent on oil wealth. The civil service, the army, the farms, the company jobs, the sheep-market, the construction work, all are ultimately dependent on oil; all their options are dependent on the present political climate continuing. Whatever happens, oil running out or Ibn

Saud disappearing or simply changing course, the Rwala are likely to be left clutching the fuzzy end of the lollipop. Against this background, camels, which look decidedly risky at the moment, suddenly appear far more attractive as a long-term investment for survival. I arrived at this conclusion in typically Western ecological fashion; the Rwala got there through political considerations.

The reluctance of the Sha'alan, in particular, to commit themselves to anything other than tribal interests, becomes more comprehensible – it is personal autonomy and self-reliance taken to the highest practicable segmentary level. With the collective caution that is the obverse of individual daring, the Rwala, as exponents of the Bedu system, prefer to spread their assets as widely as possible, to follow up many diverse options and to remain independent of any central government.

There is, of course, and always has been, the option of leaving the Bedu system entirely. This has certainly happened, can still happen and will probably continue to happen with increasing frequency. It is extremely difficult to pinpoint, as those who leave the system tend to vanish socially and leave no record behind them. The evidence for this happening in the past is scanty. The village of Sheikh Miskin in Syria is said to be populated by the descendants of detribalised outlaws (see p. 77). There is also a village in Egypt, where all the inhabitants are called Murathi and claim descent from a part of the Murath Rwala who emigrated. There is no direct evidence of the truth of their claim, but various stories about marriages to Hedjazi princesses who had to flee to Egypt and a highly circumstantial story about a Murath tribe wandering in the Sinai peninsula between the wars, give some credence to their claim. The Emir of the Rwala, who came across them by chance some years ago, considered recognising them, but political conditions changed and the matter was dropped. I only know of one Rwala whose family settled and who is still acknowledged as being a member of the tribe. The case was unusual in that his grandfather had made a deliberate decision to settle – he wasn't forced into it – and the grandson returned to the area as the head of the border police, so he had something to offer. He was reposted later and nothing more was heard of him. Among the Sba'a tribe there is one man whose family settled in Jauf some 200 or 300 years ago; he still keeps up his tribal links and enjoys a good reputation. Similarly the Muwaishir family of Jauf/Sakaka are of Bedu origin, as are several of the big trading-houses in Saudi Arabia. What prompted them to settle is unknown to me. According to Barth (1961) it was the under- and over-successful of the Basseri who left the system. This doesn't really fit the Rwala, for it is not economics but morality that determines whether a man leaves or not, except of course for those who make a deliberate decision as an option in itself. The economically under-successful have to leave because they are, by definition, morally unsuccessful; their reputation is so poor that no one wants to marry or co-operate with them. The over-successful are likely to have a similar poor reputation, for material riches imply a lack of generosity and thus a refusal to take part in the

Bedu system. This is obviously most likely to happen to the sheikhs. Ibn Rashid of Hail is an example and the Sha'alan have only avoided it by deliberate policy, as Emir Nuri ibn Hazza''s decision to abandon Jauf shows.

It is perfectly possible that present economic conditions will cause an upsurge in the numbers of those who leave the desert and cease to interact with the tribe. But now that contact with towns and villages is so much closer it is equally likely that many will leave as a deliberate choice yet still maintain their contacts with the nomadic part of their family or tribal section. Settling has become an option in its own right and one that is open to tribesmen without the necessity of cutting themselves off from their roots. It is becoming an economic option, not a moral one.

This may appear to have taken us far from the ostensible subject matter of this chapter. It hasn't really, for economic life among the Rwala is only a different facet of moral or political life. One could argue that the Rwala don't distinguish clearly between the three categories, but such an argument should, by now, be redundant; their whole life-style makes it clear. It can be said that the unifying principle behind these various sectors is Islam. In a sense this is perfectly true. However, the practice of Islam has not had the same effect on all Muslim populations; it is the way in which the Rwala have interpreted Islam that has affected their development. For an anthropologist it is more pertinent to seek the answer through a social process – segmentation.

12 Segmentation, Balance and Symbolism

Throughout the foregoing chapters there has been a continuous reference to balance and assets and options. This can be seen as the practical side of segmentation, and Rwala society is based on the principle of complementary opposition. This is easy enough to say and simple enough to see in large-scale terms, but to understand it at the individual level it is necessary to view the total society as the Rwala themselves see it. This is more difficult, as it means abandoning our preconceptions. A second theme, which runs throughout, has been individualism and autonomy. The issue of individualism in Bedu society is frequently misunderstood (cf. Ibrahim and Cole, 1978), but that individualism is real is fundamental to the Rwala version of the segmentary system. Segmentation continues down to the single, autonomous individual or even, through the concept of the generative genealogy, beyond.

The segmentary system is based on the genealogy: this is obvious to us and the Rwala, but there our viewpoints diverge. We see a genealogy as starting in the past and coming down to the present; the Rwala see it as starting in the present and receding into the past. They are firmly ego-centred. For them the main point of a genealogy is to provide a framework for legitimising present political relationships between groups. This does not mean that they seek to ratify a relationship by reference to the genealogy, but rather that an existing or proposed relationship is an inevitable result of a mutually agreed genealogy. It is not *the* genealogy leading to *a* relationship, but rather *the* relationship leading to *a* genealogy: the relationship is active, the genealogy passive. This comes out clearly in the discussion of the generative genealogy where the 'must have been' argument is considered. If groups A and B co-operate and intermarry then their f.f.f.f. or whatever 'must have been' brothers to explain the present relationship. The fact that group C claims equal relationship but doesn't intermarry or co-operate means that their f.f.f.f. 'must have been' further away, i.e. an uncle or cousin to the founding ancestor. The truth of the genealogy is irrelevant; what matters is the present and the future, so the past has to accommodate itself. In actual practice the Rwala don't even follow the argument through, they jump straight to the present, for the explanation by way of past relationship is simply an assumption, which is only brought into play when someone (in this case the anthropologist) asks for an explanation. Normally, of course, this doesn't happen. One reason for the jump into the present is that genealogy, being mostly concerned with relationships between groups, is spatial rather than temporal. Ancestors are only a link, the name of a larger segment that only has meaning in opposition to its complementary group of real, living people here and now. Groups are rarely, for the Rwala, abstract concepts; they are real living people with whom one interacts or not, as the case may be. It is difficult to get across the sense of immediacy and how little reference there is to the past. When a man says 'I am *A* son of *B* son of *C* of the Zuwaiyyid Nseir of the Murath tribal section of the Rwala Aneze', he is not thinking in terms of time, of dead individuals, but in terms of spatial, ever-expanding inclusive groups of living people. We automatically tend to think in up-and-down temporal terms; they don't: they think more in the terms of Figure 9. This diagram is ego-centred, which is how most of the Rwala think most of the time. Figure 10 allows for many egos around the edge of the outer circle. It is an anthropologist's construct, but one that the Rwala would, I think, readily understand, for they use circles within other circles to demonstrate more inclusive groups. The trouble with any diagram is that it is static whereas, for the Rwala, the genealogy and the total society is dynamic and constantly shifting. The arcs of the concentric circles should be independent within each segment, contracting and expanding in accordance with ego's intentions and purposes. But second-rate and inadequate as this diagram is, it does show two things. One, each and every man around the circumference is equal; two, generational level doesn't matter. The concentric circles are not fixed; every ego is alive and equal to every other ego and generational level is of concern to no one but himself. This way of drawing a genealogy has a conceptual disadvantage. It does not allow for two or three generations living simultaneously. This is, indeed, a complication in thinking genealogically at all. When a man can quite easily have a half-sibling fifty or more years younger than himself it is easier to think of people as living groups, unless it is necessary to think of them as individuals. Context comes to one's help. In a context where groups are being considered, generational level doesn't affect the issue: each individual is a member of the group and it is the collective that matters, not the exact relationship of each member of the group to each other member. Where the relationship of each individual is the context, then generational level is irrelevant because it is individuals who are under consideration. In everyday life generational level is rarely thought about at all. Partly, it would be extremely confusing when parts of groups exceed other parts in reproductive rate, but mostly any consideration of generational level would cut right across the principle of equality. The only concession that the Rwala make is to age and, curiously, this ranking only accentuates

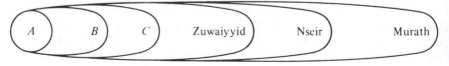

Figure 9. A Bedu genealogical diagram

152

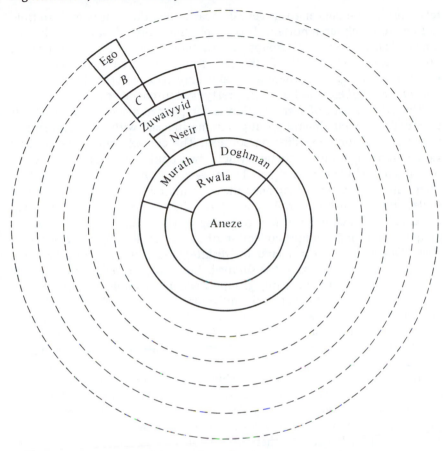

Figure 10. An ego-centred genealogy for many egos

the underlying equality. The most usual place for this to come into play is when tea or coffee are being served. In a family setting, people are served according to age, the eldest first. This does not indicate any reverence for age but simply that age is non-controversial and implies nothing but biological accident. Interestingly, sex is not a factor. If a family are all drinking tea together and there are insufficient glasses (as is usually the case), the eldest get served first irrespective of sex. The order of birth is beyond control and is therefore a safe, non-committal criterion for order of precedence among equals. If genealogical precedence were followed there would be a muddle of senior branches, junior branches, collaterals etc. Not only would it be difficult to compute, for there is no tradition of this sort, but it would imply inequality. Influence is acquired, not inherited, and the principle of primogeniture is not followed, so rank (in as far as it exists at all) could scarcely be based on genealogical or generational precedence. Thus, despite the fact that a man or a woman is identified genealogically, i.e. *A* son of *B*, or *C* daughter of *D*, and despite the fact that inter-group

153

relationships are conceived in genealogical terms, the genealogy is so fluid as to be relatively unimportant. It is simply the accepted way of explaining pragmatically determined groups, a structural framework to account for present reality. The fluidity of this structure is indicated by the paucity of terms to define groups. There are really only two below the level of tribe, *ibn amm* and *fakhdh*, and they are pretty well interchangeable.

The other aspect of segmentation is complementary opposition. This is essentially a mobile in-group/out-group mechanism, with the placement of a person or group depending on context. The context can be enormously varied, ranging from a situation where two confederations of tribes are opposed right down to a squabble between half-brothers. Even full brothers can oppose each other once they are married, for their children will (unless their mothers are full sisters) have differing assets. They are potential ancestors of complementary opposing groups. Each man and woman is unique and having a unique collection of assets can develop along different lines. This sounds like a recipe for disintegration, and it would be if co-operation wasn't necessary for survival, not just personal, individual survival but survival of the existing group of which each individual is part and of the potential group that each individual represents. While the largest and smallest context are fairly easy to determine, there is an enormous area in the middle that is confusing. In any situation the conceptual in-group can change momently, depending on new arrivals, what is being discussed and who agrees with whom, but whatever in-group is in being, it always balances the out-group to which it is in opposition. This balance seems to be absolutely crucial and is, at one and the same time, the cause and result of the fluidity of the genealogy. Just as all men are equal so must all opposing groups be conceived of as equal. All men are not, of course, equal but all start equal and their later inequality is acquired and therefore justified. Provided the superior don't try to dominate their moral or intellectual inferiors, all is well; if they do, then the mechanism of reputation comes into play and they are at once reduced to equality again. The same applies to groups, although the mechanism of reputation is not so strong nor so immediate at the more inclusive group levels. It works more slowly because a large group can co-operate and inter-marry within itself for some time and the mechanism can only operate when they seek outside alliances, of whatever nature. A large, powerful or influential group is, in practice, cut down to size by its complementary opposite growing to balance it. Again, this is a function of the fluidity of the genealogy. This is essential, not only so that opposing groups equal each other in size more or less, but also so that there are, in any context, only two opposing groups at any one level. Sons don't always come in pairs, so a way has to be found to shed the descendants of a third or later son or to include them in one of the main groups. This is amply demonstrated among the Sha'alan. For instance the Nayyif group is splitting (has split) into the Hazza' and Sattam. They are not genealogically equal for Sattam was Hazza''s b.s. However, at the moment, the number of the Sattam roughly equal the number of the

Hazza', so they are in complementary opposition. But what about the descendants of Hazza''s other brother, Faysal? They are still around, are known and even interact with the Hazza' and the Sattam. I don't know how the Sattam rationalised it but the Hazza' simply denied that Faysal was a brother; he became a f.b.s. and therefore far enough away not to distort the balance. Should either the Hazza' or the Sattam grow faster then the other, the Faysal can be reinstated to redress the inequality. There are various relationships that could be used to accomplish this. The commonest way of adjusting the genealogy for this purpose is for a father and son to become brothers or vice versa. The latter happened to the sons of Mneif ibn Gherir Sha'alan. Mneif (who died in 1760, at the latest) is nowadays said to have had two sons, Mashhur and Abdullah. The descendants of Mashhur form the group called the Mashhur while Abdullah's sons increased and now form three groups known as the Zeid, the Mijwal and the Nayyif. The groups are not obviously very equal, but an attempt has been made to even things up. Mneif certainly had one, if not two, other sons, namely Jibl and Datznan. There is no consensus of opinion as to how these two fit in; all possible permutations of son/father/brother have been put to me, depending on the informant. One point that all agree on is that the descendants of Jibl and Datznan are part of the Mashhur. So Jibl and Datznan 'must have been' sons of Mashhur. The two groups of Mashhur and Abdullah seem to have been roughly in balance the last time that they were in active opposition, 1926–34. Now the opposition is formal only, so close balance is not necessary. Nowadays the Mashhur (who are the smaller of the two groups) marry with the Muwasserin and if opposition became active again I would expect them to become, like so many, part of the Muwasserin.

This tendency to divide into two equal opposing groups breaks down at the level of tribal section. There seem to be two reasons for this. The first is that the genealogy at this level is not readily manipulable. As is shown in chapter 4, 'The Generative Genealogy and Marriage', the necessity of demonstrating unequivocal inclusion within the total system overrides the advantages of manipulation. The second reason is that the logistics of active opposition at this level are difficult. Tribal sections have rarely, if ever, actually worked as solidary groups and any conception of them as opposing groups will have a tendency to split the tribe. This nearly happened on one occasion. It was a long-drawn-out affair concerning several decades in the mid-eighteenth century. For some reason the Kwatzbe tribal section (as it now is) split off from their former tribe, the Qahtan, moved north and wished to become incorporated into the Rwala. The Sha'alan, the Murath and the Frejje wished to accept the Kwatzbe; the Doghman and the Ga'adza'a did not. This cut across the normal conceptual opposition of Murath/Doghman (known collectively as the Jum'an) as against the Ga'adza'a/Frejje (no collective name). This was a conceptual opposition only, as far as I can make out; it never had any reality. This pro- and anti-Kwatzbe division was soon confused by two other factors.

One, there was a struggle for the sheikhdom between the Mashhur and the Abdullah; and two, opinions were divided about moving north or staying in the south. This latter was never a formal choice, simply each individual's view as to which was his best option. The result was (or at least seems to have been, as I have not got all versions of what happened) that the Mashhur moved north with the Frejje and part of the Murath, while the Doghman and the Ga'adza'a mostly stayed south with the other, smaller part of the Murath. Abdullah seems to have hovered uneasily in the middle or, according to one version, sought refuge in the east, with the Shammar (his mother's tribe). I think, but again I have not got all the facts, that the leading family of the Doghman made a bid for the southern sheikhdom. This was scotched by the southern Murath supporting Abdullah and by what seems to have been the murder of several of the leading members of the Mashhur. In any event, Abdullah became the sheikh of the still-divided tribe and his son, Nayyif, presided over the reunification of the opposed sections. It is difficult to sort out the motives here. It is possible that the Rwala suddenly realised the dangers of opposing tribal sections and the advantages of remaining as one tribe with an increased area, north and south, to exploit or it may be that active opposition at tribal-section level made it difficult to operate the tribal section as a demonstration of inclusion into the total system; or it may simply be that the removal of some of the leading contenders for the sheikhdom left Abdullah in a strong position. What is clear is that putting tribal sections in a normal complementary/opposing situation gives rise to complications and that they are never thought of in this context nowadays.

Above this level the almost automatic division into two opposed groups is marked, irrespective of genealogical reality. Thus the Dhana Mislim are invariably opposed to the Dhana Bishr although they are at different genealogical levels and are only opposed because their names make it inevitable. (A few people are aware of the discrepancy between genealogical reality and wishful thinking, but they avoid explaining it or considering the consequences.) The Rwala are opposed to the rest of the Jlas; again no one can say exactly who the Jlas are (or were) or give a name to the opposing group. Those who know the tribal genealogy in some detail divide the Rwala into the Abyadh and the Asmar, but there is little agreement as to who belongs to which section. That there should be little certainty as to the composition of these groupings is hardly surprising. The opposed groups are just putting names to a conceptual image, which is a way of talking about their view of their own society; the oppositions have little reality in real life, for real life is lived at a different level.

With the exception of the level of tribal section, there is a clear conceptual image of society invariably divided in two complementary, equal, opposing segments at every level. Two factors work against the apparently divisive forces. The first is that people rarely think at one level at a time. This may sound a bit silly, but the groupings are so potentially flexible that it is perfectly possible to think of oneself as Nseir and Zuwaiyyid

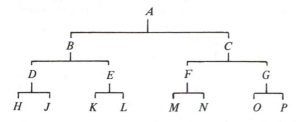

Figure 11. When is an 'ibn amm'?

Nseir and as Murath, all at the same time. Each level is conceptually different as well as actually different, but the possible choices of opposing group at each level produce a sort of *gestalt*, with the opposing group only vaguely conceptualised in the abstract. The second factor is more satisfactory and less nebulous. All groups at all levels are cross-cut by relationships through women. These factors are easier to understand with a simple model. (See Figure 11.)

H, J, K, L and *M* all camp together 'because we all belong to Group *B*'. But *M* doesn't; 'Well, we're really all Group *A*.' 'Then why are *O* and *P* camped separately?' 'Because they're not so closely related; we're all *ibn amm*.' It turns out that *M*'s mother was *E*'s sister, so *M* are more closely related in the female line – 'We're all Group *B*.' When this discrepancy is pointed out the level is switched to *A*. As the questions change the context, so the conceptual level changes to explain reality in genealogical terms. Any confusion that may arise, and it invariably does when an outsider like an anthropologist becomes involved, is brushed aside with the truthful but concealing exclamation: 'But we're all *ibn amm*.' As the total Group *A* will never be camping together, belonging to Group *A* is sufficient. When it is pointed out that not all the members of Group *A* present are camping together as one unit, refuge is sought in being 'really' Group *B*. When the discrepancy of Group *M* is pointed out, levels again switch, which brings in other criteria, in this case female lines. The people actually camping together have two explanations at their disposal, one of the formal genealogy of the total group, the other the balance of those actually there, as opposed to the group-in-the-abstract, which includes those not physically present. Provided a fairly equitable balance is achieved between the camping groups, it doesn't matter much how they arrived at that arrangement. At least it doesn't matter to any one other than the anthropologist and I suspect that some of the curious chains of reasoning, with their sudden jumps of level and context, are *ad hoc* explanations of what is really just ordinary preference. When the Rwala are forced into this position the commonest explanation is relationship through women, and it is quite clear that the divisive tendencies of the genealogy are consciously counteracted by utilising the cohesive links through women.

This brings us to the balance between public and private. If no explanations are asked for, there is a firm assumption that the official genealogy

balances. This is public. Privately everyone knows that the official genealogy is out of balance, so that in private life they redress the balance by
using female links. No outsider need know this, for women are very much
private. Thus public assumptions are balanced by private reality. It is
another aspect of segmentation, public complementarily opposed by private.
Just because the genealogy is male and public it doesn't necessarily follow
that it is true, nor does it mean that society actually works that way. This
is where the discrepancies start creeping in. Because I was male and an
outsider all explanations had to be public although the reasons were private. As soon as I was accepted I began to get the private explanations as
well. If I have shown anything it is that genealogy is a public statement
and that women play a large part in how society actually works. Our own
preconceptions about male dominance in the Arab world are reinforced by
the public statements made by the Rwala. In private women play a large
part in life, just as in our own society – we are not the only ones to have
jokes about mothers-in-law and hen-pecked husbands. This is not to say
that women are thought of as equal; they are not (though in private they
are frequently treated as equal); what I am saying is that the criteria that
apply to the male domain do not apply to the female domain, for the two
domains are in complementary opposition.

Again we are talking at different levels. The obvious opposition of
dominance–male–public and subservient–female–private cannot be made.
Dominance is a perquisite of maleness because dominance is related to
public life. The opposition of dominance and subservience doesn't come
into the private sector at all. It is a false equation, rather like converting
square feet into kilograms. In a similar manner there is no equivalent in
the private sector of the genealogy; the Rwala are not secret bilateralists.
The genealogy is male and therefore public and that is all. The genealogy is
a public statement and because it is public it must be male. I suppose that
the generative genealogy taking, as it does, female connections into account,
could be seen as the female equivalent, the private genealogy as it were, but
I don't think that the Rwala see it like this at all.

The balancing of forces within society is essential to make it work. It is
difficult to see because it is asymmetric; we see only one side of it as the
other side is private and not usually visible. The whole balancing act is at a
low segmentary level, for what is private is rarely known outside the immediate family. There is plenty of evidence for this private balancing. At
the most intimate level, names are frequently balanced: pairs of brother-
and-sister names are popular, e.g. Fahad/Fheida, Hazza'/Haza'a, Anad/
Anoud, Nawaf/Nauf, Nayyif/Nayyifa etc. Even variations on boy's names
are common for brothers, e.g. Fahd/Fahhad/Fheid, Mlih/Mliyyih, Zeid/
Zaiyad/Zaiyyid and all the Mohammad variations. Conversations are balanced in a family context. If someone makes a derogatory remark about an
absent neighbour, someone else will immediately balance it by presenting
their good points. Strangely, this doesn't run on kinship lines at all. One
can hear the same remarks a few days later with much the same people but

with the roles reversed. The one who was derogatory is now conciliatory and the one who was conciliatory is now derogatory. It is as if there were an overriding need for opposition resulting in eventual consensus irrespective of personal opinion. There is one young man with an appalling reputation and there are always new stories about his awfulness. Yet I have never heard him condemned by all; there is always someone to defend him so that a balanced assessment results. Consensus is itself a balanced decision reached by compromise. A simple decision to move one's tent can only be arrived at after long discussions within the family and with neighbours, relations and anyone else who happens to be present. These discussions are informal, conversations and ideas really, and the final decision is a compromise. There are no absolutes, no truth; no one is right, no one is wrong. Each autonomous individual is entitled to his/her opinion but modifies it for the good of the group. If they won't, they can always leave.

Resewing a tent is a good example of how co-operation is achieved. Tents are usually resewn every two years in the late summer. It would be a formidable task for one or two people, but it is always a co-operative effort. The process starts with neighbours looking up at the tent-roof while drinking tea and saying: 'Your tent needs resewing – look, it is broken there.' The owner, of course, is well aware of this. For some weeks the talk is of resewing tents but no arrangements are made beyond ascertaining that someone has some new woollen thread in the encampment. It is pointless to try to make firmer arrangements, such as: 'Can you come and help us next Wednesday?' My wife and I tried this once but none of them would commit themselves, for this would abrogate their autonomy. Then one morning the tent is emptied and taken down by the family. No one is warned beforehand, no day is fixed, no neighbours asked to help. As the women of the tent start to unpick the old stitching other women will drift across to help, but not in great numbers until the actual resewing starts. There is no right or wrong way to sew a tent; everyone is convinced that their way is better than any other. So, unless the woman of the tent is extremely strongminded, some seams will be stitched one way, some another way and some seams both ways, irrespective of what the owner herself prefers. Even this is not consistent. My wife has been shown two different 'better' stitches while working on a tent, by the same person. It is as if there must be opposition even if it entails contradiction. Putting up the finished tent is no better. Everybody knows a better way. Good-natured arguments rage over which rope to tighten first, whether supplementary poles should be put up before or after tightening ropes, in which places the strongest or longest ropes should be used. Few of these arguments are ever resolved, for while two men are arguing someone else will simply get on with the job. Again, a single person may well recommend a 'better' way that he roundly condemned last time.

What is so curious about these affairs (and other decisions too) is that the end is obtained without there being any general consensus achieved. Each individual interprets suggestions and viewpoints in his own way and

Plate 16. Resewing a tent is a co-operative job

the achievement of consensus is an individual assessment; there is no formal general consensus. We have to consider what consensus means in this context. It means that a man makes an autonomous decision on the assumption that his choice will be backed publicly by his family, as against his three-generation 'ibn amm', by his three-generation 'ibn amm' as against his five-generation 'ibn amm' and, if the need arises, by his five-generation 'ibn amm' as against any other group. In other words, consensus does not need to be reached, it needs only be seen to have been reached, whether truthfully or not. The inevitable tension between the need for autonomy and the need for consensus is masked, for each need is fulfilled at different levels. The contradictions that are so marked a feature of daily life remain private; they are never revealed publicly because the need to maintain solidarity is always at a higher segmentary level. Thus the balance between public and private is used to maintain two opposing forces that are incompatible; individuality/consensus is submerged into public/private opposition. Only consensus is publicly visible, disagreement never. The disagreement between two men as to the 'better' way to put up a tent, or the argument between two women as to the 'better' way to sew a seam, is resolved by the need for the tent to be put up or resewn. In exactly the same way, the struggle between the two brothers for the smuggling franchise was resolved, on the surface at least, by the need to present a united face towards outside intervention. (An ethnographic note: although all the literature says that women put up and take down tents, the authors are reporting a public statement. In practice anyone present, male or female, will help if he or she feels so inclined.)

The need for balance, for equalising opposing forces, is apparent everywhere. Tents are balanced between male and female sides (public and private again). The Rwala have a preference for tents with an uneven number of central poles so that the two sides are equal in size. They say that this is to show that family and visitors are of equal importance. Seating within a tent, which on formal occasions starts out in a square or oblong, always tends to assume that most balanced and egalitarian of shapes, the circle. This is more obvious in the women's side where formality is always at a minimum. The circle is always the shape assumed for eating. If there is more than one circular dish of food, then they are placed far enough apart for two complete circles of men to squat round them. The idea of an oblong table with a head and a foot is completely alien and where adopted, as in houses, gives rise to a great deal of uncertainty and unease. Unless it is a formal occasion, tables are usually ignored and every one eats, in a circle, on the floor.

Clearly, total stable balance can never be reached, for life is a process, not a state, but the Rwala continually attempt to maintain social balance. Total balance is the ideal because equality is the ideal; just as equality is never achieved, nor is total balance, so life is a tension between the ideal and the real. Even this is balanced, for reality modifies the ideal through demography and the inequality of achievement, while the ideal modifies reality through the mechanisms of reputation and the generative genealogy. This balance of ideal and real is apparent in daily life. Ideally, families camp together and never quarrel. In reality families don't camp together and quarrel as much as anyone else. Reality is modified by neighbours treating each other as if they were closely related and quarrelling being carried out extremely quietly. It is incredibly rare to hear voices raised in anger in an encampment; the offended party simply goes off and sulks. There is then a concerted effort to sort out the problem and restore harmony. If it is a case of incompatibility then one family just moves off. Everything possible is done to maintain the closest possible adherence to the ideal of harmony and equilibrium. This permeates everything. Carpets are balanced in pairs, woven patterns balance harmoniously, tattoo marks balance, tents balance, food balances not only in presentation but in texture, jewellery balances. Personal attributes and values should balance: wealth is balanced by generosity, bravery is balanced by commonsense, daring is balanced by prudence, even the protection of honour is balanced by the need to show compassion towards the transgressor. Tribal law, based as it is on *lex talionis*, is essentially balanced. In the desert they live in balance with nature, a state that they quite consciously tried to maintain. Even the ethno-botany, ethno-zoology and ethno-medicine seem to balance, although I was only just beginning to touch on these subjects towards the end of my fieldwork. (I hope to return for further research.) On an even larger scale, the Bedu system that the Rwala maintain is itself a balanced system and the relationship between the desert and the sown is seen by them as harmonious because both parties partake equally in the symbiosis.

This appears to me to be the crux of the Rwala attitude to change. The continuing tension between the ideal and the real, with the constant manipulation of assets and options, has enabled them to adapt to changing conditions with remarkable success. However the scale of recent changes has tipped the balance too heavily in favour of the townsman and it is this lack of balance that is causing the Rwala to contemplate partial withdrawal. A lack of balance indicates inequality, coercion and a lack of compromise, all of which are inimicable to the Bedu system. Having been forced by circumstances to partake increasingly in modern economics the Rwala are trying to maintain the balance by building up their herds and refusing to become citizens of any state. Autonomy is not possible where one side has the whip-hand politically and economically. Like so many actions in the desert, building up herds or refusing to settle are public statements and need interpretation, for they are at many different levels. Morally it is a rejection of Western values; wealth is not a satisfactory way of measuring worth. Politically it is a statement of autonomy; whatever the cost we will not be politically subservient to any regime. Economically it says that tradition should coexist in equality with modernity; all are equally valid ways of making a living, but neither should be imposed.

No one can truthfully say that the Rwala have avoided change or adaptation; they clearly don't, as they welcome new ideas, inventions and importations and accommodate both themselves and the idea to fit into their system. Change imposed from outside is another matter and they will resist it bitterly, not because they necessarily disapprove or dislike the change, but because its imposition does not allow them to react and partake in accordance with other factors. It implies a lack of balance between the two systems, a lack of freedom to make their own decisions and a lack of equality between individuals. That is really what the whole Bedu system is about, freedom and equality.

Postscript 1997

Any postscript starts with the words 'We would not write the book now as we did then,' and this goes for us too. It is now fifteen years since publication, and twenty-five years after the start of research. Obviously, we have more experience, more information, more understanding. However, our underlying perception of Rwala society as portrayed in *The Rwala Bedouin Today* has been maintained by repeated visits of longer or shorter duration and by work with tribal groups in other parts of the Arabian peninsula. Many Rwala, who have read the work either in English or in unauthorised and unseen translations into Arabic, see the book as an accurate portrayal of how Rwala society works. There are disagreements among them on particular points of history, but each individual realises that the knowledge and interpretation of history is effected by individuals from their own information: 'There can be no true history, because each person interprets the facts for themselves.' People have also challenged our analysis of points, in particular our statement that the Rwala approved of smuggling; this turned out to be a fault of an unauthorised translation. When we quoted Sheikh Nuri Sha'alan's words (pp. 93, 112, 129) to the effect that the smuggling from ar-Risha was traditional trading made illegal by the imposition of borders and state regulations, and that the actions of one state had taken away their livelihood so that smuggling was an honourable political – as well as economic – action, our challengers agreed with Sheikh Nuri and conceded that the translation had been inadequate.

There are a few points we would wish to change or to emphasise. Firstly, the references to 'clients' (pp. 11, 123). The Rwala insist there cannot be patron-client relations, given the internal logic of Arab tribal social practice in general and of the Rwala in particular. This emphasises individual autonomy, where each individual contracts, formally or informally, his/her particular relations with others, while generalised relations are mediated through the contexts of identity and situation. In the making of a contract, each party sees him/herself as a free agent in that contract. Even if constrained by circumstances, alternatives are always possible so constraint is not total. As each party is an autonomous individual – 'equal' and 'structurally equivalent' – neither is dominant or superior for that relation. Differences in material wealth or political power cannot enter the conceptualisation of social relationships, they are irrelevant; they may be relevant to the need for a contract to enable one party to achieve access to a resource the other controls preferentially, but both parties contribute to the enterprise, contributions made possible through the decision to make contractual relations. Such concepts negate economic and political 'structures of domination' seen to generate generalised horizontal social classes, which are then particularised by vertical patron-client ties (Doumani, 1994, p. 203ff for Jabal Nablus), or by vertical and localised lord-peasant ties of favours sought and given as in Gilsenan (1977, p. 182) for the Akkar plain of North Lebanon. Gilsenan was arguing against the use of patron-client relations as a general explanatory mechanism for Mediterranean societies. Patron-client relations are also used as a mechanism whereby centralised states attempt to incorporate tribal and other rural groups, as reported in recent discussions of the process in Saudi Arabia (al-Azmeh, 1986, pp. 82, 86; Kostiner, 1991, p. 226), the development of the Rashid polity (al Rasheed, 1989, p. 232), and French Mandated Syria (Velud, 1995), since states are founded on horizontal layers bound together through vertical ties from apex to base. The Rwala said (p. 129) that the incorporation of tribal sheikhs into the Saudi administrative system does muzzle tribal independence of action. We would now see this incorporation as capable of being used by both parties; tribal sheikhs could use incorporation for self-advancement, or for local negotiations in tribal interests. The choice is in the hands of the individual actors. The Rwala and other tribes and local rural groupings can turn these 'official' concepts around so they become local, particular face-to-face relations founded on individual autonomy and reputation.

Social relations in tribal arenas are defined in terms of closeness and distance. Public official statements of closeness and distance between known, identifiable and named bodies are contained in tribal descriptions of the structures encompassing constituent and related groups, often phrased in genealogical idioms. Private action bases itself on relationships through women, hidden in official genealogy, and an individual's earned reputation from observed behaviour measured by others against underlying moral premises and the effectiveness of actions in specific circumstances. Here, the general is the jural equality of all participants, the autonomy of each, and the capacity of each to act in accordance with moral premises. The particular lies in an individual's social relations and reputation as 'a good man' rather than in material goods. The general is expressed through being hospitable and generous to all-comers, extending protection to those who ask, and through defending one's autonomy. There are no particular returns, only the generalised of having behaved as one should that maintains one's reputation and the identity of the society (pp. 43–4; Dresch, 1989, p. 101).

Given that the Rwala and other tribal and rural groups conceptualise their social relations as between jural equals and autonomous individuals, organised in terms of closeness and distance, with general underpinnings of a shared morality, our use of clients and patrons was inappropriate. It would have been more in keeping with tribal concepts to have described *khuwa* payers, shopkeepers in the *suq* at ar-Risha, and the protected in these particular terms rather than as clients. Had we fully shared tribespeople's own confidence in their social logic, and paid more attention to remarks enlarged upon in later visits, we would have realised more fully that their emphasis on contexts of action is totally relevant to terms of social description. People are protected as *shwaya*, or *dakhil*, or through *khuwa* payments only when they are parties to a contract. When the contract ends or the context is inapplicable, the *shwaya* become Bedu (1996), the *dakhil* becomes Bedu, the *khuwa* payers are whoever they are. Tribespeople can only 'rule' an area in this manner when they are present. As we were told again in 1990, 'When we are here, this is our *dira*. When we go, our *dira* moves with us.' Thus, contexts are constructed by social actors within a conceptual framework.

For tribespeople, the general is a shared morality, there are no differentiations except through closeness and distance that maintain the horizontal dimension. The particular is mediated through face-to-face relations, which also maintain the horizontal. The opposed axis of verticality does not exist within tribal premises, which perceive it as a integral part of the conceptually opposed system of state rule. It is probable that other particular, local societies within states also emphasise such renegotiations of the structural premises of their encompassing state as in Herzfeld's analyses of Greek villages (1987).

Secondly, we think natality, where men and women (p. 58ff) remain jurally members of their natal group all their lives, is more important than has been recognised. Natality, together with the refusal to have senior and junior branches of tribes and tribal sections, appears to be a crucial difference between Arab tribes and those of Iran and Kurdistan. Natality, in one sense, is God-given rather than a social construction, and therefore a valid reference point beyond which social construction cannot go. As when, in a family setting, tea or coffee has to be served in some order of precedence, it is oldest first regardless of sex; in an arena including others, it is the most distant and/or the one who is being brought closer or the one being most honoured who is served first. In another sense, being a member of one's natal family is a jural identity of responsibility that can only be broken by actual or social death. Marriage is a linkage between families, each of whom maintains jural responsibility for its natal members, rather than transferring their jural responsibility for their women to another family on the occasion of a marriage. The acts of married women remain the concern of their fathers and brothers to be negotiated with their husbands and in-laws; women's actions give points of articulation between autonomous groups. The relevance of natality is that it is a conferral of individual autonomy within and between families; however, this is then constructed between classes of family members – in this case, men and women.

Other points arise from political and economic changes in the region since the seventies. The Rwala have shifted their foci of political action and economic interests. Or rather, Rwala whom we knew in the seventies have changed the focus of their activities, their children pursue rather different occupations, and the Rwala we have come to know in the eighties and nineties confirm these changes. These shifts are seen as the result of changes in political relations between the Syrian government and the Rwala; shifts in political relations between Jordan, Syria, Iraq and Saudi Arabia; regional economic developments following the OPEC oil price rise, the Iran-Iraq war and the Gulf War; the growth of education, especially further education in all countries; the growth in communications, especially telecommunications and computers; and changes in regulations by nation states.

Ar-Risha an-Nuri and ar-Risha al-Anwar are remnants of their former selves. Ar-Risha an-Nuri retains the *qasr* (the Sha'alan house, stores and guest-tent), an intermittently active *suq*, a flourishing garage, an enlarged primary school, and some twenty villas. These villas, well-spaced in the landscape, replace most of the one- or two-roomed houses of the seventies, used as stores and sleeping quarters by women and children, and adjuncts to the tents where men's life took place. Tents continue as men's public and family private space. Rwala and Fwaré built the villas between the late seventies and mid-eighties with profits of herding or smuggling, and the villas have changed hands many times since. Sha'alan-sponsored cross-border trade was ending in the late seventies with the return of assets or compensation by the Syrian authorities and as profits from smuggling decreased as costs rose. Many tribesmen took their profits and invested in sheep herds, land, and/or small businesses, mostly in Saudi Arabia. The Sha'alan also left, going to Damascus, Amman, Jiddah, Riyadh, Sakaka and Ar-Ar. There was little future in remaining at ar-Risha when there was no longer a political statement or a livelihood to be made, and when their children's education required good secondary schools that prepared them for university entrance.

Cultivable lands around the ar-Rishas are maintained. Rainfall is not adequate for cultivation, but in depressions with favourable soils, the moisture levels accumulate sufficiently in some rain-years for barley crops. By no means are all possible sites used or registered. Indeed, in exceptionally good rain-years, like 1994–5 in the eastern *hamad*, the area of barley cultivation is reduced since natural vegetation would provide for sheepflocks, and attempts to increase the production of preferred annuals for grazing are unnecessary. Some Sha'alan have built earth dams to allow the saturation of soils from flood flows and run-off. Barley crops are for sheep: as harvested grain, straws and stubble in one year in six; as a grazed crop in three years out of six; and with no crop sown in two out of six. Sheep herds are maintained by the sheikhs who spend short periods at the ar-Rishas. Their agents arrange for cultivation, the herding, and for preparations when the sheikhs come to keep in touch with local tribesmen and traders and to entertain local agents of state agencies. Gardens growing olives, pomegranates, vines and vegetables continue at Faydr, but have been abandoned at ar-Risha al-Anwar.

The *hamad* is used for herding. Moving herds between parts of the *hamad* that are in different states is difficult, and permitted only at official crossing points for herders. One at Tinf allows movement between Syria and Jordan, but is subject to arbitrary changes in the rules. Movement into Iraq was available during the eighties to Rwala and Sardiyya who had direct contacts, and grazing areas in west Iraq were opened to Jordanian tribes like the Ahl al-Jabal through inter-governmental negotiations. Since the Gulf War however, no herding movement into Iraq proper is allowed, although local arrangements can be made by herders habitually using border areas; cross-border trading between Iraq and Jordan continues through the official crossing point. Herders with Saudi or Jordanian passports who customarily use the *hamad* on either side of the Saudi-Jordanian border can cross at official points and must conform to national regulations, although locally negotiated decisions on the precise applications of these often contradictory regulations are possible.

Tribesmen like Rwala and Sardiyya with many Saudi nationals are able to trade pickups, lorries, and tankers from Saudi Arabia (where import duties are low) into Jordan (where they are high). Tribesmen from Jordanian registered tribes often request a particular vehicle in a certain price range from a Rwala or Sardiyya, who then sends the word out, and brings the vehicle across the border. Sheep are traded in a variety of ways. They are traded along family networks across borders in an accommodation of the earlier practice of movement from areas of poor grazing to those of good grazing, and movement to markets. Sheep are also sold when there is little grazing and the price of dry fodder rises, that is, in drought conditions; this is a normal response as flock numbers are built up above the core in good years and successively reduced by sale or dispersal in bad. Sheep supply markets in meat, dairy products, wool, and breeding animals. The sheep of the Jordanian *hamad* supply an urban Jordanian dairy product market, especially in cheese and to a lesser extent in clarified butter, and family networks; wool goes mostly to Turkey or is used within family networks; sheep for meat go mostly to the Saudi market, while breeding sheep supply markets in western Jordan or Saudi Arabia. There is a flourishing market in sheep imported from

Iraq and exported to Saudi Arabia, which was an important market for Iraqi herders before the Gulf War.

The numbers, densities and locations of herders in the *hamad* are affected by seasonal grazing and water resources over the years, and vary greatly from year to year. There are herding families who now base themselves at a location in the *hamad* for a number of years, from which the sheep are herded at distances of up to fifty kilometres or more. The ar-Rishas and Faydr, with schools and within driving distance of wells and a clinic, are used like this by Fwaré, Umur, Ghayyath and Rwala families. There are long-established Rwala clusters at Aghaban and Mingat. Long-term bases, lasting for up to ten years, are then left, and the family moves to another locality. A Rwala family based at Aghaban over many years moved to Sweir in Saudi Arabia, while the family flocks for all that period moved between Aghaban and Sweir; an Ahl al-Jabal family based in the Mahdath for eight years moved to a winter base below Irbid and a summer base between Mafraq and Jerash, and used Tell Asfar as a sort of information address. Na'im have a base near the gas-field to the east, while Beni Khalid have one south of the Syrian border at Aghaban al-Khawalid. The main Ghayyath base, Minshiyya al-Ghayyath, is west of ar-Ruwaishid (H4), on the main road. Like the ar-Rishas and Faydr, Aghaban al-Khawalid and Minshiyya al-Ghayyath have houses, a few villas, stores, and primary schools. Land has been registered for agriculture at all these locations, but no crops have been seen except at the ar-Rishas and Faydr. The establishment of Ghayyath, Beni Khalid and Na'im in the early eighties followed the crackdown on smuggling by the Syrian army and Ministry of the Interior forces and the new legal requirement for tribespeople to choose one nationality. It is said that those who moved into Jordan and took Jordanian nationality were the most implicated in smuggling. Members of the three tribes who had customarily used the Jordanian *hamad* also became Jordanian nationals; other families of all three remained in Syria.

Herders, and herding families, range widely away from these bases in good years while in poor years flock numbers are reduced and animals may be fed for eleven months of the year on supplementary feed. In wet winters, with a good growth of annual grasses and plants, additional flocks belonging to members of the Jumlan, Na'im, Muwaili and Beni Khalid from Syria may graze in the Jordanian *hamad*, as do the Rwala from Saudi Arabia. In 1995 when there was an exceptionally good spring in the eastern *hamad*, Beni Sakhr and Huwaitat (from the south) and Azazme (from Karak) grazed their herds of sheep and camels south of the Baghdad highway, leaving the area north of the road, with even better grazing, for later use by the Rwala and Ahl al-Jabal. Eastward movement by Sardiyya and Ahl al-Jabal flocks is customary in the winter. Summer movement has traditionally been out of the *badia*, but with tankers, wells and supplementary feed, many flocks stay in the *hamad* where they rest during the day under shade shelters and graze at night and early and late in the day. Shararat flocks of sheep and camels often move north from Saudi Arabia in summer, as do some Rwala flocks. Decisions as to where to graze balance information on conditions in different localities with water resources, cost of dry feed, renting crop stubbles further west, and feasibility of passage from one area to another (Lancaster, fc 1997a; fc 1997b).

Although most Rwala based in the Jordanian *hamad* in the seventies now live in Saudi Arabia, and although members of the Sha'alan are rarely present, the Rwala continue to 'rule' the Jordanian *hamad*. This is achieved by the sheikhs' negotiations with state authorities and NGOs in the interests of all tribespeople using the *hamad*. An outstanding example was the negotiation by Sheikh Nuri Sha'alan with Jordanian officials over the registration and use of vehicles in the seventies (pp. 8–9), which remains valid and has since been extended to include all Bedu and the whole of Jordanian *badia*. During the eighties, the Arab League instigated the ACSAD plan, which for the Jordanian *hamad* developed into the Hammad Basin Plan; in the late eighties and early nineties, the Royal Society for the Conservation of Nature wanted to make a Reserve at Burqa, later changed to a proposed Biosphere area, and the Higher Council of Science and Technology put in place a *Badia* Development Plan for the *harra*, with a possible extension east to the *hamad*. In the late eighties, the Ministry of Agriculture built a dam in Ghudran al-Faradis, possibly as part of the Hammad Basin Plan, and said at the time to be for agricultural development but currently to encourage recharge of sub-surface water. The Natural Resource Agency and Ministry for Energy have developed the ar-Risha Gas Fields, where Ghayyath and Na'im are employed, and made exhaustive surveys for oil and gas in the *badia* region. The government has drilled a deep well at Jisr al-Ruwaishid for water for ar-Ruwaishid, and the town, like the new Customs Post, now has electricity and piped water.

It is said that the Hammad Basin Plan, like the earlier Point Four, did not involve senior tribesmen as advisors. Senior Rwala heard of suggested projects to conserve *badia* resources and improve the quality of life. One project was to fence off a large area of the Dumaithat and Anqa in the southeast, which contains some of the best perennial grazing. Senior tribesmen, led by members of the Sha'alan, stopped this. They also advised against a project to dam the Mingat just south of the Syrian border where floodwaters enter a ravine, as the force of the water would break the dam. Their advice was rejected but the dam – for agricultural development – has not been built. Their own plan for conserving rainwater was rejected, although its costs were very low and it would have been self-sustainable; tribesmen say it was rejected for those reasons as it would not have created jobs for urban-based engineers and planners. Tribal opposition to the fencing of Burqa, a nearly reliable source of perennial water, ended the idea of fencing it off for a nature reserve; the biosphere proposal is said not to include fencing and intends to integrate herding and domestic use with conservation.

The ar-Rishas and Faydr function as addresses and are used as channels of communication between tribespeople, sheikhs' agents, local *badia* police, government officials, and the sheikhs by telephone and messenger. In the capital cities where the most prominent members of the sheikhly family live, they interact closely with senior civil servants and with members of the business communities. They are available to tribesmen in person or by phone, and frequently intervene to sort out difficulties with papers at the borders, acting as *kafila*s and guarantors. Regular visits are made to tribespeople in rural Saudi Arabia, and relations are maintained with the rulers and governments of Syria, Jordan and Saudi Arabia. Officially, the governments of nation states rule the *hamad*; locally, rule – or the keeping of the peace – is managed by negotiation between the responsible men of local groups and state agents. It is because of these activities, and the negotiations with governments and NGOs on behalf of tribespeople, that people continue to say that the Rwala rule the *hamad*.

Nathaiyyim, in al-Jubba in Saudi Arabia, was our other centre. This too has changed from an encampment of black tents, some one- or two-room houses, a few villas, and a couple of rather sparse gardens, to a place of villas, small houses and few tents, a water tower, sheep barracks, gardens with date palms, olive and fruit trees, and overhead irrigation systems for cereals. Each villa and small house is surrounded by a courtyard, divided into areas for men and women. In the men's side is the tent, now pitched permanently over a metal frame; tents have electricity, television, electric coffee-makers, and even air conditioning. Men use the tents for entertaining – women entertain in a salon in the house – and the family uses the tent when there are no visitors. A complex of small houses nearby is deserted. The houses were built for Doghman and Kwatzbe, by one of the Mu'abhil to encourage to them to settle there so that Nathaiyyim could become a *baladiya*, a self-administering settlement that, depending on population, would entitle them to certain facilities (a telephone-line, girls' school, etc.). The government refused the new-comers' title deeds to land, on the recommendation of other members of the family who had not been consulted; so the buildings remain empty. Electricity came in 1987, and the water tower was built soon after. The inhabitants are members of the family who first settled Nathaiyyim and a few families who have married in. Nathaiyyim is smaller than the neighbouring Bneyya settlement of Rifa'a, which replaced Zubara when electricity came, the Frejje settlements of Dibban and Hdaib, and the Ga'adza'a settlement of Sweir.

All around, in pockets of soil between rocky outcrops, are farms or gardens. A few farms had started during the seventies (p. 106). The Saudi government had tried large-scale settlement programmes earlier (Cole, 1975; Ibrahim and Cole, 1978; Hamza, 1982). Between the late 1970s (Lancaster and Lancaster, 1986) and the present, Rwala attitudes toward land and agriculture have changed somewhat. The baseline of their thinking is concerned with the loss of markets for camel-herding (except as supplying urban meat markets and urban dairy products; the former can be done by traditional forms of herding, the latter requires constant or at least predictable supplies of milk to processing and distribution plants); services from camels have gone, superseded by state control and technologies. To participate in current service provision, people must be citizens and highly educated; education to these levels necessitates attendance at schools offering university entrance, and then at university or colleges of further education. These are situated in cities or major urban centres. Given Arab family life, a family wanting its children to have the opportunity of participating in the opportunities of political and economic life must have a residence in a city or major urban centre or be within daily driving distance. Around Nathaiyyim, such schools are at Sakaka and Sweir.

Rwala sections owned wells at Hdaib, Sweir, Mughaira, and Shuwait-iyyah in al-Jubba, and at places in Busaita and the Wadi Sirhan. The Doghman section owned the oasis of Qara and wells at Khuʾa, and individual Rwala owned date groves in al-Jauf. Land-owning in customary and Islamic law comes from the development of land to make it more productive; undeveloped land, that is grazing lands and rain-fed arable land, is 'dead' land and therefore at the disposal of the state. (Rain-fed arable land is a tricky area, since production comes from the *tools* of production – ploughing, sowing and harvesting – and from labour rather than from improvement of the *means* of production, such as irrigation. States held that the producers owned the crop but not the land, while producers saw themselves as creating a customary right of access and use.) The ibn Saʾud held that agricultural development and settlement were necessary in the creation of the Wahhabite state. The government of Saudi Arabia thus saw all undeveloped lands as state lands to be disposed of to potential developers, which in practice were those who had pre-existing claims of customary ownership of wells, customary residence even if seasonal, and use for productive purposes. Once it was established that there was suitable water under al-Jubba, Busaita and the Wadi Sirhan, and that the technologies were available, land was developed by tribesmen who had already registered claims. Within areas associated with particular tribes and tribal sections, claimants had to be from these – or their claims unopposed by all tribal claimants. The distribution of land within al-Jauf Governate can be found in al-Sudairi (1995, pp. 161–7). Competition over land occurred at Mughaira, a group of wells owned by sections of the Mur'ath. Shararat tribesmen used the Mughaira wells when the Mur'ath were absent and on these grounds tried to claim Mughaira as theirs for land registration and agricultural use, but failed. This is a well-known example, but there are many other claims to land that are not accepted as valid; some are dealt with between claimants, others reach official levels.

All suitable soils in al-Jubba need irrigation for cultivation, other than in exceptional years. Irrigation in the early and mid-seventies depended on diesel pumps tapping into relatively shallow water tables. Crops need to be protected from wind and sand. State provision of the infrastructure for fuel distribution and electricity at subsidised prices, together with grants for the installation of pumps, water storage, irrigation systems, tractors and equipment, seed provision, and government purchase of cereals at well above world prices, made agricultural development of cereals economically attractive. Plastics technologies in drip-feed and trickle irrigation, and in sheeting for shelter, were also instrumental in developing vegetable production. Olive, vine and fruit tree cultivation, using trickle irrigation, has become common. The financing came from the oil price rises of the mid-seventies that enabled the government to pay for infrastructure and offer subsidies; the overall financial climate also encouraged private investment by individuals. Early government schemes had been unattractive to people for a variety of reasons, one of which was seen as too much overt state interference and control. This time agricultural development appears to have been much more in the hands of individual landowners, who arranged with labour importers for Syrian, Jordanian or Egyptian workers skilled in irrigated agriculture. (Arranging for labour and skills from share-croppers or waged employees has been a long-standing practice; only the bureaucratic procedures are new.)

It is said that ibn Sa'ud preferred to return some of the money from the oil price rises to the people of the countryside rather than seeing it go to the United States as payment for grain. At the same time, agricultural development was seen as a means of transforming tribespeople into citizens – as was education. The ownership of land has political relevance, since it marks the landscape; for example, it can be said 'al-Jubba belongs to the Rwala'. Ownership, or preferential access to resources, has a long tradition in the customary construction of identity by social bodies; it bestows responsibility, placing owners in a context of those who generate meaningful action. It should generate livelihood, and traditionally did so.

Currently, income is seen to derive from participation in state services, in one way almost as a *quid pro quo* for becoming an educated citizen; but people also perceive opportunities in state sectors, private business and service sectors and their participation in a wider world of international business and geopolitics as there for the taking. That is, livelihood and profits come from wealth generated from outside, as has happened at other dates in the economic history of the Arabian peninsula. The range of sources of livelihood and profit of the Rwala based in al-Jubba is wide, corresponding to perceptions of the assets and options of individuals, their families and informal '*ibn amm*' groups. People develop their livelihood as individuals; they are responsible for their decisions, but these decisions are taken with other family members and close members of the wider domestic unit. (The wider domestic unit is 'a dynamic unit toward which converge resources originating from a variety of sectors, procured and organised by *mobile* individuals belonging to a parental group whose dimensions and composition are not definable *a priori*' [Fabietti, 1990, p. 242] from Shammar information, and comparable to the Rwala informal '*ibn amm*'.) Livelihood decisions depend on ability, ambition, current opportunities and access. People change occupations over a lifetime and may do more than one thing at once; they also share family capital and need to take action to manage this capital. There is also the need to acquire and maintain a reputation as 'a good man'. Within these constraints, the Rwala herd, farm, have small businesses; work in local government; are teachers, electricians, doctors, hospital porters, lawyers, *qadi*s, accountants, businessmen, labour agents; work in government security services, in the National Guard and the armed services, in Saudi ministries at home and abroad, in telecommunications, in airport management and in highly skilled mechanical maintenance, among other occupations.

Since the withdrawal of subsidies and supported prices, many Rwala in al-Jubba with agricultural land say farming is profitable only if done on a large scale with skilled workmen and active and knowledgeable management by the owner/s, or as a garden worked by family labour supplying household needs and a little surplus for the market. Many see their gardens as sources of pleasure and household supplies rather than financial profit. Farms are organised around different crop strategies. Some use overhead pivot irrigation and concentrate on cereal cultivation, formerly wheat and barley and alfalfa for the commercial market, but some are now changing to barley and oats for their own sheep-flocks, and potatoes for the market. Others grow vegetables under polytunnels; produce is sold in the market at Sakaka, bought by local shop-owners and traders from Turaif and Ar-Ar. Many farms grow some alfalfa, some barley, some vegetables, and have some olives, vines, fruit, and date-trees; these tend to use sprinkler irrigation, and may have one or two overhead pivot systems. Some small farms grow little patches of most crops and have hens and some goats, and supply the households of their owner-workers. Some farms are worked by share-croppers or hired workmen who often have their own small-scale enterprises on site, such as rabbit, chicken or pigeon keeping. The large farms are worked by skilled teams with a specialist mechanic, crop supervisor and head shepherd, while other employees work where needed. Farms can have other spe-

cialist enterprises, such as egg production or olives. All hired farmworkers
are non-Saudi, coming from Syria, Jordan, Egypt, Pakistan, Sudan and so
on. Farm owners may own several farms in different areas, having purchased
land registered by fellow family or tribal section members who find little
interest or profit in land. From the position of the seventies, where the Rwala
who formerly herded had an almost total lack of competence in plant hus-
bandry (p. 106), some are now successful and knowledgeable farmers. Those
families who settled in Qara or al-Jauf from the beginning of the century
already had members skilled in agriculture. A Nsair woman has developed
a small farm worked by herself, and several women have small household
gardens where they grow fruit, herbs and vegetables near the house. Other
successful farmers are the sons of men who developed farms in the seventies
or later, and are driven by a desire to 'make an enterprise be successful. We
employ good workmen, and we have learnt from them about crops and soil
and so on. But I make the decisions. Really I'm a manager more than a
farmer, but I do like to know about how the crops and trees grow.' Another
man, who has around fifty plastic tunnels growing vegetables for the market
said, 'We saw this system in Jordan, and we thought it would work here. So
we found a Jordanian partner, and we provided the land and the water, and
all the equipment, and he put in his knowledge and skills. It's good, it works
well.' Some whose farms and gardens have crop failures or diseased trees
say it is because they cannot get skilled workmen and depend on their workmen's knowledge and skills.

Not every '*ibn amm*' group has land, even in al-Jubba. Most '*ibn amm*'
have members herding sheep as an important part of livelihood and group
assets, often seasonally using '*ibn amm*' agricultural land. Sheep herding is
agreed to be the most profitable investment. Most tribal sections also have
families who herd camels, sometimes with hired herders, sometimes by just
the family. Camels are sold for the meat market, and are profitable. Herding
camels is difficult to combine with education, and some families choose to
ignore education. Some Rwala see this as exemplary, others are noncommit-
tal, saying that ignoring education is to live outside the state and that is difficult. On the other hand, a highly educated Rwailiyya had doubts as to the
value of her education: 'I went to school, I did well, I went to University in
Riyadh and I have my degree. The only job I can do is teaching. I teach girls
to become educated so they can study at university and then they can teach
other girls . . . for what purpose? There isn't one. . . . I'm dependent on a
town and the state and I don't like it.' Others, men and women, think girls'
education is good because it leads to employment, more financial independence for women, and encourages companionship between marriage partners.

How much do changes in occupation, mobility, and incorporation in a state affect people's identity of themselves, the tribal structural system, and social practice?

Individual identity within the state context is as X son/daughter of Y al-Rwala; within the tribal arena, it remains as it was, contextual. Identity as Bedu is more problematic. There is a fair amount of discussion on whether or not there are Bedu, centering around on what criteria Bedu-ness is seen to depend. Some associate being Bedu with living from camels in the *badia*, and clearly not many people achieve this now – or want to. Others say the point of camel-herding was not that camel-herding and its extension into service provision made its practitioners Bedu, but that being Bedu meant providing for oneself, holding a morality of jural equality and individual autonomy; camel-herding was a viable economic expression of this morality (Lancaster and Lancaster, 1992b). Those who uphold the latter position accept that it is more difficult to construct the image of self-provision since 'trucks and pick-ups have to be bought, camels breed', but argue that given technologies have transformed economic realities, these have to be incorporated into the construction of identity based on the successful management of *badia* resources. *Badia* resources, in these conversations, include herding as the under-pinning because herding is the most profitable livelihood from the *badia*, along with transport, trade, and the provision of security. *Badia* management has always necessarily taken account of markets for exchange of *badia* products in surplus (camels, sheep and goats and their dairy products, skins and wool; collected products; labour and service skills) and for those in deficit (grain, dates, clothing, household goods and weapons) from farming areas and towns. People's skills in producing surpluses of goods and the services of providing security and restitution, through ability in execution and mediation, can be translated to changed conditions. Sheep-herding for meat, dairy products and breeding animals is what the market now demands and can be provided by using tankers for carrying water and supplies of dry feeds. Providing security is now arrogated to the state, but the state needs to recruit personnel. The multi-resource activities of the wider domestic groups, consistent with social practice, accommodates Bedu-ness. 'We have our sheep, and I have a pension, and so does he. But we got our pensions through our own actions. Our sons work for the government, it is necessary to participate. They got their employment from their educational success and by coming from families with good local reputations, and they do their jobs well. Their pay comes from their own efforts. We as a group live and use the *badia*, it keeps us, and government employment contributes. But there was income from outside before, from *khuwa* and raiding, or being a *rafiq*, or working as a harvester in the Hauran. We're Bedu because we behave like Bedu, we're hospitable and we are responsible for ourselves.'

The alternative view holds that state government has taken away from people their responsibilities of providing livelihood and security, but does not in fact provide either. In addition, the state attempts to buy support by giving some, who have no moral position/tradition, quick ways to material wealth while denying others their former wealth of social and moral action. Government actions are experienced as arbitrary, imposed, and restrictive, while government agents are perceived as unaccountable for their actions. All these are contrary to the tribal presentation, and largely supported by actions, of negotiations between partners each responsible for their actions and accountable to those who partnered them or were injured by them. State non-provision of livelihood for its citizens may well seem applicable to Syria and Jordan which are without much direct income from oil or other state resources and dependent for much of their income from aid, but Saudi Arabia is also so accused. Getting a livelihood is not difficult in Saudi Arabia for the Rwala, the trouble lies with what there is to do after that: 'It is so boring in Saudi Arabia. Once you have your flock, and the tanker and the pick-up, and the villa, and you're married, what else is there to do? Nothing, absolutely nothing except make more money, and for what? Even if you decide to make more money, and you plan a business, you have to get a licence. And they can just refuse you; they don't have to give a reason, you can't appeal.' 'I like making things work', a young Rwala said. 'I like getting the farms my father has set up to be profitable. We have five farms in different places, and there are different enterprises on each. One farm has hens for eggs, one farm grows olives, we have grapes, we grow potatoes, we grew wheat and barley that we're now changing to barley and oats for the sheep. We could have processing plants, we've applied for a licence to build a press for olive oil, a juice plant for grapes, or a drying plant to make grapes into raisins. The grapes do so well, and so many people grow grapes that the market for fresh fruit is over-supplied. But we have always been refused permission for every idea. And then a few years later, someone close to government gets permission for an olive oil press. And there's no point in applying for permission to start a potato crisp factory because someone in Riyadh has the import licence for all that sort of stuff. So we get turned down by local interests, and as well local enterprises are blocked by opposition from centrally based importers.'

It is possible for a Rwala to become rich, with astuteness, good information and connections, a willingness to take risks, a capacity for hard work and ambition. Of the few who become seriously rich, wealth is gained by the above factors together with chance – being in the right place at the right time. Wealth is used to further family and tribal interests. The expenditure of the rich and influential increases because their costs increase. To maintain reputation and standing, they must have a large and well-appointed house; they must entertain local government officials, civil servants, men from other tribes and their tribesmen, as they themselves are entertained. They must be generous with money, time and information to those who need help in negotiating bureaucracies and in sorting out disputes. They must spend time being seen at the *majlis* of local governors and leading civil servants, at those of notables of other tribal groups and urban families locally, in the capital and in other Arab cities. Their children must be highly educated, since the skills imparted through formal education are the current route to opportunities, economic and political. Having well-dispersed cores of Rwala actively participating in the political life of a state from a position of economic success means that the Rwala have a presence, they cannot be ignored. This presence enables or facilitates positions of support for (or distance from) particular policies at the regional and local level to be stated through formal and informal codes, and for negotiations on specific issues or concerning individual cases to take place.

The acquisition of wealth at this level is confined to a few. The Rwala say they are not particularly rich, as they never have been. People expect to provide for themselves and their families (i.e., informal '*ibn amm*'), to educate, marry and establish their children and to fulfill their social obligations with generosity. That is to say, their desires are materially modest and founded in social relationships; the ambition is to be 'a good man', '*rajil tayyib*'. '*Tayyib*' also has connotations of 'proper disposal of assets, management of choices'; so to be a '*rajil tayyib*' has attributes of an active pursuit of right behaviour. Under 'right behaviour' the Rwala would put achieving livelihood, but not the pursuit of material wealth at all costs and the retaining of such wealth for personal comfort or aggrandisement. Many Rwala working as teachers, policemen, accountants, or having small businesses say they live within their wages or profits only by careful management; but as members of '*ibn amm*' groups they maintain proper behaviour. Living costs have risen, while wages and profits have remained constant or declined in Saudi Arabia, partly from the withdrawal of subsidies and grants (as a result of the Gulf War and low oil prices) for electricity, water, diesel, petrol, basic foods and investment areas. People had become accustomed to being able to live well, and are now less able to replace cars and pick-ups or finish building work. Once subsidies are withdrawn from the development of farms, in many cases their economic viability is seen as doubtful. People say 'If we had had to pay for everything ourselves, we would never have developed these farms.'

Most Rwala would never have had the capital available, and regard many farms as essentially unprofitable. Soil quality varies considerably within relatively small areas. Equipment for well-drilling, water storage, pumps and irrigation, and bulldozers, ploughs and harrows, and harvesters add up to considerable sums. The technical skills of cultivation and equipment maintenance can be acquired by hire or through partnerships, but production and marketing are complicated by apparently arbitrary changes in government procedures and policies. The difficulties with developing the processing of agricultural products have been noted above. People say that only very small farms, worked by their owners for the household, and very large farms, run as highly technical businesses, are profitable. Many farms, of whatever size, supply the household with fruit and vegetables, the household or commercial flocks with grazing and fodder, and urban markets or government with stocks of cereals.

Agriculture is possible only in al-Jubba, Busaita, and the Wadi Sirhan, where Rwala wider domestic groups, like those of other tribes, combine farming, herding, employment and businesses. Rwala in Turaif and Ar-Ar used to be employed in TAP-line, are now reduced to a maintenance level; employment in local government services, business development and herding provide livelihood. Men who were welders or electricians with TAP-line are now accountants or labour agents, with interests in building land or sheep-flocks. Herding enterprises by men based in Turaif or Ar-Ar use the *hamad*, including Jordan by some, al-Labbah, al-Wudiyan, and al-Jubba. It is quite common for one member of the family to be based in al-Jubba with a camel herd, while one son is employed in Turaif, another in Qurayyat, and a third serves in the National Guard at Riyadh or Tabuk. The businesses people develop are owned by them; they provide the buildings, facilities and the licences, while the work is carried out by employed nonnational workers or Syrian or Jordanian share partners. Many provide urban services – bakeries, supermarkets, laundries, electricians, builders, restaurants, tailors, carpenters, metal workshops and so on. A restaurant sometimes links into a business importing Syrian foods, such as olive oil, olives, apricot conserves, dairy products, crystallised fruits, nuts and sweets, since most restaurant cooks are Syrian. A garage outside a town often has associated businesses of mechanics, tyre repair and fitting, car-electrics, restaurant, supermarket, and fodder store; the subsidiary businesses are sub-contracted from the developer of the site.

Many Rwala, like people of other tribes, say they wish to live their own lives, providing for their families from their own efforts and maintaining assets and options within tribal moral premises. The ways to advancement within the state system are often seen to lead only to material wealth without true morality and to a system within which men are judged only by what they own and with whom they are seen. (While there are a few really rich Rwala, tribesmen say these have high reputations within the tribe since they actively support the common weal of the tribe.) Direct autonomous economic action, apart from herding (and that too has its necessary paperwork) is difficult and mostly outside state law. An exception is the writing of praise poetry to a notable member of the Royal family, in the hope of a gift of a pick-up or car. The most common form of autonomous economic action is smuggling, regarded by its practitioners as trade across borders created by states, or in goods made profitable through the actions of states in regulations or currencies. 'If states didn't have these borders, or different currencies, or regulations, we'd be traders not smugglers.' Practitioners see smuggling and raiding as equivalent, as noted in 1981, for in both one of the attractions is that the entire responsibility for its success is 'on our head. I am responsible, that's what I like. It is all up to me. If it goes wrong, I can blame only myself, there aren't any excuses.'

In the seventies, the Rwala justified service in the National Guard, police and other government service by equating such service as helping to keep the peace as quasi-partners with state government. In general, and when talking about the position of the Rwala and other tribes *vis-à-vis* central government, this equation with keeping the peace is maintained. In particular instances, such a partnership is denied, together with indications that some consider participation in specific expressions of central government as unjustified. There is some feeling that the state has reneged on its side of a relationship of partnership between state and tribe, and that tribal moral values are seen, by the state, as being of no value. A young man who had worked in the prison service, well paid and with good prospects, had resigned because 'I couldn't stand the arbitrariness. It came to a head for me when there was a case of a tribesman who had difficulties with his neighbour, who was continually moving the boundary stones in his favour. This had gone on for years, and the owner had complained to the local land court and to the local governor. But the other man had good friends in official circles, and he was never stopped. At last, the owner got fed up and knifed the man. He died, and so the owner is now in prison. But it's wrong. The government takes away from people the right to defend their own interests and livelihood, and say we'll do that for our citizens. But they don't. They won't let us do it, and yet they don't do it themselves. And it's like that all the time.'

A sheikhly view of the relation between tribe and state was founded on the view that 'states depend for their income on external factors, on wealth from outside. Tribal wealth comes from its social cohesion, and from the assets of its members. These assets are physical, herds, land, wells, property in general, the resources available to tribal members through tribal social practice, and the generosity and good moral qualities of tribespeople. The tribal system, unlike that of a state, depends on itself, it continues since it is, at bottom, a moral system. So a tribe, if it maintains its practice, will outlast a state. This has happened before. The tribe might not be exactly the same, it might have changed its members a bit, it might have another name, but it goes on.'

This abstraction concerns the superiority of the tribal system *versus* the state system while the ex-prison service employee (echoed by many others) considers more immediate concerns. But what both tribespeople and sheikhs are doing, all the time, is negotiating between imposed formal and generalised state demands and their own locally generated informal practice. Negotiations are informed by pragmatic expectations and assessments of the motives of both sides. The results are evaluated in terms of moral values and achievement of desired aims. But while negotiations between choices of action are always an integral part of politics, the present ones are often regarded as unnecessary and invalid because negotiations should not be needed.

Such an attitude, that central government is of itself unnecessary, is widespread in the peninsula and by no means limited to the Rwala or the tribes. One does not expect a senior official of the Bank of Jordan, of an urban family, to state exactly similar views . . . but it happened. Since working with the Rwala, we have worked in two areas of Oman where the tribes or tribal sections got their livelihood by fishing (Lancaster and Lancaster 1986 & 1992b), with various tribes in the *harra* of Jordan and on the plateau north of Karak (Lancaster and Lancaster 1995 & 1996) where people are farmers and herders, and in the Wadi Dana where the people, again from a mixture of tribes, live from farming and goat-herding.

Most of these groups said they were Bedu and all that they were tribal. Bedu has implications of managing livelihood, governing and keeping the peace from one's own resources without incorporation into a centralised state. Fabietti (1994) emphasises the importance of context in using the word 'Bedu'; in the shanty towns outside Riyadh, everyone says they are Bedu; they get their livings through tribal and family connections and resource strategies, and manage their affairs in the same way. In government agricultural settlements, people say they are *hadhr*, whether of Bedu origin or not.

Bedu-ness did not of itself demand camel herding, since fishing tribes of Ja'alan and sections of the Wahiba depend largely on fishing, although they also herd camels, goats and cows, have access to date gardens and, in the past, traded. The Beni'Amr of Karak describe themselves as Bedu; they farm for the household and herd for profit. 'We are Bedu because we behave like Bedu, we are hospitable, and we know our genealogy.' Other groups in Karak said they were *fellah*, 'and always have been,' although they always had animals but made their profits from farming. One of the groups whose members said they were *fellah* was the Majali, described in the literature as heading the Bedouin or the tribes of Karak. The typologies of full-Bedouin, half-Bedouin, half-settled and so on have no relevance today and had little in the past. How people describe themselves depends on a multitude of factors; the arena, audience, context . . . and it is always in relation to 'others';

we are X but they are Y, or we and they are close and are A, but those over there are distant and therefore D, or we are all A but they are not real A. Let alone we are A because . . . but they are B because . . ., when B will say they are B because . . . and their criteria are the same as A gave for being A.

Members of these tribal groupings saw themselves as being more or less similar to each other, that all tribes and wider families were like others, and that all were founded on common principles. They also saw that there were differences between tribal groupings, in their interpretations and associated practices of common principles. Tribes and the wider families are variations on a common theme (Lancaster and Lancaster, 1992a). All say that no single landscape can provide a secure and sustainable livelihood from itself; users need access to other landscapes; there must be mobility; there have to be multi-resource economic strategies; social practice must be flexible and above all resilient. The premises of jural autonomy are expressed through hospitality, protection and honour defended by individuals identified as members of tribes or families. This tribal identity, plus individual reputation, enables tribespeople to partake in social arenas beyond those of general obligation through contracts and partnerships that depend on inputs from both parties and restitution for nonfulfillment. These processes allow for an extraordinary range of economic and political activities to take place along contractual networks between persons because their jural identity assumes individual responsibility for actions and answerability. This identity is a main function of tribal membership for an individual.

On the other hand, Fabietti (1994), using Marx's material, does not see tribe as a unified sole institution, since people have one 'tribe' for agricultural land, one for grazing, one for marriage, one for blood vengeance. Borrowing an alternative tribal identity for a particular purpose is well known and widespread; a Huwaitat visiting and in need of casual employment was told by his Amarin hosts to say he was Amarin, since casual archaeological work was available only to members of the tribes around Fainan. Harb from Ja'alan in southeast Oman always say they are Beni'Amr when applying to enlist in the UAE army, since the Beni'Amr are part of a widespread and well-known tribe, whereas the Harb are not. But this only works with outsiders.

There are institutionalised processes that have different manifestations. *Khuwa* comes from the word for 'brother', and the Rwala see the term as denoting a contract, freely entered into, between two parties following different economic and political strategies. One side, sheep or goat-herders, traders, or villagers, paid for protection or security from the second party, usually a tribe like the Rwala who herded camels. Failure to maintain security was a failure to fulfill the contract and resulted in recompense for the injured party. Herders and traders paid when wishing to use the area at that time being used by the Rwala. Villagers paid when needing security of exchange. The Rwala say that *khuwa* contracts were between an individual

Rwaili and the representative of a small group of herders, traders, or part of a village, although the relationship was talked about in terms of 'the Rwala' and 'the Fwaré' or 'the villagers of Qalamoun' or 'Qariatain' – metonymy takes over. This is consistent with *khuwa* in Musil (1928) and Thoumin (1936). *Khuwa* here is based on contracted payment for protection where restitution for nonfulfillment is guaranteed. When, for example, Fwaré herders or Qalamoun village herders were not using Rwala grazing grounds under Rwala protection, then they were not *khuwa*-payers or *shwaya*, but bedouin or villagers. Some groups, like the Ahl al-Jabal took *khuwa* from some and paid to others. It was a term used in a particular situation, and a process that allowed more productive use of resources; herders or traders paying *khuwa* did not have to provide guards as well. In the south of Jordan, Musil (1908, p. iii) describes the taking and payment of *khuwa* as a method of distributing goods between different parts of the economy in return for restitutive protection. Jaussen (1948, p. 162–4) sees *khuwa* as a tax imposed by stronger tribes on weaker ones for protected access to grazing grounds. Al-Rasheed (1989) sees *khuwa* as tribute paid by the weak (goat and sheep herders, merchants, inhabitants of oases) to powerful tribes; the economic relationship extended into providing protection, which itself developed rights and obligations between the protectors and protected. *Khuwa* thus provided security of oasis markets, agricultural lands and property, and assured the security of caravan routes. When the Rashidi Emirs took control of Hail in 1836, the Emirs centralised the system of *khuwa*, so that all revenue went through their hands and all protection was ultimately guaranteed by them; the revenue produced went in part to create a specialised military force to protect merchants and caravans, as well as Emiral power.

The identity of a tribesperson, and of tribe itself, is portrayed by members as being grounded in moral terms. People are very clear and firm about this. The obsession with power seen in writings on political science and history of the Middle East is absent from the presentation of society by its members. The power of political science and history is 'power over' by hierarchically structured classes; that of Arab tribespeople is 'power to' (get a livelihood, be 'a good man') by individuals, identified in tribal or family terms, who are closer or more distant to each other. 'Power to' is individual autonomy, just as it is 'honour defended'. 'Power to' live as a good person, and to use one's tribal identity in that way creates 'tribe', rather than 'tribe' being a straitjacket of custom and obligation. Tribal structures construct an individual's tribal identity, used to access processes for livelihood, support and security; tribal identity also provides access to wider economic and political opportunities through contracts and guarantors. These arenas of potential action are discussed in terms of various frames of reference such as closeness and distance, public and private, official and local; but all are situational and contextual. The situation within each frame of reference is negotiable within the moral premises, if the individual wishes to remain tribal. That too is a choice.

Bibliography

al-Azmeh, A. 'Wahhabite Polity', in W. E. Netton (ed.), *Arabia and the Gulf: from Traditional Society to Modern States*. Totawa, New Jersey, 1986.
Doumani, B. *Rediscovering Palestine*. University of California Press, Berkeley, 1994.
Dresch, P. *Tribes, Government and History in Yemen*. Clarendon Press, Oxford, 1989.
Fabietti, U. 'Between Two Myths: Underproductivity and Development of the Bedouin Domestic group', in E. Bernus and F. Pouillon (eds.), *Sociétés Pastorales et Développement*. Cahier des Sciences Humaines 26 (1–2). Paris, 1990.
_____. Unpublished lecture given at CERMOC, Amman, Jordan, 1994.
Gilsenan, M. 'Against Patron-Client Relations', in E. Gellner and J. Waterbury (eds.), *Patrons and Clients*. London, 1977.
Hamza, H. H. *Public Land Distribution in Saudi Arabia*. London, 1982.
Herzfeld, M. *Anthropology through the Looking-Glass*. CUP, 1987.
Jaussen, A. 1948. *Coutumes des Arabes au Pays de Moab*. Adrien-Masonneuve, Paris, 1948.
Kostiner, J. 1991. 'Transforming Dualities: Tribe and State Formation in Saudi Arabia', in P. Khoury and J. Kostiner (eds.), *Tribes and State Formation in the Middle East*. Tauris, London, 1991.
Lancaster, W. and F. Lancaster. 'The Concept of Territoriality among the Rwala Bedouin'. *Nomadic Peoples 20* (1986).
_____. 'Desert Devices: the Pastoral System of the Rwala Bedouin', in J. G. Galaty and D. L. Johnson (eds.), *A World of Pastoralism: Herding Systems in Comparative Perspective*. Guilford Press, New York, 1990.
_____. 'Tribe, Community and the Concept of Access to Resources: territorial Behaviour in South-east Ja'alan', in A. Rao (ed.), *Mobility and Territoriality*. Berg Publishing, Oxford, 1992a.
_____. 'Tribal Formations in the Arabian Peninsula'. *Arabian Archæology and Epigraphy* 3 (1992b).
_____. 'Land Use and Population in the Area North of Karak', *Levant* XXVII (1995).
_____. 'Some Comments on Peasant and Tribal Pastoral Societies of the Arabian Peninsula (with Particular Reference to the Kerak Plateau of Jordan)', in U. Fabietti and P. C. Salzman (eds.), *The Anthropology of Tribal and Peasant Pastoral Societies: The Dialectics of Social Cohesion and Fragmentation*. Collegio Ghislieri (Pavia) and Ibis, Como, 1996.
_____. 'Changes in Herding Practices in the Bilad ash-Sham', *Proceedings of the I.U.A.E.S. Inter-congress*. Lucca/Florence 1995. *Nomadic Peoples* (1997a forthcoming).
_____. 'Indigenous Resource Management Systems in the Bâdia of the Bilâd ash-Shâm', *Journal of Arid Environments* (1997b forthcoming).
Musil, A. *Arabia Petraea*. 3 vols. George Olms Verlag, New York, 1908.
al Rasheed, M. 'Pouvoir et Économie Caravanière dans une Oasis de l'Arabie du Nord: l'Éxample de Hail', in J. Bisson (ed.), *Le Nomade, l'Oasis et la Ville*. Urbama 20, Tours, 1989.
al-Sudairi, Emir Abd al-Rahman. *The Desert Frontier of Arabia – Al-Jawf*. Stacey International, London, 1995.
Thoumin, R. *Géographie Humaine de la Syrie Centrale, II: L'Aménagement et la Distribution des Eaux*. Guenther, Paris, 1936.

Postscript 1997

Velud, C. 1995. 'Syrie: Tribus, Mouvement National et État Mandataire (1920–36)', in R. Bocco and C. Velud (eds.), *Monde Arabe: Maghreb-Machrek*. Special Edition No. 147. La Documentation Français, Paris, 1995.

Other Related Publications by W. O. and F. C. Lancaster

Self help for Pastoralists. *Nomadic Peoples 6* (1980).

The Development and Function of the Sheikh in Nomad/Settler Symbiosis. *Arabian Studies 6* (1981).

The Logic of the Rwala Response to Change. *Contemporary Nomadic and Pastoral Peoples: Asia and the North. Studies in Third World Societies 18* (1982).

The Place of Peripatetics in Rwala Society. *The Other Nomads*, ed. Aparna Rao. Böhlau Verlag, Köln, 1987.

Fishing and the Coastal Communities: Decline or Renewal? *Journal of Oman Studies, Special Report 3*. The Scientific Results of the Royal Geographic Society's Oman Wahiba Sands Project, 1987.

Thoughts on the Bedouinisation of Arabia. *Proceedings of the Seminar for Arabian Studies 18* (1988).

Dhuweila: the Present Population. *Dhuweila 1986 Excavation at a Neolithic Hunting Station in East Jordan*. A. V. G. Betts (ed.). Edinburgh University Department of Archæology Occasional Papers, 1989.

Modern Ar-Risha: a Permanent Address. *Early Islamic Architecture of the Desert*. Svend Helms. Edinburgh University Press, 1990.

Anthropological Survey at Ras al-Junayz: A First Preliminary Report. *The Joint Hadd Project: Summary Report on the Third Season (October 1987–February 1988)*. S. Cleuziou, J. Reade and M. Tosi (eds.). CNRS, Paris, 1990.

As-Sahara Masdar Tabiʰwe fi Khatr. *Al-Reem: Journal of the R.J.S.C.N., Vol. 40* (1990).

Limitations on Goat and Sheep Herding in the Eastern Badia of Jordan: an Ethno-archæological Enquiry. *Levant XXIII* (1991).

Sécheresse et Stratégies de Reconversion Économique Chez les Bedouins de Jordanie. *Steppes d'Arabie*. R. Bocco, R. Jaubert and F. Métral (eds.). Presse Universitaire de France, Paris, Cahiers de l'I.U.E.D., Geneva, 1993.

Rwala. *Encyclopædia of Islam; 2nd edition*. Brill, Leiden, 1995.

Traditional Systems of Water Conservation in the Eastern Badia of Jordan. *Studies in the History and Archæology of Jordan V*. Department of Antiquities, Amman, 1995.

Mahafir: A Water Harvesting System in the Eastern Jordan (Badia) Desert. *GeoJournal 37.1*. London, 1995. (Co-authors with C. T. Agnew and E. Anderson).

Harness and Trappings, 3: the Camel. *Dictionary of Art*. Macmillan, London, 1996.

Reflections on the Social Organisation of the Arabian Bedu in Coastal Oman. *Proceedings of XIII U.I.S.P.P. Congress*, Forli, Italy, 1996.

Shawiya. *Encyclopædia of Islam; 2nd edition*. Brill, Leiden, 1997.

Sulayb. *Encyclopædia of Islam; 2nd edition*. Brill, Leiden, 1997.

Jordanian Village Houses in Context: Growth, Decay and Rebuilding. *PEQ* (1997)

Who are these Nomads? What do they do? Continuous Changes or Changing Continuities? Conference Jewish/Arab Centre. 1995. In J. Ginat and A. Khazanov (eds.), *Proceedings*, Sussex Academic Press, 1997.

Forthcoming

People, Land and Water in the Bilâd ash-Shâm. Harwood Academic Press, Reading.

Trade and Stratification among the Tribes of South-east Jaʰalan. *Proceedings of the 1991 Arabia Antiqua Conference*. ISMeO, Rome.

Postscript 1997

Social and Economic Differences between Big and Little Tribes. *Proceedings of the 1991 Lyons Conference*. CNRS, Lyon University.

Rowton's Thesis of Dimorphic Structure and Enclosed Nomadism: A Reconsideration from an Anthropological Perspective. *Proceedings of the 1992 Aleppo University Conference – Syria 3000–300 B.C.* Ministry of Culture, Damascus.

Appendix 1 The Genealogy of the Sha'alan

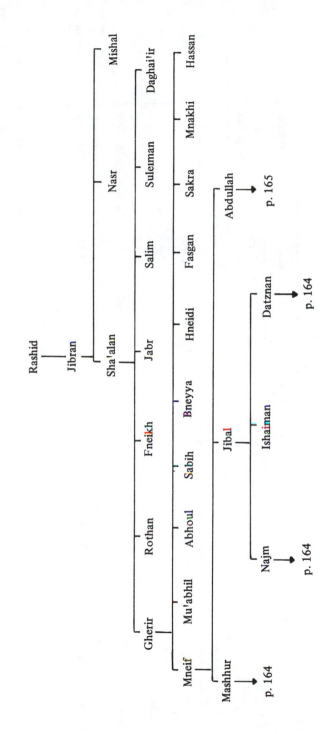

The Mashhur and the Jibal

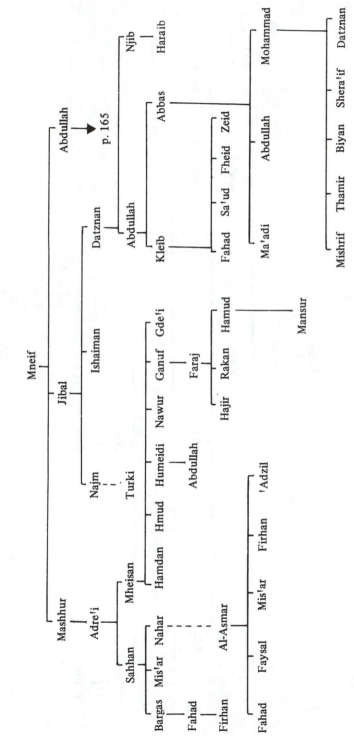

p. 165

The Abdullah and the Mijwal

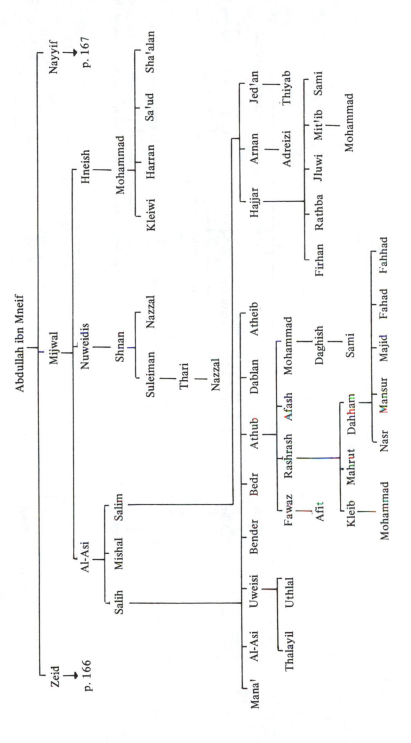

The Zeid

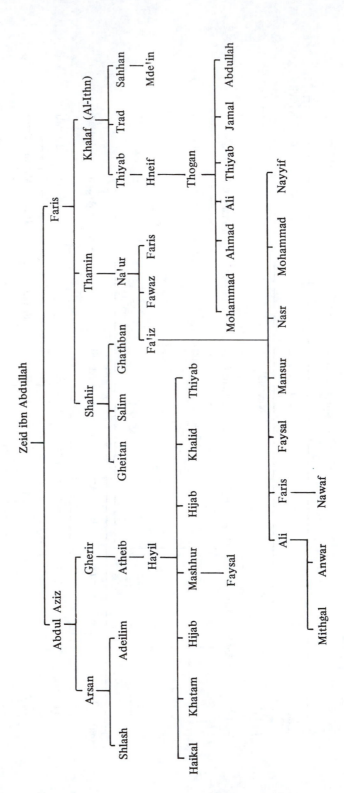

The Nayyif

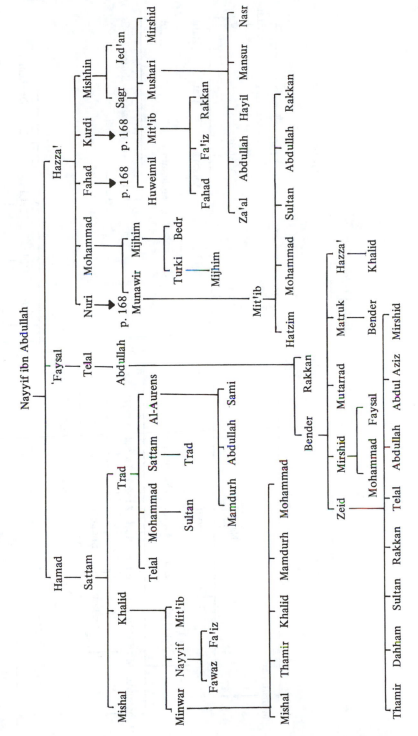

p. 168

191

The Hazza'

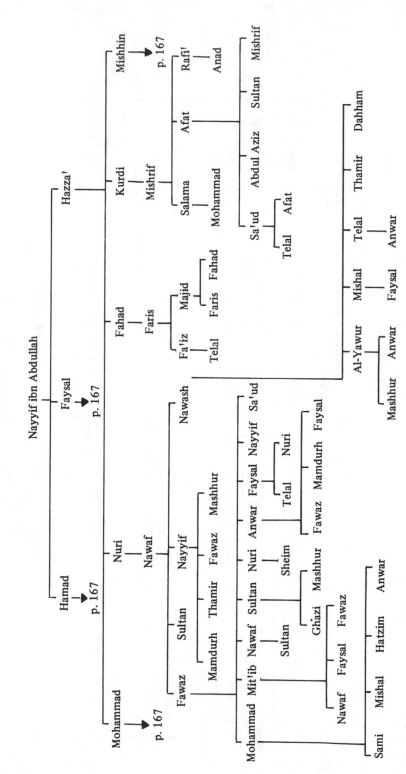

p. 167

192

Appendix 2 *Fukhudh* of the Rwala

These lists are taken from Musil (*Arabia Deserta*) and from my own field notes. Musil attempted to subdivide and group together 'subdivisions' and 'clans'. This does not seem to have been very successful and was only partially achieved. I have left his subdivisions as printed. My own lists have very few divisions, nearly all are what I refer to as five-generation 'ibn amms'. The interest lies in the fact that the lists are so similar despite some seventy or more years between them. If the patronymic ancestor of a five-generation 'ibn amm' were really five generations back, none of these group names should be the same. Actually they are almost identical. Musil used a system of transliteration all his own with a welter of accents and pointing. Rather than reproduce this I have transliterated his transliteration from German to English to make it more readily understood.

All those with an asterisk are now part of the Muwasserin.

Musil (1908)	Lancaster (1979)
The Doghman	
Haksha	Hagsha
Hasan	Hassan
Der'an	Der'an
Barabra	Barabara
The Murath	
Sha'alan	Sha'alan
Nseir	Nseir
Wheif	Uheif
Nasir	Nsir
Kbush	—
Ma'abhel	Mu'abhil*
Gaber	Jabr*
Rowzan	Rothan*
Bnejje	Bneyya*
Sabih	Sabih*
Sabte	Sabte*
—	Abhoul*
—	Fneikh*

Musil (1908)	Lancaster (1979)
—	Hneidi*
Elema	Ilama
Kata'a	Gata'a
(In text but not list)	Nuwasira

The Frejje

Khatha'	Khuthan
Fleta	Flitta
Swalha	Swalha
Sabbah	Sabah
Jufyan	Zifyan
Sumran	Simran
Hutlan	Hutlan
Sha'el	(Izoul?)
Jidran	Zidran
Mshet	Msheit
Rmah	Rmah
—	Badi
—	Mudahisha

The Ga'adza'a

Ghshum	Ghshum
Hamamid	Hamamit
Shzeir	—
Ribshan	Ribshan
Hneyyan	—
Ma'erir	Ma'arir
Wukeid	Ugait
Sab'a	—
Gerri	Jirdi?
Aweinan	Uwainan
Ajil	—
Sleim	—
Mshanna	—
Mane'	Mani'
Ka'ka	Ga'ga'
Dwerez	Dweirij
Atiyye	Attiya
Cwatle	—
Sheratin	—
Rashid	—

Fukudh *of the Rwala*

Musil (1908)	Lancaster (1979)
Rsheidan	—
	Btheini
	Rahamma
	Mustafidza

The Kwatzbe

Musil (1908)	Lancaster (1979)
Sweit	--
Mdeghem	Mdeighim
Uklan	Wuklan
Rabi'	Rabi'a
Jwahle	Juwahila
Solman	Salman
Shzeir	—
Ghnem	Ghneim
Rshud	—
Wuheib	Uhaib
Mehsen	—
Jlaidan	—
Wadi	—
Jirfe	—
Mzeibil	Nseibil
Homshi	Khimse
Arzan	Arthan
Khattam	Khattam

Bibliography

Antoun, Richard and Harik, Iliya. *Rural Politics and Social Change in the Middle East.* Indiana University Press, Bloomington/London, 1972.

Asad, Talal. 'The Bedouin as a Military Force: notes on some aspects of Power Relations between Nomad and Sedentary in an Historical Perspective', in Nelson, *The Desert and the Sown.*

Aswad, Barbara C. 'Key and Peripheral Roles of Noble Women in a M.E. Plains Village', *Anthropological Quarterly* 40, no. 3 (1967).

Property Control and Social Strategies: Settlers on a Middle Eastern Plain. Anthropological Papers, Museum of Anthropology, University of Michigan, 44. Ann Arbour, 1971.

Bailey, F. G. 'Conceptual Systems in the Study of Politics', in Antoun and Harik, *Rural Politics and Social Change.*

Barth, Fredrik. *Nomads of South Persia.* Allen and Unwin, London, 1961.

On the Study of Social Change. Plenary address to the American Anthropological Association. 1966.

Models of Social Organisation, Occasional Papers 23, Royal Anthropological Institute, 1966.

'Analytical Dimensions and the Comparison of Social Organisations', *American Anthropologist* 74, nos. 1-2 (1972).

Blunt, Lady Anne. *Bedouin Tribes of the Euphrates.* 2 vols. John Murray, London, 1879.

A Pilgrimage to Nejd. 2 vols. John Murray, London, 1881.

Burckhardt, J. L. *Notes on the Bedouins and Wahabys.* London, 1831.

Caskel, W. 'The Bedouinisation of Arabia', in G. E. von Grunebaum (ed.), *Studies in Islamic Cultural History.* American Anthropological Association, memoir 76. Menasha, Wisconsin, 1954.

Chatty, Dawn. 'From Camel to Truck: a Study of Pastoral Adaptation', *Folk* 18 (1976).

'The Current Situation of the Bedouin in Syria, Jordan and Saudi Arabia and their Prospects for the Future', in *Nomads in a Changing World.* The Institute for the Study of Human Issues of Philadelphia, 1981.

Cole, Donald Powell. *Nomads of the Nomads: the Al Murrah Bedouin of the Empty Quarter.* Aldine Publishing Co., Chicago, 1975.

Pastoral Nomads in a Rapidly Changing Economy: the Case of Saudi Arabia, O.D.I. Pastoral Network Paper 7e, London, 1979.

Dostal, Walter. 'Evolution of Bedouin Life', *L'Antica Società Bedouina* (1959).

Doughty, Charles. *Travels in Arabia Deserta.* 2 vols. Jonathan Cape, London, 1885.

Bibliography

Euting, J. *Tagebuch einer Reise in Inner-Arabien.* 2 vols. Brill, Leyden, 1896 and 1914.

Fernea, Robert A. *Shaykh and Effendi: Changing Patterns of Authority among the El-Shabana of Southern Iraq.* Harvard University Press, Cambridge, Mass., 1970.

Glubb, John Bagot. *War in the Desert.* Hodder and Stoughton, London, 1960.

Guarmani, Carlo. *Northern Najd: a Journey from Jerusalem to Anaiza in Kasim.* Foreword by Douglas Carruthers. Argonaut Press, London, 1938.

Hardy, M. J. L. *Blood Feuds and the Payment of Blood Money in the Middle East.* Catholic Press, Beirut, 1963.

Ibrahim, Saad E., and Cole, Donald P. 'Saudi Arabian Bedouin', in *Cairo Papers in Social Science,* vol. 1, monograph 5. American University in Cairo, 1978.

Issawi, Charles (ed.). *The Economic History of the Middle East, 1800–1914.* University of Chicago, 1966.

Lamartine, A. M. L. de. *Voyage en Orient (1832–33).* Brussels, 1836. (Contains *Recit de Faitallah Sayeghir.*)

Lancaster, William. 'Development and Function of the Sheikh in Nomad/ Settler Symbiosis', *Arabian Studies* 6 (1981).

Lawrence, T. E. *Revolt in the Desert.* Jonathan Cape, London, 1937.

Lewis, Bernard. 'The Ottoman Archives as a Source for the History of the Arab Lands', *Journal of the Royal Asiatic Society* (1951).

Lewis, Norman N. 'The Frontier of Settlement in Syria 1800–1950', in Issawi, *Economic History.*

Marx, Emmanuel. *Bedouin of the Negev.* Manchester University Press, 1967.

Meryon, C. L. *Travels of Lady Hester Stanhope.* London, 1846.

Monroe, Elizabeth. *Philby of Arabia.* Faber and Faber, London, 1973.

Mueller, Victor Marie Pierre. *En Syrie avec les Bedouins.* C. Leroux, Paris, 1931.

Musil, Alois. *Arabia Deserta.* American Geographical Society, New York, 1927.
    Northern Nejd. American Geographical Society, New York, 1928a.
    Manners and Customs of the Rwala Bedouin. American Geographical Society, New York, 1928b.
    Palmyrena. American Geographical Society, New York, 1928c.

Naffakh, Rabah. 'La Conception du Monde chez les Baggara', *Revue des Etudes Islamiques* 39 (1971).

Nelson, Cynthia (ed.). *The Desert and the Sown: Nomads in the Wider Society.* Research Series 21. Institute of International Studies, University of California, Berkeley, 1970.

Oppenheim, Max von. *Die Bedouinen,* vols. 1–4. Otto Hanasowitz, Leipzig and Wiesbaden, 1939–68.

Peristiani, J. G. (ed.). *Honour and Shame: the Values of Mediterranean Society.* Weidenfeld and Nicholson, London, 1965.

Pershits, A. I. 'The Economic Life of the Nomads of Saudi Arabia', in Issawi, *Economic History.*

Peters, E. L. 'The Proliferation of Segments in the Lineage of the Bedouin of Cyrenaica', *J.R.A.I.* 90 (1) (1960).

'Aspects of the Family among the Bedouin of Cyrenaica', in M. F. Nimkoff (ed.), *Comparative Family Systems.* Houghton Mifflin and Co., Boston, 1965.

'Some Structural Aspects of the Feud among the Camel Herding Bedouin in Cyrenaica', *Africa* 37 (1965).

'Shifts in Power in a Lebanese Village', in Antoun and Harik, *Rural Politics and Social Change.*

Philby, H. StJ. B. 'Jauf and the North Arabian Desert', *Geographical Journal* 62, no. 4 (1923).

Raynaud and Martinet. *Les Bedouins de la Mouvance de Damas.* Beirut, 1922.

Rosenfeld, Henry. 'The Social Composition of the Military in the process of State Formation in the Arabian Desert', *J.R.A.I.* 95 (1965).

Rutter, Eldon. 'Damascus to Hail', *Journal of the Royal Central Asian Society* 18 (1931).

Smilianskaya, I. M. 'From Subsistence to Market Economy', in Issawi, *Economic History.*

Sweet, Louise E. 'Camel Raiding of North Arabian Bedouin: a Mechanism of Ecological Adaptation', *American Anthropologist* 67 (1965).

Tabawi, A. L. *Russian Cultural Penetration of Syria–Palestine in the Nineteenth Century.* Royal Central Asian Society, London, 1966.

Volney, C. F. 'Travels through Syria and Egypt', in Issawi, *Economic History.*

Wallin, G. A. 'Narrative of a Journey from Cairo to Nejd', *Journal of the Royal Geographical Society* 24 (1854).

Winston, H. V. F. *Captain Shakespear.* Jonathan Cape, London, 1976.

Index

Abdul Hamid, Sultan, 84, 124
Abdullah ibn Mneif Sha'alan, 138, 155, 156
Adre'i ibn Mashhur Sha'alan, 128-9
affinal links, 11, 16; between ibn Sha'alan and ibn Mheid, 85-8; to other tribes, 22; within 'ibn amms', 30-2
agricultural holdings and development, 13-15, 18, 20, 84, 91, 97, 103, 106-9, 112, 115-22, 124, 130, 145, 146, 148
Aleppo, 87, 97, 124, 128, 130
Amarat (tribe), 22, 25, 86
Amman, 5, 10, 52
Aneze, 8, 23, 24, 86, 120, 136, 144; genealogy of, 25
Ar-Ar, 109
Arab–Israeli war (1967), 15
ashira, 28
assets and options, 7; basis of Bedu society, 119; change in, 144-9; devaluation of, 76; economic, 97-116, 145-6; in changing marriage patterns of sheikhs, 136-8; in genealogical terms, 15-23; in genealogical theory, 35; in marriage, 43, 52-4, 57; political, 95-6; practical side to segmentation, 151
al-Aurens ibn Trad Sha'alan, 132
autonomy, 67; generosity a statement of, 94; illustration of, 76; loss of, by ruling a town, 125; one of main functions of sheikh, 128-9, 130-1; one of the premises of the Bedu system, 73; part of the dual nature of Bedu system statements, 136; personal, 103, 159; semi-autonomy, 89; smuggling a statement of, 94; theme of society, 151, 162; version of Rwala origin, 120
Azraq, 9

Ba'ath party in Syria, 14, 15, 91, 112, 113

Baghdad, 120, 129, 130, 143
Barth, Frederick, 6, 7, 149
Bender of the Sha'alan, 33
Beni Sakhr (tribe), 22, 24, 133
bilateral links, 16; *see also* affinal links; women
bilateral ties, 40-2
Blunt, Lady Anne, 3, 82, 85, 96
Bneyya (five-generation 'ibn amm'), 63
Burckhardt, J. L., 82, 138, 141, 142

camel-herding, 8, 9-10, 18, 20, 75, 89, 99-105, 114-15, 116, 119, 123, 139, 144, 162
children, 60, 137; acquiring mediatory skills, 73; games, 69; jobs, 70; upbringing of, 66-71
clients, 11, 123
consensus, 87-9, 96, 158-60

Damascus, 6, 9, 11, 52, 67, 116, 124, 128, 129, 130, 143
debts, 99
Dhana Bishr (part of the Aneze), 35, 86, 156
Dhana Mislim (part of the Aneze), 86, 156
disputes, 20, 75, 79, 87, 160-1
Doghman (tribal section), 9, 14, 20, 25, 81, 120, 122, 155-6
drought of 1958-62, 18, 76, 100, 112, 123, 145, 148

economics, 5, 8, 15, 20-3; based on camels, 139; booming, 137; change in economic base, 84; changes in, 143-8; dependence on oil, 114; independence, 131; necessitates change in marriage patterns, 137; options in, 97-111; sheikhly options, 112-14; wealth not tangible, 143-8
education, 66-71, 102-4, 145; employment opportunities from, 105-6; of sheikhly children, 137

199

DATE